THE GREATEST
SHOW ON EARTH

THE GREATEST
SHOW ON EARTH

THE INSIDE STORY
OF THE LEGENDARY
1970 WORLD CUP

ANDREW DOWNIE

This edition first published in Great Britain in 2021 by

ARENA SPORT
An imprint of Birlinn Limited
West Newington House
10 Newington Road
Edinburgh
EH9 1QS

www.arenasportbooks.co.uk

ISBN: 9781909715967
eBook ISBN: 9781788853217

British Library Cataloguing-in-Publication Data
A catalogue record for this book is available on request from the British Library.

Designed and typeset by Polaris Publishing, Edinburgh
www.polarispublishing.com

Printed and bound by CPI Group (UK) Ltd, Croydon, CR0 4YY

CONTENTS

For Dad, and of course, Mari

ACKNOWLEDGEMENTS

Fifty years have passed since the 1970 World Cup and fewer and fewer players are alive and well enough to talk about their memories of the tournament. Fewer still grant interviews for free.

This book nevertheless contains first-hand interviews with players from fourteen of the sixteen nations who took part in the competition. The coronavirus pandemic made getting some final interviews impossible and there were many that I couldn't do personally because of the language barrier. When I was unable to communicate directly, I turned to a superb network of journalists and researchers across the globe. Without them this book would have been impossible and I owe them a huge debt of thanks.

Salvatore Riggio in Italy was superb with his contacts and speed and Omar Fares Parra in Mexico was also very helpful. Walter Arana in Peru, Alexey Yaroshevsky in Russia, Claudio Martinez in El Salvador, Metodi Shumanov in Bulgaria, Pablo Gama and Felipe Fernandez in Uruguay, Sujay Dutt in Sweden, Carim Soliman in Germany, Emanuel Rosu in Romania and Samindra Kunti in Belgium all found old players and got them to talk about what they remembered.

Thanks to my *amigão* Rocco Cotroneo for help with translating Italian TV and radio broadcasts, and to Mike Collett, Pete Hall, Ori Lewis and Anis Vijay Modi for help with contacts.

First-hand interviews alone would have barely filled a couple of chapters so much archival research was required to complete the story. Many of the quotes in the book came from old interviews found in magazines and newspapers, as well as from television and film archives. No quotes have been changed but some have been edited together from different sources for ease of reading.

The autobiographies of several players, most notably from Brazil, England and Germany, including some from those who have passed away in recent years, were also key sources of stories and anecdotes.

A special thanks goes to São Paulo's Football Museum, which granted me permission to use the testimony from its own oral history project.

Memories are fragile and on occasion friends and teammates get details wrong or contradict each other on timing or dates or names. I have left the memories as they were told to me and tried to explain any discrepancies in my text.

A big thanks goes to my editor Peter Burns, who brought the project to me in 2019 in the belief that I was the best man for the job. His cool head when I freaked out was very welcome. Likewise, thanks to my agents, David, Rebecca and Nick.

Last, but certainly not least, there is my wife Mariane, who is not just a translator, adviser, counsellor and marketing guru. She is my everything. Te adoro. (Falei isso hoje?)

FOREWORD

Winning the World Cup is one of the greatest privileges in my life. Most players don't get the opportunity to play in the finals; even fewer take home a winner's medal. The 1970 World Cup was the highlight of my professional life. I not only had the honour of playing in a team that is considered the greatest of all time, but I played alongside some of the greatest players in history.

We worked hard to win that tournament. We were all friends and there was a fantastic team spirit and that certainly helped us as we worked to achieve our goal. We knew it wasn't going to be easy. The altitude and the heat were big challenges but we went to Mexico almost four weeks before the tournament began and our preparations were exemplary. We spent a lot of time in Guanajuato, which is more than 2,000 metres above sea level, so we could get used to playing at altitude. Thanks to the rigorous training schedule put together by our team, led by coach Mario Zagallo, we were in perfect shape by the time the games kicked off. Proof of our fitness came in the fact that most of our goals were scored in the second half.

The Mexico World Cup was my first and I got off to a perfect start when I scored a lovely free kick in our first game against

Czechoslovakia. I also scored our first goal in the quarter-final against Peru and the last in our 3–1 win over Uruguay in the semi-final. They were important goals and they came at key moments.

What I remember most is the final against Italy. I can still see it all so clearly. It was a wonderful day and we played brilliantly. We won 4–1 with goals from Pelé, Gerson, Jairzinho and Carlos Alberto. But if you analyse the game, it was actually one of the easiest ones we had. It could have easily finished 5–1 or 6–1. Brazil were far superior. And it was one of the most unforgettable games in World Cup history. When the final whistle went the fans invaded the pitch. It was madness. They stripped the shirt I was wearing right off my back. I fainted and had to be helped up.

I have a picture on my wall here at home that was taken just seconds after the game ended. I am lying on the ground and Pelé is giving me an embrace. I can't remember who gave it to me, but I love that photo. It says it all. The joy. The happiness. The euphoria. Truly, there's nothing quite like it. Winning the World Cup is absolutely unforgettable.

Roberto Rivellino

PROLOGUE

The 1970 World Cup was a World Cup of superlatives.

First and foremost, it was a World Cup of modernity, as football took its first tentative steps into a new era. It was the first World Cup to be held outside of Europe or South America. The first to feature substitutes. The first to threaten players with yellow and red cards. The first to have its own ball, the Adidas Telstar, with its ultra-stylish black and white panels. Most thrillingly of all for football fans across the globe, it was the first to be broadcast live and in colour.

Thankfully, the football did not disappoint. Compared to today, it looks slow and ponderous, especially when measured against the pace and power of 21st century giants like Lionel Messi and Cristiano Ronaldo. But was there ever a more memorable tournament? At least three of the games feature on any serious list of all-time greats. England v Brazil saw the reigning champions beaten by their heirs apparent and Brazil made good on that promise by overcoming Italy 4–1 in a thrilling final. A few days previously, Italy beat West Germany after 4–3 extra–time in a semi-final so epic it was forever known as 'The Game of the Century.'

The 1970 World Cup took place at a time when foreign football was still thrillingly exotic. European fans rarely saw the Latin American sides and vice versa. National teams took short tours across the Atlantic every few years but with television still in its infancy only a few lucky supporters were able to see the entire games. Communications and travel were rudimentary and the Cold War barriers made scouting even more difficult; often coaches and players didn't know much about their opponents. The Bulgarians put together research dossiers from stories in German newspapers and via information passed on by their foreign embassies. Politics meant Israel struggled to find opponents and debutants Morocco played only one match between qualifying in November 1969 and their opening game in June 1970. Even the form of the always feared Brazil side was shrouded in mystery. Just three months before the tournament kicked off, World Soccer magazine doubted their chances and said Gerson and Rivelino were "grossly overrated."

And yet Mexico 1970 is now inextricably linked with that Brazil team, one of the greatest of all time. Names like Carlos Alberto, Rivellino, Jairzinho and Tostão were little known outside South America before the tournament began but they would soon become synonymous with power, intelligence and flair. They also had Pelé, the greatest player of all time, playing at his absolute pomp. The victorious Brazil side scored 19 goals in six games, a total that has never been bettered, even in tournaments where the finalists play seven times. Overall, there was an average of 3.96 goals per game at Mexico 70. In no tournament since has the average even surpassed three.

Impressive as all that is, it's far from the only reason the tournament is so beloved. All sporting occasions are a snapshot of the time but Mexico 1970 was a glorious sun-washed polaroid that captured football on the cusp of massive change. The world's passion for football was long established but it was not yet the true global game and the organisation reflected that reality. Only 75 teams took part in the qualifiers, far less than the 210 who sought a place in Russia in 2018. There were just five stadiums in five host cities, a far cry from the 12 used in Brazil in 2014. And in perhaps the truest illustration of how football was still run largely by enthusiastic amateurs, the draw was carried out by Monica Cañedo, the 10-year-old daughter of the head of the Mexican Football Federation.

Nevertheless, change was afoot. The 16 teams who travelled to the Americas arrived just as football was waking up to its potential as a massive money-making venture. Mexico 1970 was a World Cup of lasts as well as firsts.

There was an odd jumble of billboards around the pitches but full-on marketing rights had not been invented. FIFA still had no major commercial partnerships. Blanket press coverage was not yet a thing – there were no Matchday minus 1 press conferences or media days – and most players didn't have sponsorship deals or personalised boots. Shirts were yet to feature three lines on the sleeves or swooshes on the chest. There was not much in the way of official merchandise, no sponsor's man of the match, no statistics or heat maps to pore over after each game, and certainly no elaborately emblazoned buses to take the players to and from stadiums and hotels. Even the trophy, the Jules Rimet, was destined to make a final appearance as it was carried off by Brazil for winning it a third time.

Off the field, too, football's long-standing balance of power was starting to shift. The Latin American nations, who had won four of the eight World Cups so far and would add another to their tally in Mexico, were chaffing at FIFA's Eurocentricity and wanted more say in how things were done. In Brazilian João

Havelange they had a convincing figurehead who was preparing a campaign to unseat Englishman Stanley Rouse and end 70 years of European hegemony at football's governing body. Africa, given an automatic qualifying place for the first time after their nations boycotted England four years before, were also gearing up to exert the influence their numbers deserved and they would be followed by Asia and Oceania.

Football was changing and it has changed in myriad ways since. But the 1970 World Cup remains a benchmark, etched in the memories of all who saw it – and of many others who didn't, at least not until YouTube came along. It was, quite simply, the most iconic World Cup of them all. The stories in this book will hopefully keep those memories alive for a little longer.

ONE

PRE-TOURNAMENT PREPARATIONS

Hosts Mexico took the World Cup more seriously than anyone, with their players called together in January for what would be a five-month training camp. The home nation played thirteen full internationals between February and May and rounded off their warm-ups with a couple of wins against Dundee United, who were in Mexico on a short tour. But the time went slowly and some players paid a heavy price when they broke the confinement. Ernesto Cisneros and Gabriel Núñez were cut after sneaking out of the team base in search of R&R and then disaster struck when striker Alberto Onofre broke his leg in a training session just days before the opening match.

Alberto Onofre (Mexico): It was the last training session before the tournament started and it was raining. We were playing a bounce game; it was a Thursday and the opening game was on the Sunday. I slipped and collided with Alejándrez, I relaxed my body and he was coming in very hard so the fracture occurred. At first, I was resentful against him, yes, but as time went on that disappeared. He was also from Guadalajara and we knew each other, so there were no more grudges.

Ignacio Calderón (Mexico): We were very unfortunate that three days before the opening match one of our key players, Alberto Onofre, got injured and that was a real blow to the team. It was an accident. I remember very well seeing what happened. We were playing a training match, it was raining and midfielder [Manuel] Alejándrez went in to intercept a pass to Onofre and he slipped in the mud and broke his tibia. I was in goal and I could hear this dry crack; it was like hearing a toothbrush snap in two. We could see how he was in pain. It was just an unlucky incident, there was no malice, and it was all down to the rain that caused [Alejándrez] to slip.

Alberto Onofre (Mexico): After the operation I went to watch the opening game, and then I returned to Guadalajara and watched all the games on television. The coach had to make changes because I was a starter in all the warm-up matches. And so we didn't have a chance to play without me in a friendly beforehand.

Ignacio Calderón (Mexico): It was really sad but just because Onofre wasn't going to play didn't mean we couldn't do something. We had other quality players. Sadly that's how things go sometimes, and you have to get on with it. We knew Onofre was a key figure for us because he was at the top of his game and he was the one that inspired the whole squad. So, yes, it affected us but we kept going and we tried to put it behind us and give our all from the very start.

Javier Valdivia (Mexico): He was a very important part of the system that we were playing and it affected us because we could have done more with him in the team.

The Mexicans were desperate to put on a good show, both on and off the field. Mexico had never reached the second round before and their FA had built a brand-new headquarters and training centre to ensure the players wanted for nothing. Their fans, meanwhile, had rolled out the red carpet for most of the visitors and were warming up for what would always be remembered as one of the most passionately supported World Cups of all time. The average attendance of 52,312 would not be surpassed until 1994, when it was held in the USA.

Ignacio Calderón (Mexico): It was the first time that the national team had its own place. We had two football pitches, rooms just like a hotel, a dining room, etc. We were very happy. It was very close to the Estadio Jalisco and people were very enthusiastic about it being the first World Cup to be held in Mexico and we were also happy to be part of it. People turned out at the new training centre, the street was filled with fans, and we were delighted because we were signing footballs as part of a publicity campaign and that was the first time that had happened. I remember we signed 500 or so balls to give away. The fans were euphoric, they really believed in us. It was a really nice time to be in Mexico, the streets, with their flags, and the fans supporting us, it was a hugely happy atmosphere.

Alberto Onofre (Mexico): The atmosphere in the squad was very good, we put up with concentracion [the team's base, also called concentração in Portuguese] as was only right, we were going to the World Cup. And we were aware that we were the hosts and that we had to do well.

Javier Valdivia (Mexico): It was so satisfying to play at home and it was also great for the fans. It was a big advantage playing in Mexico in front of your home fans and it was very motivating for us.

Group 1 rivals Belgium were considered dark horses after knocking out Spain and Yugoslavia in the qualifiers. They weren't together as long as the Mexicans but they were away from home with nothing outside football to occupy their time and the strain took a toll.

Wilfried Van Moer (Belgium): We went to Mexico for about five weeks. What is the best way to explain this? There wasn't much organisation at the time. For the past fifteen to twenty years, everything is all spick and span – the staff, the hotel and everything you need and whatever you could wish for. Back in those days, it was the first time Belgium undertook such an arduous trip. Mexico isn't right next door! The heat, the altitude . . . it's a beautiful country, but it was really tough for the Belgian team. The preparation wasn't properly planned. There had been a plan to go to Switzerland for altitude training at 2,400 metres. You get thinner air, but that plan didn't come off and so we left earlier for Mexico to acclimatise, but that didn't really work out either. Yes, we struggled. The altitude was okay. We trained for three weeks, so that was manageable, but the adaptation to the climate was one of the factors . . . and the second big factor was we were away from home for such a long time that after a few weeks half the squad suffered from homesickness. They wanted to return home. You knew from the start that you would go to Mexico for at least five weeks. If you progressed, you would even be away longer from home. But, okay, nothing had been arranged in the hotel to give us any kind of distraction. You were not allowed into the swimming pool. The national team doctor prohibited this. The sun was bad, he said. Everything was bad. So you were obliged to – like we are in lockdown now – to sit in a bungalow, almost sit in a huddle, you know, and play cards and talk. You shared a bungalow with two players. What could you do? Play cards, play cards. Yes, those that wanted to play cards . . . apart from that, there was nothing. So, in Mexico, it wasn't ideal to play World Cup games. The facilities were all fine. That was not the problem. The biggest problem was that six, seven players had given up – staying such a long time. You had to wait at least three to four weeks before you played your first game. That is a very long time, especially as a group. You are there with twenty-two young players – no distraction or nothing. It was a disaster.

No team had as tumultuous a run-up as Group 1 rivals El Salvador. The tiny Central American nation qualified for the World Cup for the first time but only after a play-off against neighbours Honduras that helped provoke what became known as the Soccer War. After both teams won home and away a decider took place in Mexico City that the Salvadorans won 3–2, a result that took them into a final decider against Haiti, which they won after another three-game play-off. Honduras and El Salvador were at loggerheads over Honduras' decision to banish Salvadoran immigrants from their country and the three derbies ratcheted up the tensions. Within days of El Salvador's historic win in July 1969, Salvadoran planes were bombing their neighbours.

Mauricio Rodriguez (El Salvador): The problems we were immersed in were sociopolitical because there was a confrontation between Honduras and El Salvador that at that point was still diplomatic and verbal. Coincidentally, we had to play them in the qualifier. There are a lot of myths about it. The war over qualification was about two very independent things. Good and bad luck came together on that date. I remember that after we finished the game against Honduras, when we were still there in Mexico, someone at the hotel told me that we had just broken off diplomatic relations with Honduras. The war happened something like ten or fifteen days later, it lasted like 100 hours, and it was a more serious warlike thing. The problem is that they were expelling Salvadorans from

Honduras. And we heard about that through the media, but it never had anything to do with us or with them, because they also behaved very properly on the field. They were strong, as usual, but gentlemen.

Salvador Mariona (El Salvador): It was a coincidence that this was happening while we were trying to qualify to the next round. War was already brewing.

Mario Monge (El Salvador): The war didn't start because of our games. There was a political motive. It just happened to be during the time of the qualifiers.

Mauricio Rodriguez (El Salvador): The media charged us with patriotic responsibility, in addition to sports. We were practically soldiers of the country that were heading off to war. We felt that we had to win, that there was no room for error. The return really was perfect. I think returning from beating Honduras was as important – or more important – than when we qualified for the World Cup. People let off steam, they thought that because we had won, we had won everything . . . The truth is that for us the pressure was huge. I do not want to think about how they must have arrived in their country, because they must have gone through the same thing as we did and when they lost it must have been very ugly for them.

The hostilities were short-lived, lasting less than a week, but hundreds, and perhaps thousands, died in a conflict that scarred relations between the two countries for decades. As if that were not enough to disrupt El Salvador's preparations, they changed their coach on the eve of the tournament, did not win any of their five warm-up games, and then contrived to lose their first new strips in years before they even got to Mexico.

Mauricio Rodriguez (El Salvador): They promised us $1,000 if we qualified, because they thought we weren't going to qualify. They didn't give it to us, and before we left there was almost a strike because they didn't pay us the money. In the end they paid, but in instalments. Some players, like the goalkeeper Magaña, almost didn't go because of the strike. Don Hernán, the coach, had problems because a few days before we left they wanted to cut them and not let them go to the World Cup even though they were important players. We had to use the uniforms worn by the teams in the preceding years. So we had four of one style, five of another, and those were the strips we wore when we played. [For Mexico] Adidas sponsored us, but the strips got lost. Or they never arrived. We had to buy new strips in Mexico. The shirt that I have as a souvenir, which I wore in the World Cup, was made in Mexico and is not Adidas. We had some little badges to swap and we took the ES off them and put them on those new shirts. Adidas didn't say anything but when they got there they gave us boots and $70 for the three games. They gave the money directly to the players. But the truth is that at that time we didn't feel weird, we had been playing this same way for ten years.

Nowadays, the World Cup is a showcase to be sold, but back then, above all, it was the prestige of being in a World Cup. We were fortunate to train against some teams and teams that were better than us, that is, they helped us improve, but the problem is that we were going to compete with people who were better prepared, who had more resources. So what we did for two or three months, they did all year. We got better at a lot of things, but we weren't on a par with our rivals. Almost all our pre-tournament friendlies were at home and against clubs [rather than national teams]. It was for economic reasons, to be able to pay . . . Because in order to have the players of the national team, the federation had to pay the same wages they earned on the teams. Playing here [in El Salvador] there were no problems, because the stadium was filled with people who came to see us. The problem was if we went to play abroad, because they paid very little. I remember that once we were going to the United States and they gave us $2,000 for the whole team. And almost the airline tickets cost that . . .

Another of the teams making their World Cup debut was Israel, who qualified through the Asian Confederation. The Israelis were drawn to play qualifiers against North Korea and New Zealand but the Koreans, finalists in England four years previously, refused to play Israel and withdrew. So Israel played both their games against New Zealand in Tel Aviv. They won easily, 4–0 and 2–0, and qualified to face Australia in a play-off. They navigated that with aplomb, winning 1–0 at home and then drawing 1–1 in Sydney.

Yochanan Vollach (Israel): We left Israel at 4.00 p.m.; it was a wintry December day. We slept a night in Tehran, where it was snowing, then went to Bombay, where it was thirty-five degrees. We got back on the plane, then landed in Cambodia where it was equally hot. Then we flew to Hong Kong, spent a four- or five-hour layover there, and at night we arrived in Darwin, Australia, where it was already around forty degrees. We were all tired, but [coach Emmanuel] Scheffer decided that we would have a practice that same afternoon. At the end of the practice, most of the team were lying on the ground and only one or two of us were able to go on.

Yehoshua Feigenbaum (Israel): We went to Australia knowing we were a step away from the World Cup dream. We had goosebumps when we got there. We heard that the schools were closed back in Israel, and that everybody was hooked to their radio sets.

Zvi Rosen (Israel): It was a tough game, and the Australians felt that they were much better. How do I know that? They said they had already reserved the stadium in Australia for a third [tiebreaker] leg. They were sure they would beat us and advance.

Yehoshua Feigenbaum (Israel): The game was like a world war. We weren't worried when we conceded, we knew the game was already over. Bottom line? We let them score. At least 40,000 people were waiting for us outside. If we had won, they would've killed us. So we let them score an equaliser and left like heroes.

Israel had defeated Egypt in the Six-Day War of 1967, and three years later were still battling a coalition of Arab states in what was known as the War of Attrition. The conflicts meant football was relegated to the back pages of Israeli newspapers, even though they were making history. Their high-altitude training started in Ethiopia and continued in Colorado. They were greeted in Mexico City by a large contingent of fans from the Jewish community but because coach Scheffer did not want their rivals to see them playing before the big kick-off, he eschewed better-known opponents in favour of games against local Jewish sides and a factory team from the nearby city of Toluca. The draw, which pitted them against Italy, Sweden and Uruguay, did them no favours.

Yehoshua Feigenbaum (Israel): It wasn't a group of death, it was a group of hell. The newspapers predicted that we were going to lose big time. Some even said that with this type of draw we might as well not show up at all.

Mordechai Spiegler (Israel): Scheffer's ability was to turn us from a group of talented guys to a professional team, even though we weren't really pros yet. One of us was an Egged [bus company] member, one was a firefighter, another one had odd jobs. We just got together and practised.

Shmuel Rosenthal (Israel): The qualification to Mexico didn't start in Australia, it started in the youth national team. He [Scheffer] introduced professionalism. Before he arrived, we used to practise twice a week. He came and said we're going to practise three times a day. That was a big surprise for us.

Mordechai Spiegler (Israel): He knew how to take the best out of us for the good of the national team; whoever didn't know how to connect to his perception, his demands, just wasn't there.

Like many teams, group rivals Sweden had visited Mexico earlier in the year to get acquainted with the conditions but their return for the main event was less pleasing. The Swedes had been late in choosing their base near Toluca, just west of Mexico City, and they paid a price.

Ronnie Hellström (Sweden): We played two friendlies in Mexico City and Puebla in February. It gave us a chance to get a feel of the pitches and what it was like playing at altitudes like those. We stayed at a damn nice hotel in Mexico City, with swimming pools and the works. So we thought we'd be staying there during the World Cup, but it turned out the Italians had beaten us to it. So instead we were put up in Toluca, in what was actually an old people's home. I don't think our FA had done much research when it came to the matter of accommodation. Had we known, we would have objected. All we could do there was sleep, and we had to be driven elsewhere in a bus for all our meals and for training. We died a hotel death there. It was awful. Mexico was hot even in February, and we trained at low and high altitudes. We really had to learn to drink properly. I lost some kilos in training. It was different from what we were used to. We'd mostly played in Europe. With Hammarby we'd been once to Tunisia in 1969 or 1970. We played 0–0 at the Azteca and won 1–0 in Puebla. All in all, it was great there, particularly in Mexico City. Personally, I went on that Mexico trip in great shape. I'd spent a month in December to January at Chelsea, training with Peter Bonetti. It was fabulous to get to train with pros like him and Peter Osgood and David Webb. I'd gone with my [goalkeeping] coach at Hammarby, Sven Lindberg. Another goalkeeper friend from Sweden, Rolf Marinus, who played for Sirius, spent the same month training with Arsenal. We'd train once a day and then meet up at the pub. [Chelsea manager] Dave Sexton also brought us along to watch lots of matches in the London area.

Tommy Svensson (Sweden): Of course, we were very happy to have got the better of France, who were the clear group favourites in qualifying. Only one team from the group made it to the World Cup, so it was a lot more difficult back then. I remember feeling thrilled when we sealed qualification at old Råsunda. It was to be the first World Cup for Sweden since 1958. The world of football had made great strides since then, and we knew we'd been drawn in a tough group. Italy were huge favourites. We thought beforehand that we'd fight it out with Uruguay for second place. Israel was a team we thought we'd beat. But I don't think any of us saw us advancing beyond a quarter-final.

Ronnie Hellström (Sweden): At the World Cup we saw the opening match, Mexico–Russia, at the Azteca. It was massive of course, with 110,000 people there. Then we went back to our digs in Toluca. There wasn't much there. What we did have, in a room we used as our common area, was a dentist's chair. I guess it was used for checking the old people's teeth before our squad checked into the compound. It felt bizarre and added to the irritation of having to stay at such a place. Only once during the entire Toluca stay did we go into Mexico City for dinner. Otherwise we'd spend twenty minutes every day going to a restaurant. We spent a lot of time in the bus, with long trips to training. It was one of those old things you see in films, that would normally be carrying baskets full of live chickens and stuff on the roof. We had a narrow escape once when driving over a railway crossing. The driver only just made it over before the train rattled past, with its horn blaring. Man! That was close! We talked about nothing else the rest of that day. I don't think the press were with us then, because it didn't make the news.

We got to see more of the country in February than during the World Cup, when we just ate and trained. One thing I can say is that the Mexican people were thrilled to be hosting the World Cup. It wasn't like Argentina 1978, when people were terrified to speak their minds.

West Germany lost Günter Netzer to injury but convinced the thirty-three-year-old Uwe Seeler, who had played just four international matches in 1967 and 1968, to play in one last competition, his fourth. Seeler would end the tournament having appeared in twenty-one matches in World Cup finals, a mark bettered by only three players since. The German FA, as was so often the case, had prepared for every eventuality and unlike the Swedes the players had no complaints about their headquarters, even if they were remote.

Uwe Seeler (West Germany): The phone rang amazingly often. Sometimes it was Helmut Schön, sometimes Sepp

Herberger. They enquired about my well-being, the dog, Ilka and the children. I was also amazed that I was invited to every international match as a guest of honour. However, I didn't give in when Willi Schulz, Franz Beckenbauer, Netzer or Overath smiled at me, as if they wanted to say: 'Well, fatty, isn't it boring without international matches?' 'Very well,' I explained, 'I'm back for the World Cup and the preparation. But after that it's definitely done.'

Sepp Maier (West Germany): The team had a dream base in the middle of the Mexican desert, almost 2,000 metres above sea level and very close to León, where we played our games. You might think that there's not a lot of fun to be had in the desert. Wrong. It was a little paradise, an oasis of calm, exactly what we needed to prepare for the finals without any distractions.

Berti Vogts (West Germany): Germany, as always, was the leader as far as injuries were concerned. We had good doctors with us, good masseurs, we had at that time already two doctors and two masseurs, so Germany was very well prepared.

On the field, however, the Germans had failed to impress. Helmut Schön's team qualified thanks only to a 3–2 win in their last game against Scotland and their warm-up games against Spain, Romania, the Republic of Ireland and Yugoslavia brought two slender wins, a draw and a 2–0 loss to Spain, who hadn't come close to qualifying for the finals.

Uwe Seeler (West Germany): We attacked together in the last game qualifier against Scotland, winning 3–2. Four test games followed. Against Spain, 0–2, Romania, 1–1, Ireland, 2–1 and Yugoslavia, 1–0.

Berti Vogts (West Germany): One thing we had in mind was that we had to qualify for the World Cup in 1970 in Mexico. And we managed that successfully. What was unclear was how things would go in Mexico after that.

Wolfgang Overath (West Germany): Before we flew to Mexico, we still had three games on our schedule. But none of the three games went as national coach Schön had wished. A Bundesliga season that had been squeezed over the past few weeks had cost us a lot of strength. The football calendar had collapsed due to an extremely harsh winter, and the Bundesliga clubs – and therefore the players heading to Mexico – had to do a lot of hard work. We feared that this could come back to haunt us in Mexico. On the outside, we seemed to be optimists, but inside we expected a let-down. 'Just don't get knocked out in the preliminary round,' we told ourselves. We couldn't – and didn't – want to think any further than that.

Another one of the favourites were Italy, who were unbeaten in fourteen games stretching back to April 1968. But they too lost a key player in Pietro Anastasi, the man whose goal helped them win the final of the 1968 European Championship. The selection process was handled poorly and there was more uncertainty in the squad than there should have been for a team at the height of its powers.

Sandro Mazzola (Italy): We hadn't done well in a friendly before our opening match. We didn't know what it meant to play above 2,000 metres. After one move, you quickly got tired. You had to rest, but when you did that your opponent took advantage. We were used to playing the Italian way: defence and then counter-attack. But there, at that altitude, we couldn't play our way. We were very aware of this, how difficult it made things. In that friendly the starting team were losing 2–0 at half-time. Then, the coach, Valcareggi, changed the team to include some of those who weren't going to start in the World Cup opener. And among those who weren't going to play were many Inter players who had played in Mexico before on tour and so knew how to play at that altitude. Short runs, quick passes. So, in short, we came back to win the friendly 3–2 and Valcareggi had to alter his line-up for the first game.

Angelo Domenghini (Italy): Pietro Anastasi had had appendicitis. We found out on the morning of our departure for Mexico. Giovanni Lodetti was also on the plane with us; he was one of the twenty-two. When we arrived in Mexico, Roberto Boninsegna and Pierino Prati joined us instead of Anastasi, who was not very well. So, we became twenty-three. Then they decided to tell Giovanni Lodetti that he was no longer part of the squad. He had been very ill and we were all sorry for him. In my opinion this was a wrong thing, it shouldn't have happened. It was something that should have been decided in Italy before leaving. And then Pierino Prati never played a game. He was injured and they called him up anyway.

In addition to Brazil, only two other South American teams qualified, with Argentina missing out to Peru and failing to make the finals for the first time since 1954. Uruguay qualified unbeaten from a group that contained Chile and Ecuador and they did so without conceding a goal. But the Uruguayans looked vulnerable. They had faced European opposition only once in the previous four years and they had injury problems. Star striker Pedro Rocha, who picked up an injury on the eve of the competition, would last only the first thirteen minutes of the opening game. Moreover, coach Juan Hohberg had the task of ensuring the long-standing rivalry between the Peñarol and Nacional players was channelled towards a common goal.

Roberto Matosas (Uruguay): Uruguay's centre forwards in the 1970 World Cup were Sergio Silva, Zubía and the boy Bareño, a left winger. There was no great Uruguayan striker playing for Peñarol or Nacional. Nacional had the Argentine Luis Artime and Peñarol had Alberto Spencer [of Ecuador]. The entire [Uruguayan] team were players from Peñarol and Nacional, but neither Nacional nor Peñarol had a Uruguayan centre forward that year. Fortunately, coach Hohberg improvised Espárrago as a slightly withdrawn centre forward, giving us a fourth midfielder and that way we were able to pose an attacking threat. But the hope that we might have had for winning the championship was not the same after Rocha withdrew. Not only because of the way we played but because he was a goalscorer. Uruguay were very safe in defence, but we lacked strikers. Luis Alberto Cubilla was great, Espárrago played extraordinarily well as a deep-lying striker, and Cascarilla Morales did as well but it wasn't the same.

Ildo Maneiro (Uruguay): In the qualifying rounds, Hohberg had Héctor 'Lito' Silva, Sergio Silva and 'Pirincho' Pérez as forwards, but didn't consider them for the World Cup. If we had, for example, Luis Suárez, we would have been in with a real chance of winning the title.

Roberto Matosas (Uruguay): The coexistence was fantastic because in that previous month and during the World Cup itself the Peñarol players and the Nacional players were put together to share a room. That way we made friends and there was never animosity or cliques. I had to share a room with Juan Mujica, and we made a great friendship that lasted through time; the coaching staff chose the companions for each of the rooms. I remember in the morning I would drink mate with Luis Ubiña and sometimes [Ladislao] Mazurkiewicz would join. That is to say, between us there was nothing wrong, the only thing that interested us was the performance of the team. The expectations of both the Uruguayan fans and the Uruguayan press were positive, although not excessive. But yes, everyone was aware that we had managed to put together a good squad with quality footballers.

None of the preparations were as bizarre as Bulgaria's. For some inexplicable reason, they did their altitude training in the snow-capped mountains around Rila, just south of the capital Sofia.

Dimitar Penev (Bulgaria): With Mexico as host country and its altitude in mind, a decision was taken that our team would prepare for the tournament in the mountain sports base Belmeken, which is located around 2,000 metres above sea level in the mountain of Rila, Bulgaria. We have to give some context to the situation we were finding ourselves in – back then the Communist Party used to rule the country and it was the party that decided to be in charge of our team's World Cup preparations. But these guys committed one grave mistake – they didn't take into account the fact that although the altitude of Belmeken and that of the Mexican city of León where we later played our World Cup group stage games might have been similar, one couldn't say the same about the temperature levels. In the Bulgarian mountain it was freezing cold, while in Mexico we had to play in the scorching sun and deal with the humidity factor. That crucial difference was about to play a huge role in our performance at that World Cup. In Belmeken there was snow, and as part of our World Cup preparations we had to do some mountain hiking using ski equipment. Half of our team, though, didn't ski and that's why we just walked in the snow. The rest of the guys, meanwhile, were good at skiing and were using it as a faster way to complete the sessions. One of our teammates, Aleksandar Shalamanov, was not only a very skilful football player but he had actually participated in the 1960 Winter Olympics in the US. So I guess he had some proper fun in Belmeken.

As if that were not mad enough, the Communist Party apparatchiks leading the squad in the Mexican heat decided it would be a good idea to limit the players' water supply.

Dimitar Penev (Bulgaria): Once in Mexico, we ended up suffering from total dehydration. For some strange and absolutely inexplicable reason, we were denied free access to water. We were given a 0.2-litre cup of water each for breakfast, then another one of that same size for lunch and then a third one while having our dinner. Meanwhile, we were training in the burning sun and we were so thirsty! We needed to drink water so badly . . . At one point we started hiding from the officials and secretly going to the local shops to buy some water. There were times when we were hiding the bottles in the bushes in the courtyard of our training camp to drink from them secretly. Or because the water from the hotel sinks was too hot to drink directly, we used to pour it into some bottles and then leave these outside as the temperatures at night dropped significantly and the water cooled. Even the doctor, who was in charge of the medical team, used to buy us some water. You see, the orders to restrict our water supply were coming from above and the poor guy couldn't do anything about that. Deep down we knew that these training methods would fail our team but we were helpless. Soon we ran out of all the energy we had. It's an absolutely ridiculous situation – you're trying to make your body do something but it just ignores the commands from your brain. We were knackered.

The African nations boycotted the 1966 tournament in England in protest at not being given even one automatic berth at the finals.

FIFA listened and Morocco won through to the finals in Mexico via a qualifying tournament that featured ten African rivals. They successfully navigated three stages of the process to become not just the first automatic qualifier from the region but the first African side to participate in the World Cup since Egypt in 1934.

Allal Ben Kassou (Morocco): It was a great feeling because it was the first time Morocco had qualified for the World Cup. And in order to represent Africa and the Arab nations, we had played all the other African teams to do it. It was an amazing feeling, the fans were happy and full of enthusiasm and so were the players. To qualify for your first World Cup was a strange feeling but it was wonderful as well.

Many of the delegations were worried about crime and security. Each group was given their own security detail and Brazil were one of the most heavily guarded. Pelé was reportedly a target of Venezuelan guerrillas and when the German ambassador was seized by leftists in Rio just days after the World Cup started, security was beefed up even further. The conflict in the Middle East was ongoing, parts of Latin America were simmering, and Israel's presence was an additional factor. Mexican authorities, moreover, were not known for their light touch. Soldiers opened fire on unarmed student demonstrators just days before the Olympic Games opened there in 1968, killing possibly hundreds of people. There was tension in the air.

Martin Peters (England): I was often reminded that a potentially explosive situation could be just around the corner. Like every other national team, we were given a twenty-four-hour guard by armed agents of the Mexican government, or the Secret Service, not that they were particularly secret. Some stuck out like a hippie at the skinhead convention and it was a laugh, really, to see some of them lounging around our hotel trying to look inconspicuous and merge into the affluent background. They were present because the government took seriously that attempts might be made to kidnap star players. Two police cars stood by with every team when they went training and when it was our turn we didn't mind. It was a bit of a lark and we were in such a buoyant mood that nobody seriously thought that any of us would be held to ransom. It didn't seem quite as funny when Alf [Ramsey] called us together and said that we were not to go out alone. It was then the seriousness of the situation reached us. I cannot remember Alf's exact words, but they went something like this: 'You are all valuable property. Go out in groups and lock your doors at night.' I also read a statement by a British embassy official in one of the newspapers flown out to us. He was quoted as saying: 'Since the killing of the German ambassador in Guatemala and of an Israeli secretary in Paraguay, the Mexican Security Police have been alert to the danger of kidnapping. It is a possibility, and we must not take chances. It may not be a serious threat, but we have to take notice of it.' Our security guard was trebled. I must say I became more tolerant when things were explained more fully to me. Most important was the Mexican government's policy of giving asylum to political refugees from the rest of Latin America. Obviously, this meant exile groups with a chip on their shoulder could regard Mexico as a base where they waited for an opportunity to strike back. I don't want to make too much of this, but it happened. The tension was there and I sensed it strongly.

Another issue that worried many of the teams was the food. Mexico, of course, was famous for its 'Montezuma's revenge', the sickness and diarrhoea that sometimes beset visitors unaccustomed to the local cuisine. Some teams, including England, tried to get round it by bringing their own food and water. That annoyed the locals and it was not always a successful strategy as they would find out to their cost. Others took a more basic approach, which was every bit as questionable, as one Swedish official discovered.

Ronnie Hellström (Sweden): One funny incident took place when we were there in February. We'd been warned that we might easily pick up stomach bugs in Mexico. In those days, it wasn't considered safe to put ice cubes in your drinks because of the contaminated water. So one of our team doctors, Hans Lewerentz, he offered to try out the salad at the buffet, while telling the rest of us to stay off it until he gave us clearance. And boy, did he get sick! He definitely took one for the team!

The big concern for most of the competing teams was the altitude. All the stadiums were at least a mile above sea level. Those in Mexico City, Puebla and Toluca were higher than 2,000 metres, and the Estadio Nemesio Díez in Toluca was a breathtaking 2,660 metres high. The altitude made it difficult to recover after sprints and the players' energy levels sapped much faster than they did at sea level. Almost all the visitors worried about whether they would be able to perform to the best of their abilities.

Dimitar Penev (Bulgaria): We, the players, had no say in the way we were preparing for the 1970 World Cup in Mexico. The ruling party as well as some 'specialists' wouldn't let anyone express their opinion. We've already mentioned the high altitude that was expecting us in Mexico – in order to prepare for what was about to come, we were inhaling some oxygen from a giant balloon – its size was around ten metres by six metres – through a mouthpiece. That didn't help us too much either. By the time the 1970 World Cup in Mexico kicked off, we had already been in awful shape because of the mistaken preparations. I remember it was so hot, we were totally dehydrated, we didn't have any energy left. Some players on our team had already lost 4–5kg, while there were some extreme cases, with a few guys having lost even up to 10kg! Imagine that! CSKA Sofia striker Dimitar Marashliev was one of the guys who suffered the most. I remember some media outlets called him a 'scraggy cow' or something similar.

Ronnie Hellström (Sweden): One of the main intentions about going to Mexico in February was to get accustomed to playing at higher altitudes. Later on, in the spring, we did tests in a pressure chamber in Stockholm. They put us on bicycles to see how we'd cope with performing under strain at different altitudes. It was extremely tough. We were made to wear masks that were connected through a tube to a kind of tank. That was to measure our lung capacity, how many litres we could manage. Being an elite athlete, I did well. Goalkeepers require a different kind of stamina. We need to be able to jump up and down time and time again. When it came to running, perhaps the outfield players were stronger. We felt we were good.

Wolfgang Overath (West Germany): The memories fade away a bit but the one thing that I can still remember precisely is that we all were terribly afraid that we wouldn't be able to play football at all. There was this statement before the World Cup among the players that our bodies would not be able to take it all. We were all excited for the first training days, and they were horrible. So in the first three training sessions you had the feeling you could run some metres and then you could not run any more. This I can still remember very well.

Berti Vogts (West Germany): Because of the altitude – we played in León over 2,200 metres high – we went to Mexico four weeks before our first game to get used to the altitude. And it was very difficult for us. We didn't have any games, just training, and because of the altitude we had to start very carefully. It was our biggest challenge. We didn't occupy ourselves analysing the competitors, but we had a big complex about the altitude. I was the youngest player in the team and I didn't know how difficult it was to run forty, fifty metres without a break and to recover after that. We were not aware of that. Only three weeks before the first game, it got better. But it was our biggest challenge, the altitude.

Sandro Mazzola (Italy): We are always confident when we start a World Cup, even though we knew there were strong teams. Of course, we were playing in a new environment. We also ate different foods, even though we Italians took our own food as usual. Walking at those altitudes was also different. Therefore, we were worried because we were aware of all the difficulties that we would face.

Roberto Matosas (Uruguay): Training in Montevideo, Professor [trainer] Langlade had asked each of us to answer a set of written questions and one of them was if we were willing to spend a month before the World Cup in Mexico with the national team. We weren't used to that and most of us said we could because we all wanted to play in the World Cup finals. I think physical preparation was key because we would have suffered a lot more from the altitude if we had not prepared. Doctors said that when playing at altitude one must arrive a day early or spend a month preparing; Hohberg and Langlade decided to prepare for a month. I always say that this fourth place was largely due to the fact that we spent a month before the World Cup playing preliminary matches in Bogotá and Quito to adapt to the challenge.

Tommy Svensson (Sweden): It was different. Personally, I had no problems with the heat and never have had. But the altitude . . . Toluca lies at 2,700 metres and that was tough. One found oneself out of breath sooner, and it took longer to recover. More recovery time was needed also after training and matches. But conditions were the same for the other teams, nothing unfair about it.

Ronnie Hellström (Sweden): I'd never experienced anything like it. The other three teams were more used to the heat than us, but during the matches I don't think it mattered. What was special in Mexico was the grass; it was coarser than the kind we were used to. The ball wouldn't roll as fast along the ground as we were used to. Balls coming through the air, I don't think they travelled any faster because of the thin air.

Other teams worried more about the sun. Every one of the thirty-two games kicked off at either noon or 4.00 p.m. The early games were well timed for viewers in Europe but they were hell for players unused to such heat. The temperature was frequently in the nineties and when it rained, or threatened to rain, the conditions could also be unbearably muggy.

Berti Vogts (West Germany): Yeah, the heat. Because of the TV, we had to play at 12.00 p.m.; it was co-ordinated that it was 7.00 p.m. in Germany, and therefore we had to play in this extreme heat. I think that nowadays that would not have been allowed. I think the clubs, the countries would not tolerate that. But at that time, everything was different, we had to play at 12.00 p.m. and I must admit it was unpleasantly hot.

Wilfried Van Moer (Belgium): The altitude was quite all right, but the heat – it was thirty-five degrees. We had to play against

Mexico at 12.00 in the afternoon in the capital. The ground held 105,000 people, with a sort of huge dome around it. It was an oven. Unbelievable! All right, we were young and we could stand it, but it was impossible! It really, really was difficult. South American teams were used to playing in those temperatures, but that wasn't the case for us at all.

Allan Clarke (England): We were on twelve salt tablets a day. It's a hot climate, and in the hotel we had air conditioning but when you walked out the heat just really hit you. So the heat, just walking in it was very tiring.

Curiously, some of the Soviets – a team with a reputation for their supreme physical fitness – said they were more concerned about their own players than their opponents or the geographical or climatological conditions. Some even joked about seeking refuge from the sun in the shade of the public address systems that hung from steel cables high above the centre circle.

Anatoly Byshovets (USSR): The altitude was not much of an issue; I did not really feel any different when it comes to my functionality. And we did not put any particular emphasis on that in our training prior to the World Cup. Heat is a totally different matter though – because it was over forty degrees in the sun there, and the only shade out on the pitch was from the public address system [suspended above the pitch]. There wasn't anything particular or special we did in the run-up to the tournament, when it comes to physical training. However, we took extra caution when playing games in the Soviet league. Back in the day, we did not have yellow cards in football. So, for strikers it was particularly dangerous – they could be fouled and injured, while defenders knew there was a degree of impunity for them. Besides, zonal marking was not really a thing then – players were marked man to man, and sometimes with extra rigour. So there was a big danger for strikers to get injured in those games – and in some international friendlies too. I was so fixated on getting to that World Cup, so whenever I played in the league that year, I had a bit of a psychological block. I couldn't afford to get injured, so I took it easier. Not that I'm saying I was not motivated enough – of course I tried my best on the pitch. But I still worked very hard on avoiding injuries.

Preparations for the 1970 World Cup were tough. Lots of flights and friendlies all over the world, gruelling schedule. But it also has to do with the personal aspect – because psychology is key too. Having played so many friendlies, I felt I was beginning to burn out – not physically, but psychologically. Almost as if I started losing the hunger for the game. So I had to speak to the coach. Just ten days before the World Cup we were due to have our final friendly, and I came to Kachalin, one of the best coaches we've ever had – he won the Olympic gold in 1956 and the Euros in 1960 – and told him that I was burning out psychologically. So he agreed, took me off that game and put me on an individual training scheme. I persuaded him that this would give me a fresher hunger for the ball, which I started to lose by playing so many friendlies.

The Brazilian players met up in February to prepare for their first game in June. The CBD, the forerunner to the CBF, had arranged friendly matches in Mexico in 1968 to get the lie of the land and they came back knowing that conditioning and stamina would be absolutely vital if they were to stand a chance of winning. They drew up a training schedule that was so thorough and so effective – it was partly based around NASA's aerobic tests for astronauts – that their planning was singled out by FIFA in their technical report issued at the end of the competition.

Carlos Alberto (Brazil): It's important to remember, because people rarely mention this, that you win the World Cup with detailed preparation. Four years before, Brazil had been surprised by European football, with the so-called *futebol força*. It was what they called power football, that had at its root kicking and playing rough. Who could forget that guy with no teeth, Stiles, the Englishman who frightened everyone with his violence? The CBD did studies, they planned, and they told us on the day we met up, 'If you follow what we've planned out for you in terms of physical preparation then you'll at least get to the World Cup final. Physically, we need to be very well prepared, first because of the altitude and second because of the way the Europeans play today.' And we followed every one of their orders.

So we knew that if we were going to get something from the 1970 World Cup, if we wanted to have a good tournament and reach the final, we had to be very well prepared physically. So we worked hard on the physical side of things, and the CBD took us to high altitude a month before the tournament started so we could acclimatise. It was very well done and it worked. But there is no point in being physically fit if you don't have skill. The results were clear in every game. We got better in every match. That has a big influence on your head: we knew that if we were good physically, we had the technical ability to dominate our opponents.

We left here forty days before the start of the World Cup, we spent a few days in Guadalajara, not many, and then we went to Guanajuato and Irapuato, each one higher than the last. So when we got back to Guadalajara we spent ten, twelve, fifteen days there to play the three group games and after that the quarter- and semi-final. And we had the lungs. We were in great shape. I remember we had days off, and we always got a day off after the game. We played on a Wednesday, we went back to the concentração and the next day after lunch we were free to do what we wanted until night-time. And most of us didn't leave. 'Ah, I don't want a day off, I'll just relax here, I'll get a massage, let's win this and then I've got the rest of my life to enjoy myself.' [Laughs]

Tostão (Brazil): Everyone was freaked out because we had a kind of preparation that no one had experienced before at their clubs or at the national side. And there was time for it; we were there for almost four months, three and a half months training, so it was a long time. We had time. So it was a technological revolution in football that influenced the rest of the world.

Mario Zagallo (Brazil coach): We had a huge advantage in our physical preparation. We had trained for twenty-one days at altitude – in those days there was time for this type of preparation. We did twenty-one days because we were aware that scientifically this would stay in the organism of the players. We then went down to Guadalajara, where we played all our games until the final, but we knew that if we made it to the final then the altitude preparation was still inside the players. No one else had done it. So Brazil had prepared for altitude, even though we only played one game there. Our physical preparation was excellent – we won most of our games in the second half.

Brazil flew out with the fans on their back after an unconvincing run of friendlies and there were more questions about their line-up than their qualifying form suggested. They won six out of six in the qualifiers in 1969 but had made big changes since. Full back Marco Antônio was replaced at the last minute by Everaldo, and Piazza, a central midfielder for Cruzeiro, dropped back to play what was for him an unfamiliar role in central defence alongside Brito. Zagallo dropped Edu, the teenage Santos winger who starred in the qualifiers, and changed Saldanha's 4-2-4 into a 4-3-3 with Gerson, Rivellino and twenty-year-old Clodoaldo in the middle of the park.

Rivellino (Brazil): We left the country with everyone thinking Brazil wouldn't even get through their group.

Zé Maria (Brazil): The beginning was a bit blurry. We had a few games here in Brazil, warm-ups, and the fans weren't very confident, even though we had had some good results. So our departure wasn't one when we had the full force of the fans behind us. We started to gain that strength when we got there, in the concentração. I think the time we spent together helped a lot and it brought a consistency to the group. We left here kind of fearful.

Piazza (Brazil): I played once [as a defender] for Cruzeiro against Atlético Mineiro. We were down to ten men and I filled in in the centre of defence. It also happened at the seleção by chance. The team had Fontana and Joel Camargo. When João Saldanha left and Zagallo came in he brought another central defender in with him and I kept playing as a holding midfielder. But I began to lose some space to Zé Carlos, who played with me at Cruzeiro and was an excellent player. So I was going to be surplus to requirements. Then at training one day, two defenders got injured and there was a spare holding midfielder. Zagallo asked me to drop back and I did. It was a risk, because if the central defenders came back I'd have been cut. The central defenders in those days had to be good technically to play the ball out of defence. But it was difficult because my scope was limited. At Cruzeiro, I had more freedom and I really came off the field with my shirt wringing with sweat. There were games in the World Cup when I picked up my shirt afterwards and it wasn't heavy, wet with sweat. I always thought I hadn't played well because I hadn't run.

Felix (Brazil): Zagallo moulded the team the way he wanted it to play. The majority were intelligent players – you took a Rivellino and wherever you put him he would play; you took a Paulo Cesar and wherever you put him he would play; you took Pelé and what more do you need to say?

Piazza (Brazil): We had five men who were decisive so us defenders didn't need to go on the attack. Our team was extraordinary because we knew how to defend and how to attack. Everyone knew how to play football, down to how many scored goals. Except for Piazza, Brito, Everaldo and Felix, everyone scored goals.

The big worry, though, concerned Tostão. The Cruzeiro player suffered from a detached retina after a ball hit him in the face in September 1969 and after undergoing surgery in Houston he spent months unable to run or tackle, much less head a ball. Tostão was Brazil's top scorer in the qualifying rounds but there were questions over whether he would recover in time. Even if he did, many people, including Zagallo, wondered whether a man who played attacking midfielder for his club could play as a striker in front of Pelé. But Tostão's eye healed and he impressed the coach in that new role in friendlies on the eve of the tournament.

Pelé (Brazil): I had a particular concern in this World Cup. It was about Tostão. When we spoke to Tostão we could see that he was worried about the eye that had been operated on. He didn't head the ball in training and we were worried. It shocked us all. I was afraid that he would be worried during the games like he was in training. Thankfully he lost his inhibitions and I can tell you, it was easy to play with Tostão. He has quick reflexes as well as great ball control. He knows how to position himself, or rather, how to play without the ball at his feet. He always looked for the spaces in the opposing defence. The defenders would follow him, making it easier for me and the other players to come through the middle. Lots of our goals were created by Tostão.

Tostão (Brazil): For months I was totally sidelined, reading, resting. The restrictions diminished over time. I couldn't travel by car because it could shake, I couldn't use this or that, I couldn't run. So it was a difficult time, and there was a lot of uncertainty. And to make it worse, ten or fifteen days before the World Cup started, Zagallo changed his mind about having me start. He said he wanted Dario and Roberto. Then he saw that they weren't players who could play alongside Pelé and Gerson and he stuck me in a different position from where I played for Cruzeiro. I remember it even today, the doubts were killing him and we had a training match against a Mexican team but I played alongside Pelé and Gerson. We played this game and everyone was over the moon. So the game ended and Zagallo came up to me with a big smile and said, 'You're going to play.' [Laughs]. And a few days after that, when I was at my best, to complicate matters and make them more dramatic, a haemorrhage appeared in my eye; it was a red conjunctivitis, just like a blood clot. The doctor from Houston came down to examine me at the concentração. We were in Guanajuato, which was a long way from Mexico City, and he spent all day driving up in his car. He examined me and said, 'No, it's just conjunctivitis. The internal surgery' – the retina – 'is intact, it's cured and it's back to normal so there's no problem.' But even then there was a big kerfuffle, the team doctor, the backroom staff, the coach, all of them, they had a meeting: 'Do you think we can trust the word of the doctor, it looks . . . and the World Cup is about to start . . .' So there was a big drama.

Mario Zagallo (Brazil coach): Then there was Tostão. That was a change that was made along the way. First, there was the problem with his retina. Second, he played in the same position as Pelé, coming from behind, so normally I would have him on the bench. We had lots of players in that position.

Tostão (Brazil): Young people who watch tapes of the seleção in the 1970 World Cup see me as a centre forward who played further forward than Pelé. The truth is I never played that way with Cruzeiro. In actual fact, that was an adaptation because I couldn't play in Pelé's position. I would have had to be his reserve and so I said, 'No, in order not to be his reserve I am going to adapt my game.' So I learned a new role. But my real position at Cruzeiro was as an attacking midfielder. We agreed that I would play behind the opposing back four. That means I sacrificed myself individually to play close to the libero so he would have to mark me. For example, with the goals Brazil scored the libero should have provided cover but he didn't because he was marking me.

Felix (Brazil): For me, Tostão was tactically the best player in the team. Tostão kept two players occupied and that left Pelé free to do what he wanted, the best player in the world, that way he does things, so it was all over, man!

Brazil, of course, had already seen big changes behind the scenes in the first half of 1970. Coach João Saldanha was volatile, outspoken and a card-carrying Communist and he butted heads with the right-wing leaders and was replaced by Mario Zagallo, the winger-cum-midfielder who had played alongside Pelé in the triumphant 1958 and 1962 teams. Much onus was put on Saldanha's comment that if the military didn't try and pick his team he wouldn't get involved with choosing members of the cabinet, but it was not the main factor in his dismissal. The dictators clearly didn't want Saldanha winning the title and thus having a platform on which to criticise them. But he had become increasingly erratic and they wanted someone calmer and more pliable as coach. In spite of that decision, the Brazilian players, most of whom cared little about politics, swore that even though most of those on the backroom staff were military men, there was no political interference.

Gerson (Brazil): In 1970 we had the problem of the dictatorship and we knew what was going on but nobody put the squeeze on us, nobody went in hard. We had a seleção, we had to train, to play, and we got all the help we needed, with no problems at all in sporting terms. Naturally we knew what was happening and so you ask, 'Why didn't you walk out?' We didn't walk out because we were all representing the country in a competition that demanded commitment. If it wasn't a World Cup maybe we would have given it all up, but we went to do what we had to do, we went there and we won and the problem was over and done with. We had no problems at all when it came to pressures or any of that, we got all the guarantees we needed. We were against a lot of things, right? But we were in that context of we had to do our bit, which was sport and we did that.

Carlos Alberto (Brazil): At no moment did we hear anyone say anything, and if I had I'd tell you, no problem at all. They said the government wanted to interfere in the seleção, but we never saw anyone inside the concentração wanting to interfere or sticking their oar in. No, we did our job, we knew how important professionally it was for us to win that World Cup. For Pelé it was the last, and for Brito, Gerson, Piazza, Tostão, for the majority of the players it was their last opportunity to play a World Cup and win. And we knew we had the team to do it. We knew we had the squad to win and we knew from the planning, and work set out by the backroom staff, especially the physical preparations. We were confident that if we followed their instructions we would have all it takes to win the World Cup.

Gerson (Brazil): I am going to tell you with the utmost sincerity, if there had been pressure then we wouldn't have played. There was no pressure, not from the military, not from the backroom staff, nothing. Our work in 1970 was just. [It was a case of] this is what we're going to do, this is how we are doing it, and that is what we did. There was no interference, political, party political, military political, nothing, nothing, nothing.

Holders England went to Ecuador and Colombia to do their high-altitude preparation but it was not the thin air that left them reeling. Instead, they were caught up in what was, at the time, one of the biggest scandals ever to hit English sport. After spending a couple of weeks in Mexico to begin the process of acclimatisation, England moved to the Colombian capital Bogotá, another high-altitude city. Both the A team and the B team would take on their Colombian counterparts before heading to neighbouring Ecuador for two more preparatory games against local opposition. From there, they were to return to Mexico, via a refuelling stop in Bogotá, arriving in the Mexican capital a week before the tournament kicked off.

Gordon Banks (England): From the moment I set eyes on it I didn't like Bogotá. I was appalled by the filth on the streets. At one point we passed a dead horse lying at the side of the road. Three days later when we returned to the airport, it was still there. To us, the place looked like a living hell. Alf Ramsey had warned us of the possible pitfalls of life in this city. Under no circumstances were we to eat anything that hadn't been prepared by the chef who had been appointed to cook for the England party. Alf told us to drink bottled water only, and to ensure that the bottle was opened in our presence so we could see that the contents hadn't been topped up with tap water. We were banned from going on our customary leg-stretching walks that were a favourite way of passing the time in a foreign city before a match.

Bobby Moore (England): From the airport we went by coach to the 800-room Tequendama Hotel, an impressive skyscraper building noted as one of the best hotels in South America.

Gordon Banks (England): We were warned of the perils of Bogotá subculture. To minimise the chances of getting into trouble, Alf told us to stay within the confines of the El Tequendama. Little did he know, there was plenty of trouble lying in wait for us behind the hotel's opulent facade.

Bobby Moore (England): It all started on Monday, 18 May, when we arrived in Bogotá from Mexico City where we had been based since leaving England two weeks earlier. After being shown to our rooms and having unpacked, most of the party went to explore the hotel, which had several shops both on the ground floor and underneath at street level. I was with Bobby Charlton when we looked into the window of the Green Fire jewellery shop, one of four inside the hotel, near the main reception desk. It was more of a kiosk than a shop for the inside was very small. We looked at some rings and left.

Bobby Charlton (England): I had the idea that I might buy a piece of jewellery for [my wife] Norma. I would have made a wider investigation of shopping possibilities if we hadn't been warned to be careful about leaving the hotel because there was so much random violence and thievery on the streets of Bogotá. We'd been advised that if we did go out onto pavements that were packed with pedlars, and, we were told, pickpockets, it should never be with fewer than three companions. I saw a very attractive necklace and asked the price, suspecting that, in such a big hotel in such a place, it would probably be out of my range. A girl shop assistant unlocked a cabinet to show me the necklace and then confirmed that, at around £6,000, it was way beyond my means. Bobby and I did a little more window-shopping, but it was mostly a matter of boggling at the price tags of the items in the window, and commenting, 'That ring is worth more than my house!' and 'Unbelievable!'

We drifted away, speculating on quite who could afford such prices and how they earned their money. It certainly wasn't by playing World Cup football. We didn't have anywhere to go, or anything to do, so we sat down on one of the sofas dotted about the lobby of the hotel. Suddenly, the shop assistant appeared. Speaking in a way that seemed strange and agitated, she asked Bobby to stand up, which he did with a mystified look on his face, and then started rummaging around in the cushions of the sofa. We were baffled, as the girls spoke in Spanish, but then a man, who we presumed was the manager of the shop, appeared and announced that a bracelet was missing. He too searched the sofa. Among all the emerald rings and necklaces I hadn't seen a bracelet, and my first thought was that this was some kind of joke. But there was little humour on the faces of our accusers, so I said, 'Hey, this is serious, get our manager, get the police, get whoever . . .'

Bobby Moore (England): To our amazement, we were then approached by one of the staff from the hotel and we were then returned to the jewellery shop. It was only then we learned of the missing bracelet. We offered to co-operate as far as possible and if necessary were willing to be searched. For some unknown reason this was not done. After talking with some of the staff of the shop the whole matter seemed to have been settled. We could only think there had been some kind of misunderstanding.

Bobby Charlton (England): All hell broke loose and suddenly everyone is saying that Bobby Moore had taken this thing. And I said, 'That's nonsense.'

Before long, however, it turned into an international incident. The shop owner was convinced Moore had stolen the bracelet and called the police. Officers were on the scene in minutes and England officials quickly moved to deal with a situation they had never in their wildest dreams imagined could ever happen to them.

Bobby Charlton (England): Bobby was taken away from the hotel by police while FA officials overcame their bemusement and started making calls to the British embassy.

Nobby Stiles (England): Bobby Charlton was shocked and there were tears, mostly of rage, pouring down his face when he told us what had happened.

Gordon Banks (England): Bobby Moore, a thief, and Bobby Charlton, his accomplice. He might as well have been told Mother Teresa had been arrested for cruelty to children, it was that outlandish and unbelievable.

Bobby Moore (England): The whole world seemed to have gone crazy that day. There I was being questioned by police, then by a judge about a missing bracelet with the implication being that I had stolen it. A bracelet I had not even seen, let alone stolen. The newspaper headlines blared out all over the world – 'Bobby Moore held as thief'. And this a week before the start of the World Cup in Mexico. It was incredible, too fantastic for words. You read sometimes about people being accused of something they have not done, mostly in crime fiction, but you never imagine it could happen to you.

After realising it wasn't a joke, the players veered between thinking it was a scam, designed to get hush money out of them, and a South American plot set up to disturb their preparations for defending the Jules Rimet title.

Martin Peters (England): The lads couldn't understand why anybody could have to do this to Mooro. It was hard to know what to think, but at times like this you naturally assume somebody is organising a dark, diabolical plot.

Gordon Banks (England): I have no doubt in my mind that Bobby was stitched up by someone out to disrupt our preparations for Mexico, or someone out to make monetary gain from involving him in a trumped-up charge.

Moore was released pending further enquiries and he played in England's 4–0 win over Colombia on 21 May and was allowed to travel to Ecuador for their warm-up matches there. That, England hoped, would be the end of the affair. Moore played well in England's victory over the host nation, a game that took place in front of 36,000 fans at 2,850 metres above sea level, the highest England had ever played at that point in their history.

Bobby Charlton (England): When he was allowed to fly on to Quito and take part in the 2–0 win over Ecuador, it seemed that the whole affair had lapsed into a swiftly passing farce. I was confident enough to buy a small and quite modestly priced piece of jewellery for Norma in a Quito shop, but not before making sure that I had a teammate with me. Optimism certainly seemed to be the prevailing mood when we returned to Bogotá for a stopover at the same hotel where the problem had first occurred.

With travel in the region difficult, the England squad were scheduled to fly to Mexico via Bogotá and Panama City. The Bogotá layover was a long one and rather than have the players sit around the airport all day, Sir Alf arranged to have a bus take them back to the El Tequendama Hotel where they could relax and watch a film before returning to the airport to catch a later flight to Mexico City.

Gordon Banks (England): Back at the hotel, Alf had arranged the film show for us in the TV lounge. I'll never forget that film. It was *Shenandoah*, starring James Stewart and Doug McClure, a 1965 saga about the American Civil War and how it affected one family in Virginia.

Bobby Moore (England): Then the nightmare started.

Gordon Banks (England): About halfway through the film, two suited Colombians came into the room for a quiet word with Bobby Moore, who left in their company. At the time, I never thought anything of this. In his role as captain of England, Bobby was often called away to give interviews to the local press, or meet visiting officials from the British embassy. Even when Bobby didn't come back, we still had no reason to think there was any cause for concern. My suspicions were still not aroused when we assembled at Bogotá airport for our connecting flight to Mexico City and I noticed that Bobby wasn't with us. I simply believed Bobby had agreed to do some interviews for South American TV companies and that he would follow us on a later flight.

Martin Peters (England): I was one of the first to realise that something was wrong because as we were about to leave Bogotá for Mexico City after playing matches against Colombia and Ecuador, I was asked to carry Mooro's gear onto the plane. I gathered that he was being held by the police, but I understood that he would be released quickly after making a statement. Mooro was told that, too.

Bobby Charlton (England): Once again Ramsey was outraged – he would later say that these were the worst days of his international career – but most of the rest of us believed that the nightmare would end that morning and Bobby would appear at the airport, imperturbable as ever, the sanest man in a crazy world. When Bobby was still absent at the airport, I said to Ramsey, 'Look, I want to help all I can.' I suggested I stay behind and reiterate my statement to the police that I was with Bobby at every moment in the jewellery shop and there was no way he could be guilty of this ridiculous charge. Quite brusquely, Alf said, 'You must get on that plane, Bobby; there's no way you're staying. We'll let the politicians and the diplomats settle this.'

The players didn't know it yet, but Moore had been placed under house arrest in Bogotá. The squad set off for Mexico ignorant of the situation's gravity until Sir Alf stood up in Panama, where they were refuelling, and made an unexpected announcement to both the players and the press, who were also unaware of what exactly was going on.

Gordon Banks (England): Alf took to his feet to address the players and the accompanying press corps. I found what he said completely unbelievable. Bobby Moore has been arrested in Bogotá accused of stealing a bracelet from the Green Fire jewellery shop. The accusation had been made by the manageress of the shop, Clara Padilla. Furthermore, Padilla alleged that Bobby Charlton had covered for Bobby Moore while he stole the item.

Gordon Banks (England): On hearing Alf's statement, the journalists flapped like chickens in a hen house with a fox in residence. They were now privy to the biggest and most sensational story of the World Cup but, such was the technology of the day, being en route to Mexico City, they had no means of contacting their editors back in London. As soon as we entered the airport building the press boys ran to the telephones, just like in a courtroom drama, when they scramble to file their reports of a sensational trial. The press found themselves in a cleft stick. Here they were, stuck in Panama en route to Mexico City when their editors wanted them back in Bogotá to cover the breaking news of Bobby Moore, no less, being accused of shoplifting. Some were told by their editors to hire a car to take them back, obviously unaware that the Colombian capital was some 2,000 miles away. By coincidence, many newspapers had assigned reporters to cover the RAC London to Mexico rally [which, can you believe it, Jimmy Greaves had entered], so several motor-racing correspondents suddenly and unexpectedly found themselves taken off the rally story and rerouted to Bogotá. When we eventually arrived in Mexico City the media were lying in ambush. The Bobby Moore story was now global news and a veritable army of TV, radio and press journalists jostled for position alongside photographers whose cameras flashed and whirred away at anyone and everyone.

Back in Bogotá, Moore had avoided jail and been placed under the care of a Colombian FA official, who had agreed to look after him while authorities investigated the case. He could not train and as the opening match of the tournament loomed closer he began to worry what he thought was a daft 'misunderstanding' might keep him out of the World Cup.

Bobby Moore (England): I was allowed to stay with Señor Alfonso Senior, a leading official of the Colombian Football Association, with two security guards for company. At first, I was not too worried as I felt it would all be sorted out in a day or two at most, and I would be able to rejoin the squad in Mexico. But as it dragged on into the Wednesday I became really concerned. Our first World Cup match was due on the following Tuesday, less than a week away. I was anxious in case it had any effect on the rest of the players as I realised my predicament was receiving worldwide publicity which could possibly be harmful. I had only the clothes I was wearing when I arrived and had been unable to do any training. It was hardly the ideal physical or mental preparation for a tough World Cup competition.

Moore's worry was legitimate but when officials investigated further the case unravelled. There was no hard evidence of any theft and a judge found no reason to keep Moore in custody. Casting further doubt on the veracity of the claims, Clara Padilla had reportedly disappeared to the United States. On Thursday, 28 May, Moore was released and allowed to fly to Mexico City and rejoin his teammates.

Bobby Moore (England): I appeared only briefly on the Thursday to be told I had permission to leave the country, if I declared my willingness to go to any Colombian consulate to give any further help I could. I agreed and at last I knew the nightmare was over. I was able to have a forty-five-minute training session at one of the local grounds before catching a plane to Mexico City.

Bobby Charlton (England): We were training in Mexico without him for a long period, but he was being well looked after we were told. And we were very pleased when he came back and was able to do a bit of training and fit in.

Gordon Banks (England): When Bobby Moore arrived at our hotel, the entire England squad lined up outside the entrance to applaud him. He hadn't had a change of clothing for nearly a week, yet he looked as smart as if he were stepping out of a tailor's shop after a complete makeover. His blazer, shirt and trousers were completely unruffled, as was the man himself.

Alan Ball (England): He had missed five days of training, but looked as though not even five minutes had been taken out of his schedule.

Bobby Charlton (England): And he turned out to be probably the best defender in the World Cup. It certainly didn't do Bobby Moore any harm.

Nobby Stiles (England): Under Bobby Moore's leadership, we were strong enough to withstand the effects of a bit of noise, and this was confirmed when he returned to the team after Alf had met him with an embrace at the airport in Mexico City. 'Forget about what happened in Bogotá,' said Mooro. 'I'm fine and if we all stick together, this can make us stronger.'

Bobby Moore (England): Those four days I spent in Bogotá were a nightmare, probably the worst I have ever known. To be stranded in a strange country under house arrest, questioned about an alleged crime of which I was completely innocent while the rest of the English party had moved on back to Mexico was all so unreal yet frighteningly fact.

Bobby Charlton (England): The stigma was dreadful that it left on him. It was absolute rubbish, the whole thing. I don't know who perpetrated it or whatever but it was a nonsense. But there again it is something that affected the World Cup. Because it was the World Cup it was world headlines and a problem that we could have done without but as it turns out it didn't do Bobby Moore any harm. He was strong enough and big enough to forget it and put it behind him, which he did, fortunately. But it has made people very careful now when they prepare for a World Cup that they keep themselves isolated so that they don't give anybody the opportunity to do similar things again.

THE GROUP STAGES

TWO

GROUP 1

31 May	Mexico City	Mexico	0–0	Soviet Union
3 June	Mexico City	Belgium	3–0	El Salvador
6 June	Mexico City	Soviet Union	4–1	Belgium
7 June	Mexico City	Mexico	4–0	El Salvador
10 June	Mexico City	El Salvador	0–2	Soviet Union
11 June	Mexico City	Belgium	0–1	Mexico

The opening match of the tournament kicked off at high noon on the last day of May. A capacity crowd of more than 100,000 people turned out to see the host nation open their campaign against the Soviet Union. The teams had played a friendly 0–0 draw at the same stadium just three months previously and the opener ended the same way. It was a stolid encounter as both teams struggled with the heat, the pressure, and a whistle-happy referee. But before the game there was gamesmanship . . .

Evgeny Lovchev (USSR): We were supposed to go out onto the pitch before the game for the team presentations and stand there in the full blaze of the sun throughout the [opening] ceremony, listening to speeches and watching all the dances. However, our coach Gavriil Kachalin instead chose to send the subs out, bolstering them with our captain Shesternyov. We emerged from the cool of the changing room just before kick-off!

Javier Valdivia (Mexico): There aren't superior rivals in a World Cup, everyone is the same, the matches are all or nothing. So you have to be convincing no matter who you're playing. So it didn't matter who we were up against. Clearly, it was important because it was our first game but I think there was more pressure on Russia than us basically because they were very good. It was a tough game, there wasn't a lot of football allowed to be played, and it ended all square. We always had a positive attitude. We knew that with individual effort we could overcome some of our physical and technical deficiencies. Football is played with the mind and not with the feet so that is very important.

Ignacio Calderón (Mexico): We had many of the same players [as 1966]. By that I mean Enrique Borja, Aarón Padilla, myself, we had World Cup experience. But it's different playing a World Cup at home to playing one away, it's really beautiful. I also felt the huge responsibility that came with it because we knew that if we started badly we could probably turn things around. We spoke about it amongst ourselves, about the feeling that we had to go out there on the pitch and from the first minute show why Mexico was playing at home with such wonderful fans in front of a full Estadio Azteca.

Anatoly Byshovets (USSR): The opening of the World Cup was an event in itself. There was an unbelievable atmosphere in the stadium. It made us very excited and nervous at the same time. Your first game of a tournament is always important; it's a match you can't afford to lose.

Evgeny Lovchev (USSR): Before the Estadio Azteca I had played in front of 100,000 fans. At the Luzhniki Stadium, my native club Spartak Moscow would draw crowds that big for games against Dynamo Kyiv, Dinamo Tbilisi, Dinamo Moscow and Torpedo Moscow. We were used to that number of supporters but still it was a very different case in Mexico. Of course, everyone was shaking inside, despite the fact we had a pretty experienced side. That kind of thing is a once-in-a-lifetime experience! I dreamt of winning the World Cup for sure. But as the opening match drew nearer, we came to an understanding that we had finally reached what we had been working towards for such a long time. We felt nervous and anxious and it felt like a dream. We knew that this was the first match and there'd be more than 100,000 fans in the stands, plus we were playing the host country in such ferocious heat.

Javier Valdivia (Mexico): It was a very tight game, they never gave us much of a chance, they pressured us a lot and we didn't have many opportunities.

Anatoly Byshovets (USSR): Naturally, we were a little bit nervous. But it largely depended on how experienced a player was. I was slightly nervous, primarily because I was overly keen to play well and impress everyone. I was focused on the game and had no fear, just a little trepidation. [But that] immediately evaporated when I crossed the touchline onto the pitch. The first matches are always nervous – especially when you play the hosts of the tournament. That's why there are so many draws in that game. We were weakened by the absence of Rudakov and Papaev, but we still had a phenomenal team – which was fired up and ready to go.

Ignacio Calderón (Mexico): The Soviet Union were one of the stronger sides and that was why they were there. We had already played them . . . and we'd come away with a draw but we knew how good they were. We did really well in the opening match because the 0–0 draw helped us shake off our nervousness ahead of the next game against El Salvador and it made us stronger. The draw was good because it gave us confidence.

The match was also notable as the first game in which referees used yellow cards to caution players. After a brutally physical tournament in 1966, FIFA wanted to send a message right from the kick-off that rough play would not be tolerated and the West German referee Kurt Tschenscher was very strict. Soviet midfielder Kakhi Asatiani went into his book after thirty-one minutes, thus earning the dubious distinction of being the first player ever to be shown a yellow card in the World Cup. Two other Soviets followed him in the next three minutes. Only one Mexican was cautioned, which served to bolster a belief that grew as the tournament went on that the referees were favouring the home side.

Anatoly Byshovets (USSR): A difficult game – where it was not that important to win. It was important not to lose. So we took this result well – we shared points in a psychologically difficult game with the host nation of the World Cup. But not one I reminisce about on a daily basis.

Evgeny Lovchev (USSR): Our game against Mexico was even and fair. The opposition went on the attack and their little forward who played on the right cut inside and set himself to shoot. I was running behind him and had to stop him getting any further. I stepped across the back of the Mexican player and just barely clipped his heel. I'll remember that referee, Kurt Tschenscher from West Germany, for the rest of my life: that was virtually the only yellow card I ever got in my entire career!

Anatoly Byshovets (USSR): Of course, history showed we didn't achieve the victory we wanted. But I think the draw was a good result. It showed we could adapt to the testing conditions.

The second match of the group came three days later and was between El Salvador and dark horses Belgium. Neither side knew very much about the other and even though the fans couldn't have known much either, an astonishing 92,000 of them turned out at the Azteca. They saw a poor match in which the Belgians dispatched the Central American debutants 3–0.

Wilfried Van Moer (Belgium): There was very little information and preparation! Scouting was almost non-existent. We knew the Russians and the Mexicans because we played a friendly against them in Brussels and another match a few weeks before the World Cup. They were technically good, but not a high-quality team, but they had home advantage. Those were different times. Today, you know what each player can and cannot do. That simply didn't exist back then.

Mauricio Rodriguez (El Salvador): We didn't know anything about our rivals. I don't know if the coaches could go to see some of our rivals' games, but I doubt it because the resources we had were always meagre.

Wilfried Van Moer (Belgium): There were perhaps some nerves at the start of the El Salvador game. It is a World Cup. It is your first game and you didn't really know the opponent. You knew it was a Latin American side that wasn't too good, but that was about it. So yes, a bit of nerves, but at half-time it was 1–0 so it wasn't a problem.

Mauricio Rodriguez (El Salvador): In our first game against Belgium I remember that we could have scored the opening goal. Full back Ernesto Aparicio went forward but instead of cutting it back where Mon and I were coming through, he shot and unfortunately the keeper blocked it. That was the clearest chance we had against Belgium. And it's the thing I remember the most because I could not sleep that night for thinking that if he had played the ball backwards one of us would have scored. Belgium defended very well, they were strong and in addition to that they knew they had to be careful, so their defence played quite deep and didn't push forward much. Not that they were defensive. They scored two good goals.

Wilfried Van Moer (Belgium): El Salvador were weak and we won. It wasn't a very difficult match. You felt that we were a better team, in a different class. So you begin to think: a point against Russia . . .

Mauricio Rodriguez (El Salvador): When in doubt, it is better to wait a bit for the opponent and hit them on a counter-attack. But really the difference between us was too much, especially physically and psychologically. They ran more than us. In a sprint I could beat an opponent, because physically I was fit, but then we got tired and they didn't. It's not that we were in bad shape, but they were in better shape.

In their second match, Mexico were the overwhelming favourites to overcome the Salvadorans, a team they had beaten in four of their previous five encounters, scoring twenty-three goals in the process. As the region's footballing superpower Mexico had been the lone CONCACAF representative in the previous four finals but they qualified automatically as hosts, which meant there was space for another CONCACAF side to secure a place. The Mexicans, however, knew they couldn't get too cocky and although they eventually beat their southern neighbours 4–0, they needed to rely on some underhand shenanigans to get going.

Ignacio Calderón (Mexico): We talked a lot and we said we can't be over-confident because how many times have Central American teams beaten Mexico because we were too confident, because we thought we'd hammer them? So, from the start we went out with that mentality of wanting to notch up our first win in the World Cup.

Javier Valdivia (Mexico): [Rivals from CONCACAF] are more complicated for us because they try to drag you down to their level. We only scored the opening goal right at the end of the first half – it was a difficult situation – but the goal meant that spaces opened up.

Mauricio Rodriguez (El Salvador): The first goal came from a throw-in that should have been ours. But a Mexican grabbed the ball and took it for them as we had our backs turned. And they scored from it. But it was our throw-in. I saw the video afterwards and they had cut the incident. We were waiting for them to give the ball back, because it was our throw. But one of them took it quickly and they scored. What could we do? The referee accepted it. We were lucky, because our claims were so strong that a referee with a little more personality would have sent off four or five of our players. Mariona, the captain, was one of the most furious, also Burra Rivas. I told him to calm down, that he was not going to change the referee's decision. We were so angry that we kicked the ball into the stands three times and the referee decided to blow his whistle to end the first half when there were still two or three minutes left.

Javier Valdivia (Mexico): That was their own fault; in all honesty the goal was a good one. I got past them and I had the opportunity to score. I don't know what they were complaining about, I don't know what foul they saw to annul the goal. We know what the mentality is with players like this from these kinds of places. They look to create problems to see if you'll fall for them. It's natural, that's the essence of it. But when you are well prepared you don't fall for the mind games as easily.

Mauricio Rodriguez (El Salvador): Well, what happened here occasionally happens to us against Mexico. They are more experienced and have tricks that they didn't really need. Mexico could have beaten us easily but they wanted to make sure.

Ignacio Calderón (Mexico): That was them feeling impotent at going behind. We did what we had to do but we could feel their frustration that things were not going their way. We were delighted, and it was a situation that the referee had to decide.

Mauricio Rodriguez (El Salvador): I had a very clear opportunity before they scored the first goal. I ran on to a ball and I beat the defender for speed and I hit it. It beat the keeper, hit the post and bounced back into the goalkeeper's arms. I dreamt about that one as well. At half-time, our directors came to the dressing room to calm us down. 'What are they doing? If you are playing well, don't throw it all away being crazy,' they told us. Maybe the referee didn't notice, but the linesman did. Then in the second half they beat us with plenty to spare, they scored three more goals. It ended 4–0. With that, they qualified for the second round, something they had never managed before.

Ignacio Calderón (Mexico): Fortunately, things went well although I can't remember when we scored the first goal. It was quite late on. We had come close but once the scoreline got to 4–0 the usual nerves had gone and we were full of confidence. Both me personally and our whole defence, we felt good because we hadn't let in a goal in our first two games. It was the easiest game but when you play these kinds of countries it always gets complicated when things don't work out as you hoped and if you start to get desperate then that can work against you. So if they score, they shut up shop at the back and it's tough to find a way through. Fortunately, that never happened with us.

The Soviet Union were superb in overrunning Belgium 4–0 in their second match, a result that put the dampeners on Belgium's good start and left the group finely balanced with the last round of matches to come. It was memorable for Wilfried Van Moer's amazing double miss and Anatoly Byshovets' two goals, both of which were classy strikes into the top corner of the net.

Wilfried Van Moer (Belgium): We knew that Russia was a strong opponent. It was the Soviet Union. They could pick from a big pool of very good players. We knew that. At European level, they were one of the strongest opponents.

Anatoly Byshovets (USSR): In that particular match, I think the luck was on our side. And I also think we were better prepared in terms of heat and high-altitude training. The Belgians looked somewhat tired and like they were feeling the heat, literally. We were much fresher, much faster and managed to score quickly – which psychologically crushed them. Our pace was the key element which put them off from the start – we outran them and that essentially broke their tactical plan. That goal I scored against Belgium was historic – it made the top 100 best goals ever, somewhere around the twentieth spot. I faced three defenders and hit the far corner.

Wilfried Van Moer (Belgium): At the start of the match, I received a cross and I headed the ball straight at the goalkeeper from a few metres out and on the rebound I just wanted to connect with all my force because the ball had less resistance in Mexico because of the altitude. The ball hit the bar and bounced back and out of play! That was about ten minutes into the game and we might have taken the lead. After missing that chance and conceding the first goal, it was game over. It was a heavy verdict, but the Russians were much better. Overall, in Mexico, they were so much stronger. Perhaps the scoreline was a bit exaggerated, but we would never have beaten them. We didn't have a chance.

The results meant that both Mexico and the Soviet Union had three points from their first two games. Belgium had two but with a final match to come against the hapless Salvadorans, the USSR were almost guaranteed a place in the knockout phase and they got it with a 2–0 win in front of 90,000 people at the Azteca.

Anatoly Byshovets (USSR): Again, not the most memorable game – except maybe for the two goals that I scored. El Salvador were clearly the outsider in this group so we had no chance to mess this up – but this was probably that type of game where you can argue it was relatively easy for us. We had played them before – in the mid-sixties we went there to play. I think I even scored a goal against them then – and I scored two in the World Cup as well. That trip to them in the sixties was crazy – El Salvador was at war with one of the neighbours. And our plane was met with army patrols. It felt a bit too intimidating, but the game itself was okay.

Mauricio Rodriguez (El Salvador): They were also a good team. We didn't play badly and we had chances to score a couple of goals. I think they underestimated us, because the first half ended 0–0. They put on their best goalscorer in the second half after resting him and he scored one of the two goals. This is how our worldwide adventure ended. The truth is that we were the first country in Central America and the Caribbean to qualify for a World Cup, because although Cuba had gone to one, they had been invited. So it was something historic for our country. At the time, our fans didn't value what we'd done. They expected more from us. They wanted us to win at least one game, to score goals. Over time, reality has prevailed and they now know the true value of what we achieved. We did not do it again for twelve years, when we went to Spain. And they have not done since then, that is to say more than thirty years.

That left Mexico needing at least a point against Belgium the next day to qualify and they contrived to win both thanks to a hotly contested penalty in the fourteenth minute. Léon Jeck brought down Javier Valdivia with a high tackle inside the box, although only after playing the ball cleanly. The normally phlegmatic Belgians were outraged and besieged the Argentine referee, who was unmoved. Nevertheless, it was 1–0 to Mexico and the hosts were through.

Wilfried Van Moer (Belgium): The matches against El Salvador and Russia were far from sold out. It was a stadium that held 105,000 fans and there were about 70,000 people. That didn't really make a difference. We had played in Spain and other places with similar crowds, but against Mexico it was packed to the rafters – 105,000 supporters! That left a lasting impression. It was special, in that heat – thirty-five degrees and 105,000 people cheering and backing their team. That's something I had never experienced in my life.

Javier Valdivia (Mexico): We played well in this game, and there wasn't a lot between the sides. When we got the penalty I was right in front of goal ready to receive the ball and I got knocked down from behind. I didn't even see anyone. And then they said it wasn't a penalty! If the defender was behind me and he has no chance of winning the ball, he brought me down, he completely knocked me over, it was a clear penalty.

Wilfried Van Moer (Belgium): Léon Jeck made the tackle and he got to the ball first. The referee immediately awarded a penalty. A European or normal referee would perhaps not have awarded that penalty, but Mexico had to advance for sporting and financial reasons. It would have been a catastrophe if Mexico, as hosts, had been eliminated in the first round. They progressed and so they were happy and quite a few of us were quite happy as well that it was all over. [Laughs]

Ignacio Calderón (Mexico): If you watch it again you can see it was a penalty 100 per cent. The Belgian took Valdivia out with a scissor tackle at waist height. It was a tackle that had to be a penalty, there was no doubt about it, but they protested a lot and fortunately our regular penalty taker Peña, who had already had experience at another World Cup and who was the team captain, put it away very nicely.

Martin Peters (England): There were some eccentric decisions by referees within ten yards of the penalty area, where there was more high diving than in the Olympics, but apart from one notorious exception, penalties were not handed out cheaply. The exception was the penalty by which Mexico defeated Belgium and so qualified for the quarter-finals. I must admit that I saw the penalty awarded against the Belgians only on the box – we were otherwise engaged at the time – but it was so obviously a bad decision that television was good enough in this case. The Belgians were entitled to feel aggrieved and bitter and I hate to think of what might have happened had the penalty been given at the other end! I have no doubt at all that at the very least the game would have been abandoned after the crowd had rioted.

Gustavo Peña (Mexico): If I'd missed it, they'd have killed me [laughs]. Because it was a very important goal for the team and for me. And their goalkeeper knew my name. It was 'Pena! Pena!' because they don't have the ñ in Europe. And I ran up and the crowd went crazy. If I had missed it I wouldn't be here. I'd be in hiding, I'd have changed my face or I'd be using a mask or something.

Ignacio Calderón (Mexico): We wanted to show the fans that had got behind us that we were up for it. We knew what was expected of us. Belgium is a strong footballing nation and we knew what they were capable of. We talked a lot amongst ourselves at the training centre, as well as in the meetings with the coach. We did that to support each other and that helped bring us together; we were like a family. We roared each other on and at the end we won with a penalty. It was a rough game, hard fought, and right up to the last minutes they had us pinned back as they threw over crosses. There was one moment when we made a save as the ball was going in. We knew that we had to win and we knew that if we kept a clean sheet we'd manage it. We played very well defensively in that run of three games without conceding a goal. We were delighted because it was the first time that Mexico had reached the quarter-finals.

Losing in such controversial circumstances was too much for the Belgians, many of whom had long since had enough. What they saw as a dodgy decision to ensure the host nation progressed to the second round prompted accusations of malfeasance that did not dim as the years passed.

Wilfried Van Moer (Belgium): Against Mexico we lost because of a penalty that wasn't really a penalty. But you know, Mexico had to progress. They got a South American referee for that game and he awarded that penalty. That 1–0 was enough for Mexico. They could drop back – and we weren't good enough, because of the heat. Mentally, it was a real blow. In my view, that penalty wasn't a penalty. The referee was Latin and he knew that Mexico from a sporting and financial point of view had to progress in the tournament. We knew that the hosts would not be allowed to lose! But a lot of players were glad – it was over! We can go home! That was the mentality. It wasn't great, but I could understand it after so many weeks. Today, you know, it is so different – better hotels, better organisation. It is all professional. Back then, we were professional yes, but in reality, we were just amateurs.

The Soviet Union and Mexico progressed to the quarter-finals, with the USSR taking top place in the group on a coin toss after they both finished with five points and a goal difference of +5.

Mexico had never qualified for the second round before and the victory provoked massive outpourings of joy all across the country.

Ignacio Calderón (Mexico): It was madness. The streets, the cars peeping their horns, people waving flags and not just in Mexico City but the whole country because it was the first time we had qualified for the second round. We saw it all on television and it was unforgettable for us, seeing the stadium filled and hearing the fans and then listening to the national anthem. I had been at the 1966 World Cup but being at home was very different.

Javier Valdivia (Mexico): The feeling was indescribable; there is no way to put it into words the emotion we felt. The fans celebrated the whole night. We made Mexicans happy by doing something that Mexico had never done before and doing that in your own country, well, we were so pleased to have succeeded.

Belgium's capitulation was a surprise to the football world, but not to some of the players. The Belgians had been in Mexico for five weeks and discontent had been brewing in the Belgian camp for some time. More than a few of the squad were bored, homesick and lacked not just team spirit, but the desire to progress. Some of them couldn't wait to be on the plane home.

Wilfried Van Moer (Belgium): The main problem was that a lot of the players were homesick. [Coach Raymond Goethals] tried to do his best. He told the players that the World Cup isn't your everyday tournament, that the whole world is watching. You know, the standard sort of pep talk. But there was no desire. So you can talk and talk all you want. The FA bosses were based in Mexico City and some of them came down to Puebla to talk to the group, but after three weeks the players had thrown in the towel. So they could have talked forever but the right mentality was gone. For me, it was a disappointment. Some players did want to try and qualify for the next round, but you need the entire group [to be pulling together]. If you have a group that believes in something with 100 per cent camaraderie, you can achieve more. Belgium were among the best teams in Europe, but that isn't the point. We had the best players from both Anderlecht and Standard. From Club Brugge, [Raoul] Lambert, [Pierre] Carteus and [Erwin] Vandendaele – they were among the best players in their team as well. As a team, we should have achieved more, but the circumstances weren't favourable. I think it would have been different if the World Cup had been staged in Europe, but over in South America, no, we lacked the mentality. We should have progressed in the tournament but if you are mentally not present . . . five, six players were just thinking about going home. That is wrong and so you can't get results. It wasn't fun either for the substitutes. They were away from home for so long and they were homesick as well. When you played, you had less homesickness, but there were always eight or nine players who simply didn't play. They got homesick even quicker, you know? The FA learned a lot from everything that went wrong at that tournament.

The next few World Cup campaigns were more organised, the way it should have been. In 1982, twelve years on, lots had changed, the organisation as well. But it was a tournament in Europe and the circumstances were different. It was a good lesson for the FA. After all, the World Cup is something special in your career, but the results weren't good. I regret that.

El Salvador's elimination, meanwhile, was not a surprise to the footballing world but it was greeted with disappointment at home. Their fans, perhaps unrealistically, had expected more.

Mauricio Rodriguez (El Salvador): The thing is, people created expectations. They said that we could get a draw against Mexico and then we'd win another game. But it was all in their heads, because they didn't know our opponents. So that resulted in a false hope; they expected more than we could give them. For most people we were a failure. With the passage of time they have realised what it was that we achieved, since at that time there were only sixteen teams in a World Cup. Now there are thirty-two and [they] want to put in another thirty-two. In the long run they realised that what we did wasn't bad, but at the time it was, because they expected more from us. Having more international experience would have helped us a lot. Stepping out there is easier when you're used to playing at that level, and you take on your rivals as equals, even if you're a lesser power. We saw our opponents, some we knew from the newspapers, as big guys and we felt that inferiority. If instead of playing so many friendlies at home we had gone abroad to play, it might have been different.

The day after being knocked out we returned home. The organisers give you one or two nights after you're eliminated, and then it's goodbye . . . We were given a pass to get into the games for free, but nobody stayed. As always, the problem was that you had to pay for your hotel.

The reception at home was cold. Only relatives came out to the airport . . . It was not even the shadow of when we returned from beating Honduras and after our last game against Haiti. There were people everywhere after that match. I'm telling you, the drive from the Ilopango airport to the stadium normally took half an hour by car. It took us four hours to arrive that day because people wouldn't let the bus pass. They were waiting for us in the Flor Blanca Stadium to sing the national anthem. We took so long because the streets were full of people, we could not pass. I think people took time off work that afternoon so that they could go and receive the national team. That day when we came home from the World Cup was fast; we arrived in less than twenty minutes.

	P	W	D	L	Gls	Pts
SOVIET UNION	3	2	1	0	6-1	5
MEXICO	3	2	1	0	5-0	5
Belgium	3	1	0	2	4-5	2
El Salvador	3	0	0	3	0-9	0

THREE

GROUP 2

2 June	Puebla	Uruguay	2–0	Israel
3 June	Toluca	Italy	1–0	Sweden
6 June	Puebla	Uruguay	0–0	Italy
7 June	Toluca	Israel	1–1	Sweden
10 June	Puebla	Sweden	1–0	Uruguay
11 June	Toluca	Italy	0–0	Israel

Group 2 always looked like being a battle between Uruguay and Italy, the two teams who between them had won the first four World Cups, and so it turned out. Uruguay, champions in 1930 and 1950, started the tournament in the worst possible fashion, with star man Pedro Rocha forced off with an injury just thirteen minutes into their opening game against Israel. But the experienced Uruguayans were still too strong for the newcomers and a goal in each half made certain they began their pursuit of a third World Cup with a win.

Dagoberto Fontes (Uruguay): We had played 4-2-4 and that became 4-4-2. We lost a forward, who was Pedro [Rocha], and the whole system changed. Pedro was the man that organised everything. He was, in inverted commas, the Uruguayan Pelé.

Ildo Maneiro (Uruguay): Uruguay had the misfortune to lose Pedro Rocha to an injury that he picked up and played through on the preparatory tour in Quito and Bogotá. Our acclimatisation was very rigorous and very good, but Rocha was already struggling and his injury eventually forced me to take on other responsibilities. The man who took Rocha's place was [Julio] 'Pocho' Cortés. Pedro had great ability in the air and an impressive shot. Cortés was extremely hard-working, he never stopped running and always helped out. We complemented each other very well with Cortés and Víctor Espárrago or Dagoberto Fontes, both of them improvised centre forwards. In addition, together with Montero Castillo we did a good job in midfield. There was also Luis Alberto Cubilla, who was a phenomenon, but Julio César Morales played little because he picked up a serious injury before the championship started.

The game was Israel's first ever in the World Cup finals and they admitted they had not prepared sufficiently — and nor were they ready to face a team as cunning as the South Americans.

Mordechai Spiegler (Israel): We were the biggest underdogs ever seen in football. We knew they had great players, Rocha, Mazurkiewicz. We did not build any big dreams, big hopes. It was about participating to do our best and if we're lucky we might qualify but it was hard because every team of the [other] three were better than us. But we did not want to fail, and we wanted to play to prove that we are here because we are a solid team.

Shmuel Rosenthal (Israel): Our legs were shaking. The Uruguayans pinched and bit us, and we weren't used to that intensity. It was a baptism by fire, after which we knew how we should be playing.

Tommy Svensson (Sweden): They were a physically tough team – South American in a different way than the Brazilians. These guys used more physique, more force. While English football was always physical in the sense that the teams ran a lot, Uruguay played physically when challenging for the ball, and in how they marked their opponents. It was tough, but nothing out of the ordinary.

Roberto Matosas (Uruguay): We were never nasty. I do not remember any unfair action. I mean, we're talking about fifty years ago, so there are some little things that escape my memory.

Ildo Maneiro (Uruguay): I got off on the right foot because I scored the first goal and created the second. The first was a cross from Juan Martín Mujica on the left. It was drizzling and the pitch was wet. The ball bounced in front of the near post, Espárrago hadn't arrived and I came in at the back post and the ball hit my head and went in. And the second goal came from a rebound after my shot from outside the area. The loose ball fell to Mujica who was coming in from the left and finished it off to make it 2–0.

Mordechai Spiegler (Israel): [Coach Emmanuel] Scheffer said that if they had let him watch Uruguay play beforehand, the score would've been different. He told me, 'Motke, they [the IFA] didn't let me go. I swear if I did, we wouldn't have lost.'

Roberto Matosas (Uruguay): The only thing I remember from the game against Israel is that we played at the level we wanted. It was not a great level but winning the first game is always important.

Mordechai Spiegler (Israel): Uruguay was far better. We lost 2–0 and it was thanks to our wonderful goalkeeper, [Itzhak] Vissoker. He had a very good day. They covered the pitch, but they played against a schoolboy team; the difference was 5–0, not 2–0.

Italy faced Sweden in their opener a day later, with the Scandinavian side appearing at their first World Cup finals since losing in the final at home to Brazil twelve years earlier. For the Swedes, this was the match that counted, the match they had prepared for, but it turned out to be a disappointing one. The game kicked off in Toluca, which, at 2,667 metres above sea level, was twice as high as the highest mountain in Great Britain. That inhibited any real expansive play and the Italians scored early and then shut up shop. The winning goal, which came in the eleventh minute, resulted from a goalkeeping error. At altitude the ball moved faster than some players expected and it caused all sorts of problems for keepers. Angelo Domenghini's shot went straight under Ronnie Hellström's body. Other keepers would suffer a similar fate as the ball performed erratically in the thin air.

Ronnie Hellström (Sweden): We thought we'd have a chance to progress from the group, but that Italy would be the strongest side in the group. We had been to Israel for training camps and I'd played against them then. We counted on beating them. Uruguay looked like a tough challenge. Still we thought we'd beat them too. One always does. We went to Mexico with the intention of winning our matches but knew that it would be difficult to repeat 1958. We'd be far from home this time. Their [Italy's] big star was Riva. There were stories about him and his shot; some said he struck the ball with such power that he injured keepers in training! It got to the point where we nearly forgot about ourselves, and that we were pretty good too. I hadn't heard of Riva much myself, but we talked to the Swedish press every day, and they told us to watch out for him because he was so f-ing good. Maybe it got to [coach Orvar] Bergmark because he put Jan Olsson to man-mark Riva. We'd never man-marked any single player as extremely as we did with Riva. I was not by any means a sure starter, as there were three of us keepers fighting for the spot. None of us knew who the hell would get to play. And so the outfield players didn't know who the hell would be there behind them. The night before the Italy match, Orvar came into my room and said, 'You're playing.' Why couldn't he have told me fourteen days before? Having twelve hours to prepare was not ideal.

Tommy Svensson (Sweden): We got off to an unfortunate start, with [goalkeeper] Ronnie Hellström making a real blunder. The match was even and there weren't many chances. Italy of course knew how to defend a lead. They kept possession and took few risks. We couldn't counter-attack and didn't manage to unlock their defence. Perhaps the heat was a factor. In conditions like that, it's easier to defend a lead than to be on the chase. There was never much of a tactical plan in those days. We never discussed much how the opponents attacked or how they acted on set pieces. In hindsight, our mistake was that we man-marked their best man, Riva. Jan Olsson was given that job. Focusing on Riva meant that we never found our own game and rhythm.

Ronnie Hellström (Sweden): The match began and after ten minutes came that damn shot that of course I should have saved. I've seen it on TV afterwards, how they take a corner and the ball gets to Domenghini. After that, I did well in the match. And we didn't play badly. But the pressure was on me, and the rest of the tournament I had to watch from the terraces; I wasn't even on the bench. That was a damn hard blow. From number one to number three. And then those bastards [laughs] went on to reach the final.

Sandro Mazzola (Italy): The fact that we beat Sweden was very important, especially bearing in mind the mistakes we made in England four years earlier.

Angelo Domenghini (Italy): It was not an easy game to play. I had scored, thanks also to a mistake by the goalkeeper. Then we managed to defend the result. Winning the first game meant we had a very good chance of going through.

Ronnie Hellström (Sweden): We didn't know then how far Italy would go; we didn't know how good they actually were. But looking back, we had focused too much on Italy. That wasn't the match we had to win, Israel was the one.

After Italy and Uruguay both won their opening matches there was a barely acknowledged understanding that a draw would suit both sides when they met in the second round of games. Italy were banking on defeating Israel in their final match and content to play for a draw so they strung men along the eighteen-yard line. Uruguay, who had a dozen corners to Italy's two, were the more attacking side but they could not make a dent in the Italian rearguard and did not seem overly worried about it. The lacklustre 0–0 draw might not have pleased the fans but both teams appeared satisfied.

Sandro Mazzola (Italy): The captain of Uruguay, or their most important player, was the father of Paolo Montero [later of Juventus]. We looked at each other at the start of the game. When players look at each other in a certain way they understand each other. The game started off very calmly, it was very slow. Bertini took a shot and Montero came up to me and said in Spanish, 'What are you doing?' I said to him, 'He's a crazy man, don't worry.' And Montero said, 'Well, now we're going to have a shot at goal as well.' After that we didn't speak again. We kept playing, very slowly and we knew that a draw for both teams would practically guarantee we'd go into the second stage. That is football.

Angelo Domenghini (Italy): I think it was normal that it was played that way. In case of victory, one of the two would have gone home. Playing offensively was a risk. Objectively this was an unnecessary risk. The draw would have qualified both, but we did not agree. It is a psychological thing, it's unconscious. The history of football is full of such episodes. They also happened in editions after the World Cup or the European Championships or any other tournament. It must be said that we also hit a post in the second half against Uruguay, and we went close to scoring.

Enrico Albertosi (Italy): We went there just to secure qualification.

Ildo Maneiro (Uruguay): It was a game where a draw was useful for both teams. I'd never heard about Mazzola saying that until now, fifty years later, but I don't think Montero or Mazzola had so much influence on the group. Yes, both teams played very speculatively. They complained a lot about the heat, but they had a very good squad; at that time everyone was talking about Italian football: Gianni Rivera, Gigi Riva, Roberto Boninsegna. Everyone knew who they were.

Sandro Mazzola (Italy): We were thinking of qualifying and also in saving our energy for the next stage.

Roberto Matosas (Uruguay): Then we drew goalless against Italy, a match in which two quite conservative teams turned up. There were not many scoring opportunities and the draw suited both of us as we had already won our first game.

Ildo Maneiro (Uruguay): Italy got better as the championship went on and they played a great match against Germany in the semi-final. The reality is that we did not have great offensive power; Morales did not play that game either. Given that we both had two points at the start, with a draw we were golden. We thought that we were going to beat Sweden.

For their second game against Israel, Swedish coach Orvar Bergmark dropped goalkeeper Hellström. Both teams knew a win was vital if they were to have a chance of progressing. Sweden had beaten Israel three times in the previous three years and were confident of making it four in a row. Instead, the Israelis surprised their more illustrious opponents. Although Sweden took the lead eight minutes into the second half, Mordechai Spiegler, who would go on to play first for Paris Saint-Germain and then alongside Pelé at New York Cosmos, deservedly equalised with a thirty-yard shot that even today remains their only World Cup goal. The 1–1 draw was not great for either side but it did leave both teams with an outside chance of qualifying with the final round of matches still to come.

Mordechai Spiegler (Israel): It's a pity that football is not like basketball, because I scored from a distance, it should be three goals, like three points. Stephen Curry always gets three points, and me from a bigger distance only one [laughs].

Tommy Svensson (Sweden): We knew we still had a chance to progress, having Israel in the upcoming match. Actually, we'd been to Israel both in 1968 and 1969 for training camps, and we played the Israelis both times. So we were familiar with them and knew who their best players were. But we didn't analyse them the way that one does nowadays. All in all, we knew them better than we knew most teams. And they were familiar with us too. We prepared for the match with a talk, but then focused mostly on our own game.

Ronnie Hellström (Sweden): All we talked about after Italy was winning against Israel, which would put us back in the race. The problem was that everyone had only focused on that damn match against Italy. There was no plan for whatever might happen if we lost to Italy. Israel had two good guys – Spiegel and Spiegler – who we had studied a bit. Otherwise the team was average. We'd beaten them both times that we'd played them over in Israel. We were there in 1968 and 1969 for training so knew a bit about them. A mediocre team.

Mordechai Spiegler (Israel): When we got to know that we were playing against Uruguay, Sweden and Italy, I stood up and made this [raises arm in the air]. And I said when I score, this is how I will go back to the midfield. When you score four goals against the United States in the preparation for the World Cup – in sixteen minutes I scored four goals – you feel okay to talk about when I score; I did not say if I score. And when the moment came and I scored this is what I remembered in my head. So I did not run back crazy, I was just doing this and people said what is it and I just said this was a promise to my family.

Ronnie Hellström (Sweden): That was a match that we should have won nine times out of ten. We absolutely should have won this one too, but we couldn't quite get going. I won't say we underestimated them, because we knew we had to win. But we didn't play a good match. Israel saw their chance and took it. Conceding an equaliser only three minutes after going ahead was not good, of course.

Yochanan Vollach (Israel): Years later, I met one of the Swedish players, and he said to me, 'In '68 we came to Israel and easily beat you 3–0. When we came to the World Cup, it was already totally different. How did that happen?' I told him: We were raised like an army unit. We spent a year and a half in training camps, sometimes Sunday through Thursday. We'd only show up to the regular league to play on the weekends.

Tommy Svensson (Sweden): I was the captain on that day since Björn Nordqvist had got ill and couldn't play. It was my first match as Sweden captain. Once again, we conceded a goal that the keeper [not Ronnie this time] should have saved. From then on, there was only one thing that mattered: to score. Israel's goal made us disappointed and angry but not panicky. We thought we were the better team. Tom Turesson got our goal. But to only get a 1–1 draw was disappointing.

Mordechai Spiegler (Israel): Some could say, if, if, if, we could win and I say if, if, if to the other side we could lose. The story was 1–1. Next page.

The Swedes were miserable. Not only were results not going their way, they were stuck in a cheap hotel, far from the action, with nothing much to do. Even speaking to their families on the phone was a major hassle.

Ronnie Hellström (Sweden): At our compound we'd sit in the evenings trading stories. But mostly we just waited for that damn phone to ring. In those days one would order a long-distance call and then wait up to six hours to be put through. I think we probably got our accommodation when all the other teams had had their picks. We also had quizzes. They were on general knowledge, and the organiser was always Tommy Svensson. He was a schoolteacher after all and had the best general knowledge, no doubt about it. He also filmed a lot with his Super 8 camera. Wherever we went on our trips, Tommy's camera was there to film. He'd show us films from past trips whenever the team got together for new matches. At the camp we'd get Swedish newspapers every day. They were three or four days old by the time they arrived, and that's how I got to read all the shit after the Italy game. That wasn't much fun. For a few days people back home had been saying, 'It wasn't only your fault,' but then the newspapers finally arrived. I still have the papers. My dad would save all clippings, even the mean ones.

The 1–1 draw between Israel and Sweden a day after Italy and Uruguay had shared the points meant that Italy were almost definitely through. The Swedes could only leapfrog Uruguay if they beat the South Americans by at least two goals. They were buoyed by moving to a new hotel at a lower altitude but although they scraped a win with an injury-time goal it was not enough to take them into the last eight.

Ronnie Hellström (Sweden): We must have talked about having the chance by beating them by two or three goals. When we got to Puebla we stayed at a better hotel, which had a pool and activities. That cheered us up. The old people's home where our World Cup base was had nothing. It also felt good to come down from Toluca [altitude 2,600 metres] to Puebla [2,100 metres]. It made things a little easier. I don't remember much about [the game]. That's where our chance went up in smoke. We really should have scored earlier in the match. Uruguay weren't bad either, and they ended up playing West Germany for the bronze medal.

Tommy Svensson (Sweden): We knew beforehand what we needed to do. A 2–0 win would get us through. It was an evenly contested match, by far our best match in Mexico. We reached the level that we felt we should have been playing at all along. We scored one and had chances to score even more. One more goal and we'd have gone through to the quarter-finals. We were disappointed in the end. Particularly for not having beaten Israel. That would have been enough. Our problem at the World Cup was that we didn't get as much out of our attacking game as we'd hoped.

Ildo Maneiro (Uruguay): At that time Sweden were totally unknown to us, but they had a great aerial game and they made it very difficult for us. Physically they were powerful and after they made it 1–0 we didn't have the capacity to fight back and get a draw.

Tommy Svensson (Sweden): We knew it was going to be tough but the chance was still there, absolutely. We knew that. We also knew that we'd be going down to Puebla at an altitude of 2,100 metres, a 600-metre difference [from Toluca]. We noticed the difference straight away.

Roberto Matosas (Uruguay): And then we suffered a lot against Sweden, we suffered a lot; we knew that with the draw or losing by one goal we had enough to qualify for the next phase.

Sweden's tepid 1–0 win left the door open for Israel, who could qualify for the quarter-finals with a comprehensive win over Italy. It was an unlikely scenario for the group's final game, especially one that ended up with just six goals in six games, the lowest total of all the groups and a remarkable four times less than the twenty-four goals in Group 4. Israel, though, performed creditably and were not the whipping boys many thought they would be. Winning points against both Sweden and eventual finalists Italy was a considerable feat for the semi-professionals. Their spirited performance in the 0–0 draw with Italy won them the backing of the Mexican crowd who, with a shower of bottles and cushions, let the Italians know what they thought of their toothless display.

Mordechai Spiegler (Israel): We hoped more than we thought [we could win].

Zvi Rosen (Israel): We got dressed before the game and walked down where there was a smaller field. The Italians were already there warming up, and they're all tan and full of muscles, wearing fashionable black underwear.

Yehoshua Feigenbaum (Israel): We stood in two lines to go up to the stadium. As I'm looking over, I see Facchetti scratching the floor with his shoe, and he has aluminium cleats, sharp as knives. I said, 'Man, I'm not going there.'

Giora Spiegel (Israel): We felt the Italians wanted to play fast, so we played slower than the train from Jerusalem to Tel Aviv to drain the joy out of their game.

Mordechai Spiegler (Israel): It was a good game. We had a couple of chances. I had a good chance to score and I did not. We competed well.

Angelo Domenghini (Italy): They were an experienced team, and they had put us in difficulty. We were unlucky against them.

The referee ruled out two of our goals, one for me and one for Gigi Riva, but both were regular. We understood that something was wrong.

The Uruguayans squeaked into the quarter-finals thanks to goal difference. Sweden and Uruguay both won one, drew one and lost one but the South Americans qualified because they had conceded only one goal to Sweden's two. The top two sides managed a paltry two goals each in their opening three games and Sweden went home nursing a bitter feeling of what might have been.

Mordechai Spiegler (Israel): So we needed one more point maybe to qualify. But if is not a factor in football. We went home happy to be at the same World Cup where Brazil are the champions and Pelé is the king. At the end of the day Italy went to the final and Uruguay went to the semi-final, both from our group.

Ronnie Hellström (Sweden): I committed my blunder against Italy. After that game Orvar didn't say anything in particular or give an explanation, but from then on, I was his third choice. If at least I'd been on the bench from then on, I would have maintained a connection with the team. Being sat on the terrace was the worst. Why remove me altogether? I should have at least been allowed to compete for a place. I think it was his way of trying to protect me, that he was afraid that if I committed one more error I'd be damaged for life. But having to watch from the terrace gave me the sense that I was to blame for losing to Italy, when in fact ten other players could have done something to turn the match around. But I wasn't the only one to be dissatisfied. A lot of players lost their places from one match to the next. Normally, there's a core in a team. That didn't seem to be the case this time. Maybe the outfield players were just as annoyed as I was with not knowing if they had a sure place or not. That probably wasn't good for the morale in the squad. Nobody else in the squad commented on my demotion. Strange. There was no one that I could share my thoughts with. From being in the thick of things, I was outside of the group. The rest of the World Cup wasn't much fun, and when I got home again everybody just asked: 'How could you concede that goal?' For a long time afterwards in Sweden, whenever a keeper let in a soft goal, the saying was that 'he did a Hellström'. The Mexico World Cup was an anti-climax for me. But I learned a lot, about digging in and keeping up my training.

Tommy Svensson (Sweden): I was rather pleased with how I played myself. Actually, I was named the best Swedish player by the organisers. I don't want to go into individual critique of players. One positive example was Bo Larsson, who always did a great job out on the pitch. Ronnie Hellström didn't get to play the rest of the World Cup after the error against Italy. It was a pity that he was benched, as he really should have continued for us. But I guess the experience lit a fire in him, because he would go on to prove what a class keeper he was. By 1974, he knew what a World Cup was all about, thanks to the experience in Mexico.

Enrico Albertosi (Italy): In the group stage we were a little stuck. Our goal was to qualify for the next round, so when we won the first game with Sweden, then the aim against Uruguay and Israel was not to lose. We were blocked and shut down and the two games finished 0–0. Then from the quarter-finals, things changed. We played differently because if you lost, you were immediately eliminated. So we scored four goals against Mexico [in the quarter-finals] and four goals against West Germany [in the semi-finals] and we managed to score a goal against Brazil too.

On the other hand, even though they departed as early as everyone expected, in some ways it was a triumph for Israel, who acquitted themselves admirably with two draws and only one loss, to Uruguay. Individuals in the team caught the attention of scouts and several of their players signed for bigger clubs overseas. It also presented the beleaguered nation in a different light after years of headlines that only seemed to scream of conflict.

Mordechai Spiegler (Israel): We were very much anonymous underdogs and suddenly people say, 'Israel, where? Israel who?' and you say a country in the Middle East also plays football. It was an opening. We all had a chance to go and play professionally as the gates were not really open to us before then. I went to Paris, Paris Football Club and Paris Saint-Germain. [Then Cosmos]. We had one player who went to play for Mönchengladbach. My friend Spiegel he played a couple of years in France, in Strasbourg and Lyon, and later every generation had more opportunities as the market became more open and that began at our time.

	P	W	D	L	Gls	Pts
ITALY	3	1	2	0	1-0	4
URUGUAY	3	1	1	1	2-1	3
Sweden	3	1	1	1	2-2	3
Israel	3	0	2	1	1-3	2

FOUR

GROUP 3

2 June	Guadalajara	England	1–0	Romania
3 June	Guadalajara	Brazil	4–1	Czechoslovakia
6 June	Guadalajara	Romania	2–1	Czechoslovakia
7 June	Guadalajara	Brazil	1–0	England
10 June	Guadalajara	Romania	2–3	Brazil
11 June	Guadalajara	Czechoslovakia	0–1	England

The term 'Group of Death' had yet to be coined but Group 3 was undoubtedly the strongest in the competition. Not only did it feature the holders England and the joint favourites Brazil, there were two strong European sides present also. Romania were many people's outside bets to do well, and the Czechs, while perhaps not the powerhouse they were in 1962 when they reached the final, were still a team worthy of respect.

Pelé (Brazil): When we finally went to Mexico, there were many both at home and abroad who felt Brazil didn't have a chance. They felt we were insufficiently trained, that the disagreements that led to a change in our coaching staff, even though resolved, had led to dissensions that would be difficult to overcome. Those critics also had an unfortunate tendency to believe the statements of the managers of competing teams. In our group, for example, were Czechoslovakia, England, Romania and Brazil. The head of the Czech commission, Jozef Marco, made endless statements to the press that his team was unbeatable, certainly in the group elimination rounds; Sir Alf Ramsey, of England, never noted for modesty, insisted that England would not only win our group, but would go on to repeat their victory of 1966. But Zagallo never said a word about our chances; he was a firm believer in the old proverb that a shut mouth catches no flies. If Saldanha had been coaching us, he would have taken Marco's bragging and Ramsey's boasting as a personal insult, and probably asked the two men to step outside into the alley. And the animosity he would have earned us with such tactics would scarcely have helped our cause.

England began their defence of the title against Romania, a side they had met twice in the previous eighteen months. Both games, in London and Bucharest, had ended in draws, and were an indication of how strong the little-known Romanians were. The

East Europeans had talent, strikers Florea Dumitrache and Emerich Dembrovschi and midfielder Cornel Dinu chief among them, but here in Guadalajara they spent much of the game hacking at the legs of the England forwards. It was only thanks to Geoff Hurst's superb penalty box finishing that England escaped with both points.

Bobby Moore (England): Our match against Romania, on Tuesday, 2 June, was the first of Group 3 and so vitally important. Everyone looked towards Sunday and our clash with Brazil but we knew victories over the other countries were equally significant at this stage of the tournament. We had played Romania twice recently and both games – home and away – were drawn so we did not underestimate their strength. They also reached Mexico by defeating 1966 World Cup semi-finalists Portugal, which again gave a clear indication of their ability. I don't think anyone who stepped onto the pitch at the Estadio Jalisco was quite prepared for the reception we received from the Mexican crowd. The jeers and whistles that greeted our entrance were almost deafening. You would have thought we were playing the Mexicans themselves.

Alan Mullery (England): They were quite a dirty side actually. They were a bit nasty at times and there were a few things going on off the ball. The Romanians were a really tough side to play against, they were a physically tough side to play against. I think we had more skill and quality than they had. And that should come out in the end but doesn't always come out in the end. I think we were better at certain things than they were.

Francis Lee (England): It was a hard match. We had quite a strong dominance. They didn't look like they were going to score. And they kicked a few lumps out of us and that was it.

Bobby Moore (England): We kept the defence-conscious Romanians pegged in their own half for most of the first forty-five minutes, but without success. Our perseverance finally paid off in the sixty-fourth minute when Tommy Wright gave Alan Ball possession. His cross was back-headed on for Geoff Hurst, who swerved past one defender before slotting the ball home. It was a great relief to see that ball in the back of the net.

Gordon Banks (England): We failed to sparkle in our opening match against a physical and defensively minded Romanian team. We won, thanks to Geoff Hurst who latched on to a super pass from Francis Lee to score the only goal of the game with a shot that passed through the legs of their goalkeeper Adamache.

Francis Lee (England): Before the first game against Romania we hadn't had an alcoholic drink for four weeks and when we got back to the hotel after the game, we all thought we'll go and have two or three beers, sneak round the hotel or something. You didn't want a beer. You just lay on the bed sipping water, you were just absolutely knackered. There is a big change in your metabolism. It took a day or so to get over it, you know. After that game, I was lying down, and I felt like I'd been pulling a cart for a week.

Allan Clarke (England): I know against Romania players lost a stone in weight. I lost half a stone against Czechoslovakia, but I was trim so I didn't have a lot of weight to lose.

A day later Brazil and Czechoslovakia met in their opener in Guadalajara. The Czechs started the stronger of the two teams and opened the scoring after twelve minutes, but once Brazil got into their stride they were unstoppable. Rivellino equalised with a nicely worked free kick twelve minutes later and then they overran their opponents with three goals in the second half to run out worthy 4–1 winners.

Pelé (Brazil): Our first game was against Czechoslovakia on 3 June. Czechoslovakia had been called one of the strongest teams at the games by the press, and they got off to a good start with a goal by Petras just eleven minutes into the match. He moved past Brito and feinted Felix out of position to put the ball in the net. But I was not worried. It was evident shortly after play began that the Czech team, regardless of the pronouncements of Jozef Marco, were certainly not the excellent team they had fielded in 1962. And while I knew our defence had its weaknesses, I couldn't believe that our strong attack could not more than compensate for that. And, as if to prove my point, Rivellino, with a swerving free kick, equalled the score not long after, and the game was tied, 1–1.

Edu (Brazil): I remember the first game well because it is important. You're always a bit nervous. No matter how experienced a player is he feels the first game in the World Cup. And Brazil were kicking off against Czechoslovakia, a very good team who played nice football. They scored the first goal but we were so confident that we said, 'Keep calm, we'll turn this around.' We all thought we were going to be world champions. And we thought that even though we lost a goal we'd score more, because we had such a great forward line.

Felix (Brazil): The first game is the worst because no one knows what's going to happen. And we started by going one-nil down. We conceded the goal just as we were starting to grow into the game. We were just settling down, fifteen minutes into the match. From then on, we let ourselves go. And it ended 4–1. I had two or three difficult saves to make but Brazil attacked more than we defended. And after that first game, we really took off.

Bobby Moore (England): For a brief moment it looked as though Brazil might suffer the indignity of defeat against the Czechs. In fact, if the Czechs had taken full advantage of their early opportunities they could indeed have put themselves en route to victory. Their brilliant little striker Ladislav Petras weaved his way past three Brazilian defenders in the sixth minute only to aim wide. He put his head in his hands, knelt and begged forgiveness. He took up a slightly different pose soon afterwards, having taken the ball off the feet of Clodoaldo and planted it into the net. He knelt again, looked up to the heavens and made the sign of the cross. A single and moving scene which will always stand out in my memory. So the mighty Brazil were on the brink of disaster – but not for long. Pelé won a free kick just outside the penalty area and Rivellino curved the ball around the wall of defenders into the net. The issue remained in doubt until Gerson, who had already hit the post with a scorching drive, floated over a wonderful cross-field pass in the sixtieth minute for Pelé to crash into the net. The stadium erupted; Pelé had signalled his presence. Five minutes later Gerson again provided the outlet for Jairzinho cleverly to flick the ball over the head of the approaching goalkeeper Viktor and route it towards goal. In the closing minutes Jairzinho scored again after ghosting past two defenders and Brazil had sent out their warning to the rest of the world – and us in particular. The Czech hopes faded completely when, three days later, Romania defeated them 2–1.

Bobby Charlton (England): This Brazilian team had not only kept pace with the game but was threatening to define a whole new dimension of it. For many of us, the free kick converted by Rivellino was most disturbing. We had heard about his ability to do extraordinary things with the dead ball and his 'banana kick' was already a key part of his fast-rising reputation, and here he and Jairzinho were showing themselves brilliantly equipped to make practice on the training field come to life in the heat of match conditions. Jairzinho forced his way on to the left side of the Czech wall and Rivellino appeared to drive straight at his teammate. As Jairzinho flung himself away, the Czech goalkeeper, Ivo Viktor, could only brush the ball faintly with his fingers as it flew into the net. I turned to Martin Peters, who was sitting next to me, and the look on his face perfectly reflected my own feelings. Here was the reality of our next opponents. They so often made a fantasy of football, but they were clearly just as happy to deliver a killer blow as basic as a left hook.

Pelé (Brazil): The second half was all Brazil. I caught a long, high pass from Gerson, trapped it on my chest and volleyed it into the net before it touched the ground, or before Viktor even knew what was happening. Then, a short time later Jairzinho, certainly not nervous any more, took the ball down the field after Czechoslovakia had given away the ball on a corner kick, and broke through to score our third goal. Before the end of the game, Jairzinho did it again, shaking off three defenders and an attempted foul to cut back in smartly and shoot the ball past a frustrated Viktor for our final goal. And that was the way it ended: Brazil 4 Czechoslovakia 1.

That match was as memorable for a goal that didn't happen as for any of the five that did. Not long before the end of the game, Pelé spotted Czech keeper Viktor off his line. Pelé had long wanted to score from inside his own half, a feat that had rarely, if ever, been done before and certainly not on football's biggest stage. And so when he looked up and saw his chance he went for it.

Pelé (Brazil): It was during this game that I came close to making one of the most unforgettable goals of my career. In watching tapes and in playing friendly games in Europe, I had noticed that many European goalkeepers had a tendency to stray from their positions in front of the goal whenever the play was in the opponent's half of the field. In this particular game I noted that the Czech goalkeeper, Viktor, had this same tendency. He seemed assured that there was no danger so long as the activity was distant, and that he had more than ample time to get back to his position to guard the goal area if the play should come close. At this particular moment I had the ball in my possession well on our side of the midfield stripe, and the defence was making no great attempt to tackle the ball from me. Viktor was off to one side, watching the play, ready to return when required; the moment I had been waiting for arrived. It was a moment to demonstrate [my father] Dondinho's advice to 'play instinctively, almost without thinking' and almost without thinking – but with full knowledge of what I was doing – I launched a powerful kick for the goal. I am sure that most of the spectators must have thought I was insane . . . but they changed their minds when they saw the ball curving in towards the goal and Viktor many yards away, helpless, without the slightest chance to defend. Unfortunately, the ball just slid past the post on the outside, but the roar of approval from the crowd at least partially compensated for the miss. It was the most commented-upon play of the 1970 games. The tragic thing was that from then on Viktor kept near his net no matter where the play was, as did the goalkeepers of our subsequent opponents, so that I later wished I had saved a shot like that for the game with England, or for a more difficult adversary than Czechoslovakia!

When the draw was made, the Brazil v England game was the biggest match of the opening round. It was a mouth-watering prospect, featuring the winners of the last three World Cups; the country that invented the game against the country that perfected it. It was a contrast of styles, of tempos, and of attitude. And before the teams even got near the Estadio Jalisco, the fun and games had begun.

Gordon Banks (England): We were staying at the Hilton Hotel in Guadalajara and hardly got a wink of sleep on the night preceding our game against Brazil. Hundreds of Mexican supporters held an all-night anti-England vigil in the street outside. They constantly chanted 'Bra-zil' honked car horns and bashed dustbin lids together.

Bobby Moore (England): Some of the Brazilian supporters – and I believe many of them were Mexicans – went too far in their fanatical loyalty and apparent anti-English feelings. When a crowd of them formed outside the Hilton Hotel sounding car horns, yelling and screaming and keeping several of our players awake most of the night before the game, it was hardly harmless and good-natured patriotism. I was lucky enough to be sleeping at the rear of the hotel so I was unaffected.

Martin Peters (England): Their aim was clear, to stop us from sleeping – and, unfortunately, they had a good deal of success. Bobby Charlton hardly slept, Gordon Banks was kept awake until about 3.00 a.m. and many of the team were forced to change rooms in the middle of the night and move to the back of the hotel. Why we couldn't have been placed there from the start beats me.

Bobby Moore (England): Harold Shepherdson and Les Cocker, helped by a group of England supporters, tried to lure the mob away from the hotel. Disguised as players, they trooped out and into our coach and were driven around the block. Unfortunately, the Brazilian fans were not fooled, did not give chase and continued their vigil.

Gordon Banks (England): The England party had taken up the entire twelfth floor of the Hilton but the constant noise kept us awake all night. I was sharing a room with Alex Stepney of Manchester United. At one point a group of Mexican supporters gained access to the floor and banged on our door. I jumped out of bed and swung the door open just in time to see half a dozen Mexicans in their late teens and early twenties being chased down the corridor by a furious Jack Charlton.

Mario Zagallo (Brazil coach): While all that was going on our concentração had turned into an Aztec paradise. Not just inside but at the gate as well, where the samba was played daily. Whenever possible Brazilian players joined in and that went right to the hearts of the Mexican fans. Brito, Jairzinho, Pelé and Paulo Cesar didn't just put on a show on the football field. They were the kings of samba. Our players didn't take to the field for training matches or games in the early rounds without a bouquet of flowers in each of their hands. The flowers were handed over to fans. All the initiatives we adopted as a way of showing the Mexicans our friendliness were received with the utmost gratitude. The fact was that the Mexican people liked the seleção. The only thing they preferred was their own side. That festive expectation did not extend to the English. They gave the impression that they were Greek gods, two-faced ones.

Gordon Banks (England): We had only snatched a couple of hours of fitful sleep, but such was our motivation and state of mind, we couldn't wait to get out there and face the Brazilians.

England's decision to bring their own food and water, and even their own team bus, had infuriated the locals, who interpreted it as an offence. The anti-English feeling had long been present in Latin America and many of England's rivals had not forgotten Alf Ramsey calling the Argentines 'animals' after their bad-tempered clash at Wembley in 1966. Many in the region interpreted his words as a slight on the entire continent and saw Ramsey as the archetypal haughty, stuck-up Brit. Before the game, the always nationalistic Zagallo used those factors to rouse his players.

Pelé (Brazil): England came into this game with a further disadvantage; they were actively disliked for having called the Argentinians 'animals' in the 1966 games. In our game with England the stands were full of Brazilian flags, held not just by Brazilians, but by Mexicans who wanted to see England beaten.

Mario Zagallo (Brazil coach): They arrived in Mexico carrying water, food and they even brought their own bus. They were so sure of themselves and they didn't communicate much with anyone. The fans on the streets almost never saw them, because they only left their hotel if people begged them to. They gave the impression that they didn't want to mix. The coach of the team went further; in interviews he went out of the way to be arrogant.

Bobby Moore (England): 'The Mexican football fans need a devil and an angel,' I was told. 'Unfortunately, England was selected as the devil.' Perhaps that explains in some way the attitude we encountered. I would like to stress that, as individuals, we were always treated with courtesy and warmth and made lots of friends. It was only when we stepped out onto the pitch that we were looked upon as Public Enemy Number One. The jeers, boos and whistles had no effect on our performance and perhaps they even increased our desire to do better.

Pelé (Brazil): The stadium was jammed when we got there, and we arrived in a festive mood. In the bus from our hotel to the stadium we had a little batucada going; batucada is the Brazilian word for the carnival rhythms beaten out on any object by any other object close at hand, such as fingers drumming against a matchbox, or hands slamming against a windowsill, sometimes while one is humming a carnival tune as accompaniment, sometimes not. Batucada has a beat to it; it is always morale-building to a Brazilian – and we needed all the morale-building we could get.

Mario Zagallo (Brazil coach): The feelings of affection that the Mexicans felt for the Brazilians was obvious, as was the antipathy they felt for the English. I even warned our players in the dressing room before the game against England. The warmth of the Aztec fans could have affected their focus, and lead them to take their eye off the ball.

Players with both teams knew this was a match that could potentially decide the outcome of the group, and because it would decide who went where in the next round, by extension the whole tournament. Zagallo told his players the match was 'the final before the final' but the England side was not at all overawed. In fact, some of them believed they were the favourites going into the match.

Pelé (Brazil): This was really the most important game of the tournament. This was the 'final' so to speak. This was the meeting between the champions of 1958 and 1962, Brazil, and the present world champions, England, and it promised to be a great battle. People were looking forward to seeing how the Brazilian style of football – and attacking game – would fare against the English style of football, which was primarily defensive. But Zagallo decided that we would play their game. It would be a game of patience, he told us; a game of chess. The first one to make a mistake would pay for it, probably with the championship.

Carlos Alberto (Brazil): What happened was they drummed into us as a group, the players, that the most important match of the tournament was against England. And we were like, 'Eh, what do you mean the most important game of the Copa?' Because the team that finished first in the group, Brazil or England, with all due respect to Czechoslovakia and Romania, the first place in the group was going to be Brazil or England. The winners of the group would stay in Guadalajara, practically at sea level, and the runner-up, what was going to happen to them? They were going to leave Guadalajara and go to a higher altitude to face who? Oh, West Germany was there, waiting on them. And that was exactly what happened. We beat England, we stayed in Guadalajara, and England had to play West Germany and were knocked out. Zagallo, Chirol, Coutinho, they all said, 'If we win that game, we're definitely going to the final. Winning it was another thing, because we need to see who we're up against but we'll definitely be there in the final.' And that was what happened, so our work was well thought out, you know, well planned, the importance of the physical preparation, the importance of coming first, of beating England.

Bobby Charlton (England): Estadio Jalisco, Guadalajara, 7 June – the place and date were foremost in all our minds. Brazil, champions-elect in the opinion of most neutrals, would be our opponents – and the litmus test of our progress as a team through all the convulsions that had come since we set foot in Latin America. Here, potentially, was the match of the tournament, even though it might not be decisive to the progress of either team. Better than that, it might just possibly be one for the football ages.

Martin Peters (England): That afternoon in June was more than a football match. Anybody who was there will tell you the same. We were the symbol of English austerity and coldness and Brazil were the happy-go-lucky, heroic crusaders with right on their side.

Pelé (Brazil): It was generally considered in 1970 that England had the best defence, while Brazil had the best attack. People said that if a team could be made up combining English defence and Brazilian attack, it would be the perfect unbeatable team. Possibly. Or possibly not. One has to remember that England's defence was strong precisely because their attack was weak. With only two or three men in front it automatically gives the defence one or two more men. Conversely, critics of Brazil's style of play constantly claim that the defence is weak. This claim is based on the fact that Brazil puts four men on the line, thus depriving the defence of the possible assistance of those men. But the difference in style between the European style of play and the South American style of play is far more than the difference in one man more or less on the line. Regardless of style, it must always be remembered that the object of the game is to score goals, not merely to prevent your opponent from scoring them. Scoreless ties do not win games, or tournaments.

Mario Zagallo (Brazil coach): Our confidence as we sought to win the World Cup got much stronger after that win against the Czechs. Not just because we had hammered them. More important was the superb football we played. That demonstration of power and the proof that we had what it takes to respond on the pitch were encouraging signs. Our goal difference of three was also useful. It constituted an auspicious reflection, above all in defining our supremacy over the English. The British were never going to get a goal difference of more than plus one.

Francis Lee (England): I thought we were a better team than them. The challenge was to beat them playing football and to dominate them. There are certain parts of the game you won't beat them at like the Rivellino dribbles and things like that but there were other parts of the game they wouldn't beat us at. It was a contrast of two different styles, both high quality. I don't think they've got the same ability to cover the pitch and to pass it and support and everything like that. They played a different type of passing game, they passed it and somebody would control it and then stop. And they'd pass it back to somebody and they'd stop and they would gradually work their way up to the last third of the field and then they would speed up. Whereas we tried to play it quickly from the back and get them caught out of position.

Mario Zagallo (Brazil coach): The team we would face were very strong, and they played marvellous football. They arrived there as world champions. The glory of winning the title in 1966 had maybe turned English heads. I am convinced the English overestimated themselves.

Piazza (Brazil): England, of course, had to believe in themselves and that they were capable of winning another title. But I think they were so aware that they went too far. They arrived, as they say, too sure of themselves.

Pelé (Brazil): Right from the start we could see that our worries were justified. It wasn't easy to break down their defensive barriers. The British defence, and that was their strong point, worried me. I thought if they score then we'll struggle to equalise. It was going to be a game of patience, almost chess. The team that lost concentration would lose the game, and Zagallo knew that.

Both teams made changes to their starting line-ups. Brazil rested Gerson, who was nursing an injured thigh, and replaced him with Paulo Cesar, a mercurial winger. England, meanwhile, began with Tommy Wright in place of Keith Newton, whom he had replaced in the game against Romania after Newton was hacked down ruthlessly.

Gordon Banks (England): A couple of days before our game against Brazil, Alf Ramsey made an uncharacteristic faux pas. Following a training session, he gathered us all together and told us that the eleven who had finished the game against Romania would start against Brazil. Full back Keith Newton had not recovered from the injury he had picked up against the Romanians, which meant his Everton teammate Tommy Wright was to continue at right back. Chelsea's Peter Osgood had replaced Francis Lee and Ossie could not contain his joy at having been selected to face Brazil. Later that day we had a team meeting and Alf began talking about the roles of Francis Lee and Bobby Charlton, only for a perplexed Franny to point out that he hadn't been selected. 'But you are in the side, Francis,' said Alf. For some reason, Alf had completely forgotten that Peter Osgood had come on for Franny Lee against Romania. Alf was very embarrassed and Peter very disappointed.

Alan Ball (England): Sir Alf made one of his memorable speeches. 'Would you give gold away?' he asked, somewhat mysteriously. Before anyone could answer he added: 'Well, the ball is gold today. Don't give it away and you will defeat these Brazilians, but if you give it away in this heat you might not get it back.'

Bobby Charlton (England): We couldn't sit back against these Brazilians because that would be like inviting in the sea. Never forgetting the ability of Pelé, for instance, to change everything in a flicker of an eyelid, we would be ourselves and we would make a match of it, uncontaminated by any hint of fear or resignation. That much, unquestionably, we achieved.

Terry Cooper (England): I can remember at quarter to twelve the buzzer going to come out into the passageway to go out together, and looking to my right to see who I was walking out against, and it was Pelé. I remember thinking, 'Bloody hell, he's like a pocket battleship. Look at his thighs. Jesus, if you run into him . . .' And then I turned round and looked at the others! That stood out, how physically strong they were, as well as technically superb.

Alan Ball (England): I looked across at the Brazil side and thought, 'You'll not get a much better side than this ever, ever, ever.' Just awesome. I remember thinking, 'We've got to be on our knock here today.'

Pelé (Brazil): The Estadio Jalisco was full. It was a really hot day, something that bothered the English more than it did us, as we were used to it.

Gordon Banks (England): The heat was so withering I was sweating buckets just standing in line.

Pelé (Brazil): In this game between the champions of '58 and '62 and the champions of '66, that the whole world was watching, more than just a win was at stake. First and foremost it was about world footballing hegemony.

Tostão (Brazil): Dr Roberto Abdalla Moura, who operated on my eye and was present to watch all of the Brazil games at the invite of the backroom staff, tells a story in two chapters of my most recent book: Estadio Jalisco, Guadalajara. Midday. It was boiling hot. The stadium was good, but there was only electricity in one of the dressing rooms. That night, with the players already having gone to their rooms, someone said: 'We need to get there early tomorrow to get the dressing room with the electricity.' Someone said, 'What if the English get there before us?' So we looked at each other and someone said, 'Let's get over there now.' Dr Roberto went on: 'So four musketeers went off in the middle of the night to the stadium. They woke up the security guards and after explaining what was going on, they were let in to grab the ideal dressing room, with their Brazilian flag and all that. The result was that in that infernal heat the English team didn't even go into the dressing rooms at half-time. Brazil 1–0. They say the World Cup is won with tiny details and we proudly felt like we had contributed to the victory.'

Bobby Moore (England): The atmosphere at the Estadio Jalisco was electric, with bongo-playing Brazilian supporters adding a real South American calypso flavour to the proceedings. It was as though everyone knew they were seeing what was thought to be the two great soccer powers of the world.

Pelé (Brazil): Outside of Brazil I'd never seen so many Brazilian flags in the one place. It seemed like we were playing at the Maracanã or the Mineirão, or the Morumbi, or the Beira-Rio.

Alan Ball (England): We knew we could match them at keep ball, passing the ball, holding the ball up, which is what we've got to do in that heat and play a different style to how we would play in England. We *knew* we could match them at their game, in their climate.

The game kicked off at midday in blistering heat. Both sides were content to feel each other out and England had the best of the early stages with Peters and Lee both testing Felix. Neither side wanted to take unnecessary risks and England paid particular attention to Pelé.

Gordon Banks (England): Franny Lee tried to find Hurst but Brito extended the leg and Brazil leisurely wandered upfield. Brito to Paulo Cesar to Clodoaldo to Pelé. Whack! Alan Mullery dumped the great man on the ground. Mullers held up the palms of his hands to the referee in recognition of his cumbersome tackle and kept on the right side of the official by extending a hand to Pelé, offering to help him to his feet. Pelé ignored it. Mullers smiled and rubbed the top of Pelé's head with his hand. 'You okay, mate?' enquired Mullers. 'I am not . . . your . . . mate,' replied Pelé. 'It's best that you are,' said Mullers. 'Believe me, yer don't wanna make an enemy of me.' Pelé simply shook his head and smiled to himself.

Alan Mullery (England): You can't do that today, give him a few whacks. It doesn't work today; people fall over if you pass wind. They fall over and the referee gives them a free kick. In those days you had to take those knocks and he took them and came back for more. And when you think he played what, 1,600 games, 1,300 games in his career and there were people trying to kick him all that time to try and stop him winning games. It wasn't the first time I'd played against Brazil. The first time was in 1969 and that was in the Maracaná Stadium and at that stage the Maracaná Stadium held 200,000. So to play under that and then to go to Mexico and get 60,000 people it didn't bother us. But the first time playing against him at the Maracanã was something really special, to chase him all over the place, trying to catch him was quite difficult. But I learnt a lot from that game and a year later we were playing against him again.

I think I did the job that Alf Ramsey wanted me to do, which would be to stop him being the footballer he was, which was very difficult, and we'd have a better chance of winning the game than if we let him just do what he wanted to do. So I followed him everywhere he went. I think I hit him a few times. In those days they were tackles. Today it would be assault. People asked me how do you stop him and I said you buy a gun and you shoot him and that was the only way you could do that because he was the Lionel Messi of today. The year before the World Cup you could see how good Brazil were. Many, many years later I met Pelé in London one day and he said the only team they feared in Mexico was England.

Pelé (Brazil): It appeared to me that England was playing for a tie, possibly hoping to beat Czechoslovakia by a large margin while Romania contained us, thus putting England into the quarter-finals.

Nobby Stiles (England): It was nothing less than daunting to see the ease with which Pelé held off his marker. Repeatedly, Mullers tried to hustle Pelé off the ball. Repeatedly, he failed. He just couldn't get close enough, and at throw-ins and corners Pelé exerted tremendous leverage with his strong arms. When you looked at him in his maturity – and his performances in Mexico surely represented his prime – you saw a talent that he had honed down to all the essentials of winning football. If a simple pass would work best for the team, he would play it. It was only if he was under pressure and lacking other options that he would launch some outrageous initiative. He was both the engine and the heart of Brazil, as well as being the ultimate example of that nation's superb feeling for the game.

Gordon Banks (England): The opening ten minutes of England's match against Brazil are best described as footballing chess, with both sides sounding each other out. Then, just when I thought the game was settling down to a rolling, strolling classic, it suddenly exploded into life.

The England–Brazil game is unusual in that it is remembered not for the goal that was scored but for the goal that wasn't. With ten minutes gone, Jairzinho hit the byline and when Pelé got on the end of his cross the header looked goalbound. Until, that is, Gordon Banks sprung across his goal to touch the ball over the bar. Even today, fifty years later, it is still remembered as one of the greatest saves of all time.

British TV commentary: *'There goes Jairzinho, he's onside, that's a good cross ball, it's Pelé. And a fantastic save by Banks. What a fantastic save by Gordon Banks. A glorious header from Pelé.'*

Bobby Moore (England): One point no one could argue about was that we had the greatest goalkeeper in the world. Gordon Banks gave undeniable proof of his mastery with a save of pure magic in the tenth minute.

Gordon Banks (England): It started with a fantastic pass from Carlos Alberto who played right back and he hit it with the outside of his right foot and he actually bent it round the full back right into the path of Jairzinho. I moved two feet off my line, expecting him to cross to the penalty spot, in the belief that, since Pelé had now just entered our penalty area, I'd be first to the ball. Only Jairzinho didn't aim for the penalty spot. He whipped the ball across to a point just outside my six-yard box, a yard or so in from my right-hand post. As I turned my head I saw Pelé again. He'd made ground fast and such was the athleticism of the man, he'd already launched himself into the air. As an attacking header, it was textbook stuff. He rose above the ball and headed it hard and low towards my right-hand corner. The moment the ball left his head I heard Pelé shout 'Golo!'

Carlos Alberto (Brazil): When Pelé prepared to jump and head the ball I think we all thought that it would be a goal.

Gordon Banks (England): Faced with a situation like that your mind becomes clear. All your experience and technique take over. One thing did flash through my mind: if I do make contact, I'll not hold this. The ball hit the deck two yards in front of me. My immediate concern was how high it would bounce. It left the turf and headed towards my right-hand corner, but I managed to make contact with the finger of my gloved right hand. It was the first time I'd worn these particular gloves. I'd noticed that the Mexican and South American goalkeepers wore gloves that were larger than their British counterparts, with palms covered in dimpled rubber. I'd been so impressed with this innovation that I'd invested in two pairs. Those little rubber dimples did their stuff: the bouncing ball didn't immediately glance off my hand and I was able to scoop it high into the air. But another thought flashed through my mind. In directing the ball upwards, I might only succeed in flicking it up into the roof of the net. So I rolled my right hand, slightly, using the third and fourth fingers as leverage. I landed crumpled against the inner side netting of the goal, and my first reaction was to look at Pelé. I hadn't a clue where the ball was. He'd ground to a halt, head clasped between his hands, and I knew then all that I needed to know. Ninety-nine times out of a hundred Pelé's shout of 'Golo!' would have been justified, but on that day I was equal to the task. It was really just about being in the right place at the right time – one of those rare occasions when years of hard work and practice combine in one perfect moment. As Pelé positioned himself for the resulting corner he turned to me and smiled. He told me he thought that he'd scored. So did I – and I told him as much. 'Great save . . . mate,' he said. At a critical stage of the game, it was 0–0, if the ball had gone in at that particular stage I think the heads would have gone down.

Pelé (Brazil): Banks made what was to my mind the best save of the World Cup. Not because it was my header. I just am recognising a fact. The header was hard, surprisingly hard, and in the corner. The keeper's dive was instantaneous and efficient.

Nobby Stiles (England): When he saved from Pelé – more brilliantly it seemed than any goalkeeper had ever saved before – we leapt up from the bench and shook our heads in wonderment. Banksy, in his rather dour way, said that he didn't really know what all the fuss was about. He was merely doing his job and, if anyone cared to remember, he had made equally good saves back at home in bread-and-butter league games.

Gordon Banks (England): That save from Pelé is considered by many to be the greatest I ever made. Such opinions are always subjective. I believe the reason my save against Pelé has received so many accolades is largely due to the fact that it was made in a very high profile match in front of a global TV audience.

Ado (Brazil): I modelled myself on him, Banks. I really liked that guy. My uncle sent me pictures of him from Italy, because it was easier when you were in Europe. In Brazil we had very little access to newspapers and television. And so I looked at how they trained because in Brazil we didn't have goalkeeper coaches; that began in 1970 with Carlesso. The guy who trained me at Corinthians was Dadson, an ex-boxer, and he used to throw medicine balls at me. I was pretty damn strong. [Laughs]. So I tried to model myself on these guys.

Gordon Banks (England): Pelé always says to me when he comes over here, he says, I travel all over the world and they talk about the goals I scored but when I come to England all they talk about is that save. The TV footage of the game shows me laughing as I turned to take up my position for the corner. I was laughing at what Bobby Moore had just said to me. 'You're getting old, Banksy,' he quipped. 'You used to hold on to them.' Like hell I did.

The save boosted England but they could not get a goal and just moments later there came an incident that many Brazilian players believe was the turning point of the match. Tommy Wright sent over an inviting cross from the right flank and Felix made a point-blank save to stop Francis Lee's diving header. The Brazilians thought Lee kicked Felix as they fought for the loose ball on the ground and they set out to take their revenge as soon as possible.

Bobby Charlton (England): After the Banks save, our feeling was that we had become impregnable. All that was necessary now was one moment of precision in front of goal. Agonisingly, it didn't come.

Bobby Moore (England): During the tense conflict there was only one moment when it appeared that tempers might become frayed. This came when Francis Lee dived to head a Tommy Wright cross goalwards. Felix let the ball slip from his hands and Lee swung his foot in an attempt to push it into the net but instead, he caught the goalkeeper. Several Brazilian players surrounded Lee but fortunately only angry words were exchanged and, after all, the Manchester City forward was only attempting to play the ball.

British TV commentary: *'Tommy Wright made a good run and a good cross. It was Lee. And I think he's kicked the goalkeeper. And the goalkeeper is spark out. Let's see that again. A great bit of running by Tommy Wright. Francis Lee coming in on it, the header, saved. Lee falling. The ball is free, the goalkeeper hadn't got it. And Lee kicked him in the head.'*

Francis Lee (England): I knew what he had done and I knew why he'd done it. But it was still an accidental kick on the goalkeeper. The thing is, the goalkeeper made a very good save, a blind save, he didn't know what he had done. I knew what I'd done, I'd missed a golden opportunity. But I'd headed it exactly where I wanted to head it but he flailed his arms and saved it and then it just dropped on the floor and I just had a swing at it as it dropped and he went for the ball at the same time. I think I kicked him on the shoulder or something like that. He was acting.

Felix (Brazil): He came in with a nasty challenge. He had already hit Everaldo. There was a cross, and I thought it was Bobby Charlton who headed it but it was Lee. The cross came in from their right – our left – and Lee threw himself through the air to head it. And I saved it; it was a great save actually, with one hand and then dived on it and smothered it. Lee was on the ground too and he turned and thinking he was going to get the ball he got my face, right on my face and knocked me out. I saw the tapes later . . . and I hit the ground and was knocked out, I was shaking. Mario Américo came running and he took care of me. So I got up and kept playing. It was just like if I was a boxer being knocked out, but I was back on my feet. I was on automatic after that, you know when you can see everything that you are doing but it's like you're watching someone else. Then the first half ended, it was all square.

Francis Lee (England): It was a great save. It was a bad miss but I did exactly what I wanted to do and he sort of flailed himself and put his arm up and it hit his arm and came down and dropped on the floor. I had a kick at it when it was on the floor, the ball. I was pissed off that I never scored because I thought I should have scored. And I know that someone once told me that the Brazilians rated that as good as the save that Banks made from Pelé. Everybody said that Felix was not a good goalkeeper and we thought wow, here's our chance and he turns out to make a save like that; if that had gone in it was over.

Carlos Alberto (Brazil): There was still the remnants of what we saw in 1966. The game against England, they tried to impose their style of play on us, which was going in hard, and we weren't having it. That guy Lee, on two separate occasions, Felix had gathered the ball, twice, not just once, and he kicked him, he could have stopped short, the ball was with the keeper, so what was he doing kicking the keeper in the face? He did it once and then the second time I was there challenging too. I remember, I said to Pelé, 'Pelé, we've got to . . .' and Pelé knew how to dish it out. I wasn't good at it, I went over the score and I risked getting sent off. So I said to Pelé, 'Hey, Pelé . . .' and Pelé said to me, 'Leave it to me, leave it to me.' But the game restarted and the first loose ball was right there between me and him. And I said to myself, 'I'm not waiting on Pelé.' I was a bit clumsy, but I thought, 'Shit, I've got to make him feel it.' So I hit him here on the thigh and it went bright red, because he was very white, really pale. And immediately I thought, 'Shiiiiiiiit, I'm going to get sent off.' But it seemed as if the referee sort of recognised that the guy was playing dirty and he just gave me a yellow card. I remember that from then on in the game got better. They had a great team, they started to play football, real football, and I'll tell you, we were very lucky in that game, because after we went 1–0 up . . .

Felix (Brazil): Carlos Alberto shouted to Pelé, 'Hey, Negão, you need to sort that guy out.' And Pelé said, 'How am I going to sort him out if he's there and I am here up front? How do you expect me to get back and sort him out?' Pelé had been kicked about for so long, the poor guy, so he knew how to get someone back. I saw Pelé start in football, because I was at Portuguesa at the same time that he began. So I saw how he was treated. He learned to dish it out without the referee seeing. So in this case, Carlos Alberto called him over. And then suddenly the ball went to Lee and so Carlos Alberto put him up in the air. Lee was lucky because he never caught him cleanly.

Mexican TV commentary: *'No, Carlos Alberto. No. No. No. You don't do that here. There's no need for that, Carlos Alberto. You have to play fair. A very strong and very bad challenge by Carlos Alberto. My good friend Carlos Alberto, the captain of the Brazilian team, you can't be doing that.'*

Francis Lee (England): He clattered me, but okay, you got clattered all the time. Nothing new.

Edu (Brazil): The England game was the hardest, because they came after us. An important moment was when Lee was harassing us and he went in hard on Felix. Carlos Alberto got him back and he got a bit freaked and it calmed him down.

And England were done. Because he was their danger man, he created for them. It changed the game.

The incident confirmed what many people saw but few were prepared to say outright, that for all their talent and ability the Brazilians were no angels, and they knew how to mix it when they had to.

Martin Peters (England): I reckon the game itself took years off my life. At half-time I was convinced there wouldn't be any goals. We were both wary of each other and a draw would have suited us both – not that there wasn't much physical combat. The Romanians were hard, but as far as I was concerned the Brazilians were harder; and if that seemed difficult to believe, I had the bruises and soreness to prove my point. Jairzinho went right over the top of the ball and kicked my shins, and I also had a dust-up with Pelé right on the final whistle. He had a go at me, and I landed one back, so that was twice I lost my temper which is unusual for me. I know that Brazil prospered because they had men such as Pelé, Tostão, Jairzinho and Rivellino, but it would be foolish to overlook that they were essentially a team, and apart from their eccentric goalkeeper they were not so badly equipped at the back as some thought. They could dish out the stick when it was wanted, as I know only too well.

Alexandru Neagu (Romania): Pelé was very good, but he was a liar, and he didn't have manners on the pitch; he used to dive and try to trick the ref and his opponents.

Nicolae Lupescu (Romania): At one point, I tackled Pelé hard. He spat on me and told me something I never understood. I spat back.

The game was very evenly poised at the halfway stage and both teams believed they could edge ahead in the second period. Brazil had the advantage of being more at home in the heat but England remained confident.

Martin Peters (England): At the interval we were level and I just couldn't see them scoring. Pelé was superbly marked by Alan Mullery and Tostão and Jairzinho were being contained. We had every reason to think that if anybody was going to grab one it was us, for their defence, especially their keeper Felix, were a bag of nerves.

Pelé (Brazil): The English worked hard defensively to annul our attacks. Alan Ball fell deep, as did Bobby Charlton, all so that their defence wouldn't be breached. Because of that the English attack hardly bothered our defence. I got the impression they were playing for a draw.

Gordon Banks (England): On entering the dressing room at half-time I was surprised to see non-playing members of the squad, such as Jack Charlton and Peter Osgood, along with Peter Thompson and Brian Kidd, hacking at large chunks of ice with knives and chisels. Alf had instructed them to place broken ice in towels, which we were then told to drape around our necks to cool us down. It felt great so I asked Peter Thompson to hack off some more ice and place it in a polythene bag for me. I intended to take the bag of ice out with me on the pitch, place it behind one of the goalposts, and when play was down in the Brazilian half of the field use it to cool myself down. Less than ten minutes into the second half we were on the attack so I went over to the polythene bag anticipating a brief but welcome dip into my store of ice. I couldn't believe it. All I found was a bag of tepid water. In little over ten minutes every chunk of ice had melted.

The only goal of the game came fifteen minutes into the second period and while it could not be described as slick, it featured much of the individual brilliance that Brazil would be remembered for: a nutmeg from Tostão on Bobby Moore, a no-look pass from Pelé, and a goal from Jairzinho.

Martin Peters (England): Then they hit us with a goal that was their speciality. It was great to watch, I suppose, but what few people realised in all the hysteria was that they had three lucky rebounds before Jairzinho whacked it in. Still, the ball went into the net and that's what counts.

Brazilian radio commentary: *'Goooooooooooooooooooooooooooo ooooooooal! Jaiiiiirziiiiinho for Brazil! Fourteen and a half minutes. Jairzinho after a cross by Paulo Cesar. After a dummy by Pelé. Who rolls the ball to Jairzinho. Who dribbles and the keeper comes out. The Brazilian shoots from close in. The English goalkeeper is livid. But there's no point in crying now. Brazilian goal in Mexico. To the delirium of the Brazilian fans. The fans of our beloved Brazil. Brazil 1, England 0.'*

Pelé (Brazil): Tostão's move was genius. He dribbled past two defenders and then crossed to me inside the area, almost without looking. I could have taken a shot. Cooper could have blocked my shot. I saw Jair free and I gave him the ball. Cooper closed me down and I gave it to Jair. It was fatal. The shot was strong and angled. Brazil, 1–0. We all felt that goal was worth the World Cup.

Jairzinho (Brazil): It was a marvellous move by Tostão on the left. Beating one, two, three, four English defenders, he passed it with his right into the penalty area. It came to Pelé, I called for it, he passed it to me and I was running in to hit it. My marker

Cooper threw himself, Banks came out and I hit it. It was a beautiful goal. I celebrated that goal for about five minutes. I never jumped so much in my life.

Tostão (Brazil): In the second game against England it was tough and there were few chances to combine moves with Pelé. I looked over and saw Roberto warming up and I thought, 'He's coming on for me.' I'm sure that gave me the stimulus to try an individual move and I went on a dribble that helped set up the only goal – looking at the tape I admit I fouled Bobby Moore with my arm. But we scored and even though Roberto came on for me afterwards, it was then that I sealed my place in the side.

Mario Zagallo (Brazil coach): Until that point in my time in Mexico I hadn't experienced such euphoria. That moment was worth so much that even when I think of it now I don't know whether to laugh or cry. Five minutes later Dr Antônio do Passo asked me if we would win the game. I answered that it was a game of giants, two evenly matched teams. I said, 'Dr Passo, in a game like this, whoever scores the first goal wins.' And we had scored the first goal. I was calm but I was thinking that the moment of truth had arrived for our much-criticised defence – 'My God, Brito and Piazza, will they hold out? And Felix. How will those three hold up? Did the critics get to them? No!' The rest of the game proved that we could be champions: a superb attack and a magisterial midfield. Added to that, we were putting on an extraordinary defensive performance. Felix was a wall. Brito and Piazza grew and were giants. And not only them. Everyone.

Bobby Moore (England): One look at the relief in the faces of the Brazilian players when they scored was enough to convince me that they were more worried about us than anyone.

Alan Ball (England): It was a wonderful match to play in and I have only one grouse. I will maintain until the day I die that Tostáo elbowed me in the face just as I was about to nick the ball from him. He turned back on to his right foot and crossed the ball. It went straight to Pelé. With Brian Labone facing him and Terry Cooper straining to get across, Pelé decided against a shot and elected to slide the ball almost gently at an angle for Jairzinho. Cooper lost his footing as he went for a last-ditch interception and Jairzinho hammered his cross-shot high into the net with his right foot. I don't want to sound grudging but there should have been a free kick awarded against Tostáo.

England dominated the last half hour of the match as they pushed forward in search of an equaliser. They had a string of half chances and some that were even more clear-cut. The best fell to substitute Jeff Astle, who scuffed a shot wide from ten yards. Alan Ball saw his drive from outside the box clip the bar and go over and Felix struggled as the crosses rained in from all angles. As England threw men forward, spaces started to open up at the back and Brazil counter-attacked. But neither side could get another goal.

Martin Peters (England): For the first time things were not under control, probably because we were pushing forward more and leaving a few gaps behind. The rest of the match was nothing but pure agony for us. Poor Jeff Astle, who came on with Colin Bell for Lee and Bobby Charlton, laughed off the moment when he put the ball past the right-hand post with virtually a free shot when a Brazilian defender dropped a terrible clanger. I say he laughed it off outwardly but I wouldn't like to guess what he felt inwardly. Jeff just turned away and beat the air with his fist. It is unfair, however, to single out any one miss. There were plenty of others.

Terry Cooper (England): To be fair to Jeff Astle, he'd only just come on.

Gordon Banks (England): Jeff had finished the season as the leading goalscorer in the First Division and he had been presented with the sort of chance that was normally meat and drink to him. Whether it was because he had only just arrived on the pitch and was yet to be properly adjusted to the pace and intensity of the game, I don't know. Whatever the reason, he missed the sort of chance he normally gobbled up. With Felix stranded, Jeff scuffed his effort wide. The chance was gone, as was our chance of taking something from an even and exhilarating game. We gave it everything we had. Bobby Moore was imperious. Alan Mullery indefatigable. Alan Ball unlucky when he cut in from our left and saw his shot cannon off the Brazilian crossbar with Felix well beaten. Towards the end, I thought we would deservedly equalise.

Jairzinho (Brazil): The English had lots of chances to open the scoring. But for me this was the best game our goalkeeper Felix had.

Bobby Charlton (England): We couldn't get the draw that was, I will always believe, the least we deserved, but we could continue to show that we were authentic world champions. It was a superb match and there was no question that we provided the hardest opposition Brazil faced in the tournament. Franny Lee had one chance, but from close in he could only head straight at the Brazilian goalkeeper Felix. Martin Peters had an opportunity earlier, after a typically subtle run, but his header went too high. A shot by Alan Ball flew off the crossbar. Finally, the ball fell to Jeff Astle, who had replaced Lee. Astle was brilliant in the air, less so on the ground, and his left-footed shot flew wide.

Pelé (Brazil): What gave a real value to our win was the way the English played. They gave everything to try and stop us winning.

Piazza (Brazil): Sometimes, against Uruguay for example, we were terrible in the first half. But we managed, truly, to always play better in the second half. Now, against England, they were the holders. They really had an extraordinary team. So the game was end to end. That win, it was all down to chance. A chance arose and we took it. England had a chance to level, they had a chance to score the first goal, but that's natural. We knew England were a strong side.

Ado (Brazil): It was the final before the final. I followed England a bit and I liked their midfield and the goalkeeper; England had an impressive side. I said, if we beat them then there's no way we're going to lose after that. And we managed it, but it was a tough game. And that was confirmation of what we could do in the rest of the games to come.

Bobby Charlton (England): It was a great match and was always going to be settled by one roll of the ball, one little bit of fate. If I could go back through all the games I played for England and wish again for one of the defeats to be transferred to the win column, it would be this one, because if we had won it, I do not believe anyone could have stopped us.

Bobby Moore (England): I don't think it would be unrealistic to say that we deserved at least a draw with Brazil. We had outplayed them for much of the game, particularly in the closing stages. We did everything right except in that so important department in front of goal. I suppose that, in the end, we only had ourselves to blame. We created numerous scoring chances yet threw them all away.

Francis Lee (England): How many should we have beaten Brazil by? We should have beaten them 4–3 or 4–2. I'd have loved to play against them on a chilly night in Manchester. Or at a nippy night in Wembley. Then we might have seen some real action.

Pelé (Brazil): Credit must be given where it is due. The English team had some outstanding players. Men like Banks and Bobby Moore and Cooper and Bobby Charlton and Jack Charlton. They can play on any Brazilian team at any time – and that is no light compliment.

The match ended with another iconic moment. As Pelé and Bobby Moore swapped shirts, a cameraman caught them together in what both men said was an exchange of words that summed up the enormous regard in which they quite clearly held one another.

Bobby Moore (England): At the end I swapped shirts with Pelé and told him: 'See you in the final.' He nodded and grinned and replied: 'I think you will.'

Nobby Stiles (England): If there was ever a perfect picture of what football represented at its best, at its purest, it was the one taken of him and Pelé embracing and exchanging their shirts at the end.

Bobby Charlton (England): When, at the end, Pelé and Moore exchanged jerseys, it was entirely appropriate. When I thought of what our captain had come through, and how he had handled it, and the lift he gave us all when he returned to the squad, I could only marvel at the quality of his performance that day in Guadalajara. He was a giant in a game that I will always rate among the best, if not the best, I ever played in.

Gordon Banks (England): It was, I'm sure, Bobby's intention to go up to Pelé and congratulate him. But the Brazilian beat him to it. The victor saw fit to lavish praise upon the vanquished, because Pelé knew Bobby had been outstanding, and that Brazil had been as fortunate to win as we had been unlucky to lose. There had been little to choose between the two teams, but there had been one telling difference. Finishing. Brazil had taken their best chance and we had missed ours. At that level of football, the consequences of missing a chance can be catastrophic.

Terry Cooper (England): Probably the best team I've ever played against. Probably the best team I've ever seen all round.

Jack Charlton (England): Everybody after that game thought it would be an England–Brazil final. Everybody thought it. And we thought it, to tell you the truth.

Martin Peters (England): My first reaction to our defeat by Brazil, a defeat that had unwanted consequences, was of utter dejection. I was sick. I have been in the game long enough to have discovered there is no reason to believe you will always be rewarded for effort and I suppose by now I ought to have learned you can't win them all. The fact is I don't think I will ever look back on this match without feeling sorry for myself and all the lads. So much work, so much spirit, so much preparation down the drain. Self-pity has no place in a professional's make-up, but we are only human and we were all inconsolable. Maybe that was why we enjoyed ourselves with a vengeance that night in the hotel. Alf gave us an extension and we had a few drinks to try to forget. We didn't go mad, but now I know how people can use alcohol to try to wash away unpleasant memories.

Pelé (Brazil): When we got back to the hotel after the game, happy and excited, there was a mob of Brazilians and Mexicans there, all wanting to continue the celebration through the rest of the afternoon and far into the night. Sleep was almost impossible; automobile horns never stopped blowing and the crowd never stopped singing and shouting. One would have thought we had already won the World Cup, whereas we hadn't even made the quarter-finals with any assurance.

The result meant that with four points from four Brazil were almost certainly through. Romania could still qualify for the quarter-finals with a win but they were another side whose preparations left something to be desired. First-choice goalkeeper Necula Raducanu was dropped for indiscipline and had to wait until twenty-eight minutes of their third match against Brazil to get a game. It was the first time a goalkeeper had been substituted in a World Cup match. That behaviour was indicative of greater problems in the Romanian squad. Nicolae Dobrin, the Romanian footballer of the year in 1966, 1967 and 1971, was another who was dropped because of off-the-field behaviour.

Nicolae Lupescu (Romania): Dobrin didn't play in that tournament because he loved beer too much. He used to drink one, but because of the heat he would ask for the second, then for the third and so on. That was it. Dobrin was saying the weather is too warm, so he's not training. In the night, he was out in the bars, he was leaving the hotel. I liked him as a person, but it wasn't unfair to him that he didn't play. He didn't deserve to!

Angelo Niculescu (Romania coach): I didn't talk to Dobrin after the tournament about the reason behind my decision not to use him. He knew I liked discipline, and players should have given their all ahead of such an important tournament. I couldn't spend the entire day asking him to behave, to give everything. He was complaining about the heat all the time. I told him: 'Dobrin, there was never a player born with an umbrella to protect him!'

Nicolae Lupescu (Romania): And regarding Raducanu . . . What could the manager do if he didn't find him in his bed at 3.00 a.m. in the morning?

Pelé (Brazil): We were fortunate that their fine keeper Raducanu was not in for the full game; rumour had it he was still being disciplined for having pushed someone into the hotel pool in a moment of high spirits.

Mircea Lucescu (Romania): The shirts we wore against Brazil were bought by me! Brazil was playing in yellow, just like we did. I went to a market and bought the blue shirts we played in. I then attached the national symbols with a pin! I still have Pelé's shirt; we exchanged shirts. I didn't wash it, I kept it as he gave it to me. It's now like a painting for me! It still has some sweat on it, you can see it.

Nevertheless, Romania were no pushovers. Pelé and Jairzinho put Brazil 2–0 up after twenty-two minutes but Romania, by now with their new goalkeeper in position, fought back valiantly. Florea Dumitrache made it 2–1 twelve minutes before half-time and even after Pelé restored Brazil's two-goal cushion midway through the second half, Emerich Dembrovschi brought Romania back into contention once more with seven minutes remaining.

Pelé (Brazil): Romania had beaten Czechoslovakia in the interim, to everybody's surprise, and had automatically gone up in everyone's estimation. Dembrovschi and Dumitrache, two powerful forwards, were proving themselves to be players of international calibre. We started off playing excellent football against a team that quite obviously was nervous to be playing us, with our record and reputation. With the game only nineteen minutes old, the ball was passed to me; I took it through the Romanian defence and kicked our first goal, an easy goal, and just one minute later Jairzinho dribbled the ball through the Romanian midfield and easily scored our second goal unassisted. It appeared to us that we could make as many goals as we wanted, whenever we wanted, and we allowed this feeling to relax our guard somewhat. Shortly thereafter, Dumitrache made a brilliant goal, passing our defence as if they were not there and completely fooling Felix at the net. The second half had scarcely started when I scored our third goal, and immediately we became the same euphoric team, convinced that some divine inspiration would lead us to overwhelming victory – but after that the Romanian defence tightened and we could make little headway against them. Then, with eight minutes left in the game, Dembrovschi took a high ball perfectly and headed it past Felix to score the second goal for Romania. The game ended that way, with Brazil winning 3–2, but it was far from the runaway victory we had expected and I am convinced that a bit more of that euphoric over-confidence in the first half could have led to a tie, or even to a defeat.

Nicolae Lupescu (Romania): At half-time, against Brazil, our coach told us to attack, no matter if its Brazil we're playing against. He shouted it clear. We were close to doing something major in that game. If it had lasted ten minutes more, I think we would have equalised, and then we would have won the game.

Necula Raducanu (Romania): I could have played in Brazil. I was there in 1969, in Rio, and I became friends with Pelé. We met in Guadalajara, at the World Cup. We kept in touch over the years, and we have some pictures together. He used to call me Ricardo. He scored against me in 1970. After the game, the journalists asked me: 'How did Pelé score against you?' I said: 'I let him do it because he's my friend!'

That result meant England took on Czechoslovakia needing just a point to qualify for the last eight and Ramsey made several changes, prime among them giving a debut to Allan Clarke, the twenty-three-year-old Leeds United striker who was tickled by his coach telling him he finally thought he was ready to don an England shirt.

Allan Clarke (England): The day before we played Czechoslovakia – I can remember it as if it was yesterday – Alf came up to me and said, 'I am going to play you tomorrow,' and I said, 'That's great.' Alf said, 'I think you're ready now, son.' And I thought, *Alf, I've been ready for three years.*

Bobby Moore (England): We needed only to draw against Czechoslovakia to enter the last eight. This we were confident of doing. Wishing to keep his players fresh for Sunday's quarter-final, Sir Alf made several changes for the Czech game. He gave Allan Clarke – on his wedding anniversary and wife's birthday – his first full cap and brought in Jackie Charlton, Jeff Astle, Colin Bell and the now fit Keith Newton. There were significantly few words in the team talk beforehand when Sir Alf asked for volunteers for the job of penalty taking, with Geoff Hurst out of the side. No one responded so Allan Clarke said he would take them as he had done at Leicester and Fulham. And as it turned out his decision gave him the opportunity to score on his debut.

Alan Ball (England): We left that [Brazil] game undaunted, knowing that we had the team capable of retaining the trophy. Brazil defeated Romania, which meant they topped the group. Plenty of folk were indulging in the mathematics of the situation as we went forward to our final group match, but the bottom line was that we must not lose. Brazil could relax. If we lost by a goal, points and goal difference would put us absolutely level with Romania and lots would have to be drawn. If we lost by two goals then Romania would go through. Sir Alf decided to rest some players and introduce recruits. He must have been feeling confident.

The match itself was poor, with neither side showing much flair and the winning penalty aside, goalkeeping errors at both ends were the closest thing to goals. England could be forgiven for losing their focus and thinking ahead to the quarter-final date with the top team in Group 4, but their insipid showing was not a good omen for the rest of the tournament.

Allan Clarke (England): We were having a team meeting before the game and we had this fellow called Les Cocker, who was a trainer with our great Leeds United side. And he said, 'If we have a penalty, who'll take it?' I'm making my debut and I was waiting for a more experienced player to volunteer and it seemed like a long time [was going by]. So I said, 'I'll take it.' And Alf said, 'Good lad.' We won 1–0 and I scored the penalty. After the match I was drying myself off and Les Cocker came up to me and said, 'Alf was funny when you were placing the ball on the spot.' Les was in the dugout with Alf and the subs, and he said that Alf said, 'Will Allan score?' and I said, 'What?' And he said, 'Will Allan score?' and Les said, 'Alf, you could put your mortgage on it.'

Martin Peters (England): Our policy has always been to take one match at a time and not bother what others were doing, but at this stage it was almost impossible not to think about the many permutations, because to some extent we knew our future could lie in somebody else's hands. Being knocked over by Brazil, unjustly or not, had virtually made them certain of heading the group and staying in Guadalajara for the quarter-final. We were now fighting for our lives to come second and go to León, about 160 miles away, and go to a ground that held only 25,000. Fortunately, our third qualifying match against the Czechs came after Brazil had beaten Romania, so we knew that a draw would be good enough.

Alan Ball (England): We were not at our best. These things happen from time to time; days when everything you try just seems not to come off. Thankfully, we scored after forty-eight minutes, when Colin Bell was fouled in the area and Allan Clarke dispatched the penalty. I went on twelve minutes later in place of Bobby Charlton, whose appearance took him level with Billy Wright's record 105 full cap appearances for England.

Bobby Moore (England): We would be the first to admit we played badly that day. Whether it was the changes that were made that disturbed the rhythm of the side or not I do not know. Nothing seemed to go smoothly and we even had a scare when a drive from Karol eight minutes from the end slipped through Gordon Banks' hands and onto the bar. Mind you, Colin Bell, who replaced Bobby Charlton, hit the bar at the other end just earlier. We won and that was what really counted at that stage.

Gordon Banks (England): We dominated the proceedings against the Czechs, but it was no classic. An Allan Clarke penalty gave us a 1–0 victory, but that was enough to see us qualify from our group. Towards the end of the match, the Czech full back Dobias tried his luck from twenty-five yards. The ball swerved through the thin air and what should have been a comfortable save for me, suddenly became a problem. I managed to get the fingertips of my right hand to the deviating ball and push it upwards. I immediately spun around and was astonished to see the ball return from the crossbar and straight into my waiting hands. 'Brilliant!' said Jack, 'and what are yor gonna dee for yer next trick against them Jormans?'

The Mexican press may have warmed to us a little, but the Mexican public were still very hostile when we took to the pitch for our final group game against Czechoslovakia. I had more trouble with the crowd during this game than the Czech forward line. They pelted me with orange peel, apple cores and coins throughout the first half. I complained to the referee, who drew the matter to the attention of the FIFA officials present. They in turn asked the Mexican police to stand behind my goal and that changed things drastically: about five times the amount of orange peel and coins rained down. I wouldn't be short of change for the telephone after this game.

Bobby Moore (England): Sir Alf Ramsey took one look at our dejected and mournful faces and said, 'Go out and get the kiss of life.' It was after our defeat by Brazil in Guadalajara and he knew how badly we felt. So, for the first time since our arrival in Mexico over four weeks earlier, we let our hair down. And I mean a little because, back home, one newspaper printed a story about some of us having a wild fling and being put on the carpet by Sir Alf the next morning. This was pure fabrication.

	P	W	D	L	Gls	Pts
BRAZIL	3	3	0	0	8-3	6
ENGLAND	3	2	0	1	2-1	4
Romania	3	1	0	2	4-5	2
Czechoslovakia	3	0	0	3	2-7	0

FIVE

GROUP 4

2 June	León	Peru	3–2	Bulgaria
3 June	León	Morocco	1–2	West Germany
6 June	León	Peru	3–0	Morocco
7 June	León	West Germany	5–2	Bulgaria
10 June	León	West Germany	3–1	Peru
11 June	León	Bulgaria	1–1	Morocco

Closed and secretive, the Iron Curtain countries were always shrouded in mystery when they arrived at World Cups. In 1970, four of Europe's nine qualifiers came from the Soviet bloc and not much was known about them. One of them, Bulgaria, were taking part in their third consecutive World Cup finals and still hoping for their first win. This year they were highly rated, having knocked out Poland and the Netherlands in the qualifiers. They retained several of the players who had taken them to the final of the Olympic soccer tournament two years earlier and as those games also took place in Mexico they had the added advantage of experience in the heat and altitude.

Dimitar Penev (Bulgaria): You know what, we had a great team back then. And it had all started two years earlier in 1968, when, coincidentally, Mexico hosted the Summer Olympics. Bulgaria managed to finish as runners-up in the Olympic football tournament, losing to Hungary in the final. Some of the guys who played in that Olympic tournament then returned two years later to Mexico for the World Cup as Bulgarian internationals. Players like my CSKA Sofia teammate Petar Zhekov took part in both events and were thus already familiar with what playing in Mexico was like. As you already mentioned, we did great in the 1970 World Cup qualifiers and we wanted to show the world that Bulgaria was full of talented players. Besides, Mexico was Bulgaria's third consecutive World Cup appearance and given our success at the already mentioned 1968 Olympics it was something we wanted to build on. Unfortunately, things didn't work out for us . . .

In 1970, before regular television coverage, the internet and the globalisation of newspapers and magazines, it could be difficult to find out details on your future opponents. That was definitely the case when it came to the Communist bloc nations that were largely cut off from the West. It was easier for their European neighbours, who at least could see the top clubs in European competition and the national side in regular qualifiers for the European Championship and World Cup. But the non-European nations knew little about their Iron Curtain rivals and Bulgaria knew just as little about their South American and African opponents. What they did know came from sources that did not necessarily take current form into account.

Dimitar Penev (Bulgaria): We went to Mexico in order to make ourselves familiar with the climate, the country, the surroundings. Back then our national team had a B side – and that second team travelled to Brazil at the same time. Later some of the guys who used to play for that B side joined the A team for the World Cup. So, despite the fact we were living behind the Iron Curtain, those kind of football visits were not as surprising as it might sound now. We managed to beat Peru 3–1 in the first warm-up friendly you've just mentioned, but a few days later we lost 5–3 to them. We thought we could beat them once the moment of truth arrived and we have to play the Peruvians at the World Cup but it wasn't meant to be . . . By the time the 1970 World Cup in Mexico kicked off, we had already been in awful shape because of the mistaken preparations. Back then learning the strengths of your upcoming rivals wasn't an easy job to do. We mainly gathered information through fellow countrymen who were living in the countries we were to play against. In the early seventies we already had embassies all around the world and it was often the case that we received some useful information through our diplomatic missions. We also managed to get our hands on some German newspapers – they were always full of interesting facts related to teams you might come up against. That's how things used to be done back in the day.

Berti Vogts (West Germany): It wasn't like nowadays; we didn't have a chance to look at their games, to do video analysis, etc., etc. Our assistant coach watched the games and then we discussed it.

There were games on television, but there was no analysis that is presented to the players, like nowadays. Such a thing didn't exist.

The first game of the group was Bulgaria against Peru in León. The match was significant for all sorts of reasons. It was the first time Peru had qualified for the finals since the inaugural tournament in 1930 and expectations were high for a team that had secured their place at the expense of Argentina with a thrilling 2–2 draw at the Bombonera stadium. More tragically, a massive earthquake rocked Peru on the eve of the finals. However, news of the damage and the thousands of deaths were kept from the players for as long as possible so as not to upset their preparations.

Hector Chumpitaz (Peru): In reality we did not know the magnitude of the earthquake. The director José Aramburú Menchaca, who was president of the National Sports Committee [CND], which today is the IPD [Peruvian Sports Institute], he was the one who encouraged us and told us that it had been a small thing, that it hadn't really hit Lima very hard. He lied to us and told us a story so we wouldn't worry.

Reliable news reports were hard to come by. Some fans relayed snippets of information to the players but officials downplayed the scale of the tragedy. When the players found out the gravity of the destruction some of them wanted to return home immediately but officials coaxed them into staying, telling them they could do more for their compatriots by performing well and giving them something to smile about.

Hector Chumpitaz (Peru): It was a day before the match against Bulgaria, because we went to take a look at the León pitch. We went to train, to check out the playing surface, see what the conditions were like. And it was there that we learned from Peruvian fans who had come to see us play. We didn't believe everything that they said happened because they told us things only briefly, and it was not good for the players to worry. We knew that some people had died, but we did not know the rest. It was at a time when communications were more difficult. It is easier now with social networks where they explain everything, but back then they only said what had happened. Some players were very worried because they were from provinces, like Nicolás Fuentes, who was from the Camaná province. There were others, also the late Julio Baylón, and 'Perico' León, there were several, but we had to calm them down, because we knew that even though we were worried and felt their pain, we had to be calm. The president sent us a telegram, telling us that everything was fine, that everything was under control. He asked us to keep calm because we were representing our country, and he wished us good luck. Apart from that I knew that despite all these problems that we were going to take the team forward in the World Cup matches.

Peru, wearing an unfamiliar red shirt without their trademark sash, won the opener, although only after a shaky start. They lost one goal to a superbly worked free kick after just twelve minutes and then another at the start of the second half when goalkeeper Luis Rubiños let a long-range free kick squirm through his hands into the net. But the Bulgarians wilted in the humid conditions and Peru charged back to win 3–2. The South Americans were rampant in the second period and their winning margin could have been greater as they had three goals chalked off.

Hector Chumpitaz (Peru): The game started and they scored this goal as if it was cooked up in a laboratory. Very, very, very well planned. At the start of the second half they scored another, 2–0. We turned things around from 2–0 to 3–2. The first one was Gallardo, the second one was mine from a free kick, and the third was from Nene Cubillas.

Dimitar Penev (Bulgaria): We played a fantastic first half – we managed to take an early lead, then we scored another one right after the break. But by that point we already knew that something was wrong. When we got to the dressing room at half-time we felt really dizzy because of the altitude and the fact we hadn't drunk enough water. The wrong preparation had taken its toll. Despite that, we doubled our lead early in the second half but then we fell apart. We saw it coming – the Peruvians outplayed us completely after the break. They outran us and were winning every tackle. The day after the game we admitted that we had made some big mistakes in the build-up to the tournament. We were exhausted. It was so hot, the humidity was unbearable and on top of that, we were dehydrated!

Hugo Sotil (Peru): The first half ended 1–0 and at half-time I was told to warm up. I was hotter than a chicken on a grill and then they scored to make it 2–0. I wanted to go on. When I did, three gringos marked me as I had scored three goals against them in a friendly not long before. And they forgot about Gallardo, who was on the other side of the pitch and he made it 2–1. Then I was fouled inside the area but the referee gave a free kick and Chumpitaz made it 2–2. Then my man Cubillas played a one-two with Mifflin and put us 3–2 ahead.

Hector Chumpitaz (Peru): I remember an anecdote when we were losing at half-time in the first game, 1–0 to Bulgaria. We were in the dressing room and a pot of earth appeared with soil that we were told had come from Peru, from Huaraz. And Aramburú Menchaca started to throw it on the ground, and onto his suit and his shoes. And he said we had to do the same thing. And would you believe it, as luck would have it, we turned the match around and beat Bulgaria 3–2. It became a lucky superstition for us and that is why we came from behind.

Hugo Sotil (Peru): It was unforgettable. Following the tragedy, we were able to give Peru a victory in such a great way against Bulgaria, after being 2–0 down. It wasn't going to save lives but we were able to calm the tragedy in some way.

Teofilo Cubillas (Peru): Knowing that we'd brought a little bit of happiness to the country was a feeling that is impossible to put into words.

Hector Chumpitaz (Peru): I remember that later I contacted my wife. Back then it was via a landline, or they sent telegrams, and they said a few words and that was it before you got cut off. That was when I found out it had been stronger than we had been told, but this was after the Bulgaria match. I felt very worried like everyone else, but I also didn't know exactly everything that had happened. She told me that in Lima she had not felt the quake as much as in the epicentre of Huaraz. Already after a few days she was already learning everything, the number of dead, the houses that had fallen, she even told me that there was a hill where there was a cross, and after the earthquake the hill had disappeared and the only thing that remained was the cross. From that point on we worried a little more.

Runners-up in England in 1966, West Germany retained many of their top players from that tournament and were firm favourites to win the group. Morocco were playing in their first World Cup, having withdrawn as part of the African boycott in England four years previously. They were Africa's first World Cup finalists since 1934 but nobody gave them the slightest chance of overcoming the all-powerful Germans. Even the Moroccans went into the match doubting themselves but the game got off to an unexpected start when they took the lead after twenty-one minutes. All of a sudden, one of the tournament's first shocks seemed a real possibility.

Allal Ben Kassou (Morocco): We were confident and also unafraid even though we had a very difficult opening game. The German team of the 1970s had a huge reputation and some of the biggest names in football, like Beckenbauer, Seeler, Müller and the goalkeeper Maier. As far as we were concerned we were representing Morocco and Africa. But this was an opponent that we had to treat with the utmost seriousness. It was going to be a difficult match but we wanted to try as hard as possible to get a result that would please us as well as the Moroccan fans.

Wolfgang Overath (West Germany): Our confidence wasn't boosted during those first few days in Mexico. We trained but it was stop-start. The unusually strong heat and the thin air hit us hard at the start. After half a minute of effort, you needed two or three minutes of rest.

Berti Vogts (West Germany): Yeah, we used to train at noon. We also trained at 8 a.m. and then we had our main training session at noon so we could get used to the heat. But for the whole week before the first game, we didn't train at 12.00 because we needed to preserve our strength and Germany lives from its strong football; we require that for the whole ninety minutes. So for that week before we played Morocco we didn't train at 12.00.

Morocco's goal came from a mix-up in the German defence. A cross from the left sailed over Maier's head but as the keeper scrambled to make it to his back post a German defender nodded it back across the six-yard box where Mohammed Houmane Jarir was standing all alone in front of an open goal. Maier slipped and Jarir hammered the ball into the roof of the empty net.

Said Ghandi (Morocco): Our first goal really shocked the

Germans. Only God knows what they must have thought when we were in the lead.

Berti Vogts (West Germany): It was a big mistake from a player from our defence. And I think we went in at the break losing 1–0. We all said, 'If we get one goal, Morocco will be afraid, the Africans usually get nervous, therefore we need to get an equaliser.' And we did, and it was a very happy win for us. If you look at the overall game, Morocco played better than Germany.

Allal Ben Kassou (Morocco): Honestly, we really didn't think that we could beat them. They attacked right from the very beginning of the game and I had to make quite a few important saves. All their attacks seemed like they would definitely produce goals and after something like that, and after defending with your backs to the wall, your confidence can become fragile. But when we scored that all changed. Our confidence grew again and we felt great, but we had to stay focused and keep hold of our lead.

It was still 1–0 at half-time but the introduction of winger Jürgen Grabowski roused the Germans in the second half and set a pattern for the rest of the tournament. The Germans scored twice in the second period, both goals coming from the Uwe Seeler–Gerd Müller combination up front. There was considerable unease about the pair leading up to the tournament with many believing the thirty-three-year-old Seeler, playing in his fourth World Cup, and the twenty-four-year-old Müller, playing in his first, could not gel together. Having been coaxed out of semi-retirement Seeler returned as the father figure in a team that was transitioning between the finalists of 1966 and the winners of 1974. The Germans were lucky against Morocco but the comeback was the perfect riposte to critics who thought the ageing Seeler and the young Müller would not hit it off.

Sepp Maier (West Germany): They always said the Müller-Seeler combination wouldn't work, that one would crowd out the other. In addition to that, there was an unfortunate comment from Gerd about our first game: 'Either I play or Seeler plays.' Helmut Schön drummed it into his head, he released a storm that Gerd had to handle. And lo and behold: we never had a stronger storm than the tandem of the two great 'bombers of the nation'.

Berti Vogts (West Germany): Before, you used to have a centre forward, and then you had the right winger and left winger. Then came the midfielders, but for the first time we played with two attackers, and that surprised our opponents. Both Gerd Müller and Uwe Seeler were world-class players, and, above all, two nice guys and that made the whole thing so much fun. I was the youngest of all our twenty-two players and Uwe Seeler in particular helped the young players, which was great.

Uwe Seeler (West Germany): First game, first win: 2–1 against Morocco. Double joy and confirmation for Schön's chess move: a goal from Gerd, a goal from me.

Siegfried Held (West Germany): Gerd Müller was a natural goalscorer. He was so clinical. Uwe Seeler was very strong in the air and he threw himself into the fray. Gerd Müller was probably a little more shrewd.

Jürgen Grabowski (West Germany): We played in the extreme heat of 12 noon and there was such an enthusiasm that you just put that away. It was a dry heat, and we came out [of this situation] brilliantly.

Wolfgang Overath (West Germany): The Moroccans coped with the heat much better than we did and they played more rationally. I think you can get used to it, and after a while you realise that. They let the ball run, while we wanted to do too much on our own as individuals. That was a fundamental mistake and so we soon had to pay the price. The minnows, the supposed minnows, went 1–0 up in the twenty-first minute. Would that be the end? Dark suspicions crept up on me because nothing seemed to want to go right. Helmut Schön and Jupp Derwall tried to lift our mood at half-time and convince us we could still win, but the spark didn't really want to take.

Allal Ben Kassou (Morocco): We lost 2–1 and no one likes losing but when you lose to one of the best footballing nations in the world, who at the time were playing some great football, 2–1 wasn't such a bad result. It was a great experience. We were happy and still enthusiastic.

Germany were fortunate and they knew it. They had won but they had got out of jail and some of them later admitted they hadn't shown the Africans enough respect.

Berti Vogts (West Germany): We knew very, very little about the Moroccans, and in this game we had a lot of luck in winning 2–1.

Wolfgang Overath (West Germany): Thank God the first opponent was Morocco. That was a small comfort. For us it was clear: if we don't hammer the North Africans, who do we want to stand up to? So we went into the game a bit arrogant.

Berti Vogts (West Germany): I played three World Cups, and the first game was always the most difficult one for the German team. You haven't found your rhythm yet and you don't know where you stand. They were the most unknown rivals for us. We got little information from them, and we also discussed at that time, why we players got so little information, but it was another era. That is why.

Wolfgang Overath (West Germany): We won with a little bit of luck. Uwe and Gerd Müller managed to help us avoid a fiasco with the goals. We had got away with it again. Who didn't get away it, though, was Helmut Haller. He showed in this game that he was not in good condition after he had missed out on a lot of training because of a serious shoulder injury in the game against Romania. He had to give up his place in the team and there was no chance of him playing against Bulgaria. Haller was as an example for us and it became clear that we all had to be in excellent condition. Under the abnormal conditions we encountered in Mexico we had to remain fit.

Siegfried Held (West Germany): It was a very rough game. The reaction at the time was not good. I was one of the players who didn't play in the next game as a result. The press was not happy and so changes were made.

Peru captain Chumpitaz ended his sixteen-year international career in 1981 with 105 caps, which is still the second highest total for a Peruvian player. In Mexico he was already a dominant personality in the dressing room and his belief in the lucky soil worked so well, or so he believed, that he followed a similar routine in their second game against Morocco. Morocco's best player in their opening match, goalkeeper Allal Ben Kassou, played thanks only to a painkilling injection for an ankle injury, but even he could do little to halt the rampaging South Americans. Peru won 3–0, with Cubillas getting two of their three goals in a ten-minute burst during the second half. The defeat prematurely ended Morocco's chances of progressing.

Hector Chumpitaz (Peru): Then came the second game against

Morocco, and it was 0–0 at the break, and I also took the earth at half-time and in the second half we won 3–0, and also took the ground for the third match against Germany, but there yes we lost 3–1, but those are stories that suddenly gave all the players peace of mind, and more than anything, we were more aware of what had happened.

Said Ghandi (Morocco): Peru had an earthquake in their country and the players initially decided to leave the tournament and return home. This would have meant that we would have been awarded the match. Our coach gave us a break from training but the Peruvians decided they would play after all. We had a day off from training and lost the psychological edge. The team lost focus and were completely thrown off balance.

Hector Chumpitaz (Peru): After all that had happened, and because we had never played in a World Cup before, the joy of singing the national anthem was fabulous. Because of that and because of the earthquake in Huaraz, I cried some tears. It was very emotional.

The Germans, meanwhile, again lost the opening goal in their second match against Bulgaria, and again they were saved by the Seeler-Müller partnership. Coach Helmut Schön withdrew Seeler into a deeper position and it worked like a dream against a team that was paying a heavy price for their comical preparations. Together, Seeler and Müller scored four of Germany's five goals in a comprehensive 5–2 victory. Reinhard Libuda scored the other and provided two assists for Müller, whose poacher's goals were known in Germany as 'small goals'.

Berti Vogts (West Germany): They were both top players, but it was a big question for the journalists. Who is the best player, Gerd Müller or Uwe Seeler? But we had known for a long time that Helmut Schön had spoken with Uwe Seeler, and Uwe said to us: 'You will be surprised; I will withdraw a little deeper into midfield and from there I will support Gerd Müller.' Gerd had problems in the running area, and Uwe Seeler was a real fighter, but Gerd Müller was the player who had the real nose for goal, and they were two of the greatest forwards in the World Cup, the way they played with each other.

Uwe Seeler (West Germany): The duo was always called the young Müller and the old Seeler. 'Little fat Müller', twenty-four years old; 'our Uwe', thirty-three. The press described me as a running field horse, Müller as the man of the small goals, Franz Beckenbauer as a general in shorts. We felt infinitely strong.

Wolfgang Overath (West Germany): Against Bulgaria we knew we had to score the first goal and watch out for their free kicks. But understanding that was not much of a help. Before we knew it, the Bulgarians were 1–0 up. Thanks to a free kick. Good night, German football. I saw myself being cursed by angry German fans. To our big surprise going a goal down did not put us off. The change in the team seemed to have worked. Uwe, who did not quite mesh as a second striker with Gerd Müller against Morocco, was reborn as a midfielder. In front we had two real wingers and both Libuda and Löhr were key players. Libuda, who played for Schalke, was caught in one of his big days. Irresistibly he always got away from his markers and became the favourite of both Mexican and German fans. At first, he scored the equalising goal in a somewhat lucky way when his shot at Bulgaria's goalkeeper Simeonov slipped through his arm to make it 1–1. Then he fed Gerd Müller with such a beautiful pass so that Gerd couldn't miss.

Dimitar Penev (Bulgaria): We all knew that Germany were the team to beat in our group – and we even managed to score first against them. Just like the game against Peru, we got the goal, this time thanks to Nikodimov, shortly after the first whistle. But just like the match against the team from South America, we then collapsed and lost 5–2 in the end.

Wolfgang Overath (West Germany): We had the bad start we are used to having as a German team. [Laughs].

Uwe Seeler (West Germany): Second game, four days later on 7 June: second win, 5–2 against Bulgaria. Another nice confirmation: three goals from Gerd, one goal from me.

Wolfgang Overath (West Germany): At the end of the match we had won 5–2, qualified for the next round and, more importantly, regained our confidence.

Berti Vogts (West Germany): Bulgaria was not a big problem, they were Europeans, we knew their strengths, we knew their weaknesses, they were defensively oriented, so it was not an issue.

The Bulgarian players knew they had the ability to cause a shock and they proved it by taking the lead in each of their three games. But the order not to drink water was a hard one to break for players used to such an authoritarian regime. Playing at altitude and in great heat without the required hydration was too much of a hurdle for them and they gave up their leads as they succumbed to the conditions. They, like Morocco, saw their chances disappear after two defeats in their first two games and the teams played their final match to a collegial 1–1 draw in front of fewer than 2,000 fans.

Dimitar Penev (Bulgaria): Unfortunately, the situation was already irreversible. We had already lost so much weight – we were looking like shadows of ourselves, and nobody felt well.

These World Cup preparations turned out to be one huge mistake which the ruling party and the governing football body were to blame for. Football-wise, we had a great team. It is no coincidence that in every group stage game we were the ones who opened the scoring. We were creating clear-cut chances, and it was a pity we couldn't play that way throughout the entire ninety minutes. I remember we were training a lot of free kicks – if you look at late Dinko Dermendzhiev's fantastic goal that gave us the lead against Peru, you'll see it was a fantastic team effort we had been working on in our training sessions . . .

Wolfgang Overath (West Germany): The Bulgarians had to deal with two defeats against Peru and against us and they were labelled the World Cup losers. For me, their one-month preparation was a big mistake. It felt like the players were happy to finally go home. They looked so indifferent.

Dimitar Penev (Bulgaria): Let me tell you a funny story. Ahead of that game against Morocco we coincidentally met half of their team as it turned out they were based really close to our hotel. So we greeted each other, and we even drank some tea and coffee with their players. The atmosphere was unbelievably friendly. You could say that the Morocco players didn't feel any pressure – they were happy just to be there and participate in that World Cup. We, on the other hand, were in a totally different situation: a lot was expected from us, including to claim that first ever World Cup group stage win. We drew 1–1 with Morocco although we managed to open the scoring for the third game in a row. They were very happy with the result, while we were in such a bad mood. We had already lost our first two games in Mexico, then we couldn't win the third one either. Physically and psychologically speaking, we were feeling really awful. Curiously, we had to wait another twenty-four years for that long-anticipated debut World Cup win – and it came at the 1994 World Cup when we beat Greece 4–0 in the group stage. By that point I was already the head coach of Bulgaria.

In the Peru v West Germany game that would decide who topped the group and stayed in León, the Europeans came out on top. The Germans were in pole position and could have been forgiven for taking their foot off the pedal but they were keen to avoid Brazil in the quarter-finals and went all out in a blistering first half. Müller got another hat-trick, all of them coming in a nineteen-minute spell towards the end of the half, and although Cubillas got his fourth goal in three games, it was the Germans who ended up 3–1 winners in yet another end-to-end match in what was undoubtedly the most entertaining group of all.

Berti Vogts (West Germany): We had a very strict trainer called Helmut Schön and he wanted to win every game. The first half we played with our complete main team. After that he made a few changes and we had something clear in mind: we wanted to be the first in our group. We were looking at the other groups. We wanted to finish first to avoid Brazil. That was the problem.

Wolfgang Overath (West Germany): Our new goal was clear: we had to become group winners by defeating Peru. I knew that the South Americans' style of play suited us because they did not defend well. We calculated that if we beat the Peruvians, we would stay in León and continue to play there. If we came second in the group we would have to travel to Guadalajara. Against Peru we got straight down to business. Gerd Müller grabbed the hat-trick in twenty minutes and the game was already over. It was only in the second half that Didi's protégés got the opportunity to show their artistic skills. In anticipation of the group victory, we let the reins slide a bit and the Peruvians came back with full power. I couldn't help but think of the second half of the Bulgaria–Peru game, in which Bulgaria's 2–0 lead turned into a 3–2 victory for the Latin Americans. But we managed to survive a period of exerted pressure by our opponents, who had great individual talents in Cubillas, León, Gallardo, Sotil, Mifflin and Challe, and we left the stadium with a 3–1 win. We were group winners. If someone had dared to predict that after the opening game against Morocco, he would have been laughed at.

Berti Vogts (West Germany): Peru was for us the most unknown team. As I said, against Morocco we were not good and we didn't know how well the Peruvians could play football. Besides they have an advantage, because Peru is located in the altitude, and we knew they would play in a fast rhythm, and we had to be careful. We were a bit inhibited and we wanted to be the first in the group at all costs, and in terms of football, the Peruvians totally surprised us how well they played.

Uwe Seeler (West Germany): Third game: third win, 3–1 against Peru, three times Gerd.

Hector Chumpitaz (Peru): There were several people who calmed us and more than anything, what calmed us the most, was winning our opening match. There was Didi, who was the coach, there was Alejandro Heredia, who was the assistant, the same manager Aramburú Menchaca. We always tried to communicate with our family members but it was very difficult. Apart from the fact that we were far from the city, that was difficult for us. Even knowing that our relatives in Lima were fine, we were still grieving over the people in the provinces who had died.

Their perfect showing of three wins from three games meant West Germany would avoid Brazil in the quarter-finals but that good news was tempered by an almost as daunting reality of a replay of their 1966 final against England. Peru would go to Guadalajara to face the favourites Brazil. Morocco were happy to have acquitted themselves well but Bulgaria, who despite having played three World Cups in a row were still without a win to their name, faced the uncomfortable prospect of returning home to the Communist nation empty-handed.

Allal Ben Kassou (Morocco): So we didn't qualify for the second round but we played some good football and showed the rest of the world that African football had to be taken seriously. We got a lot of recognition from everyone, all our families, friends and the fans. And when we arrived back home there were thousands of fans waiting for us at the airport. That was because they wanted to show how happy and thankful they were for all that we'd achieved.

Dimitar Penev (Bulgaria): Here's another good story to put things into perspective. Our 1970 World Cup appearance was already over and on our way back from Mexico we had to change flights in Germany. Upon entering the plane on German soil, one of the stewardesses told our team: 'Prepare yourselves for some heavy criticism once you're back home. They're just waiting for you to return . . .' The FA officials, who were drinking some whisky during the flight, got scared by this lady's words. And they started considering different scenarios. They were even thinking of landing in Romania to avoid the public anger. In the end, when we finally approached the border between Bulgaria and Romania, it was decided we would be landing in Sofia nevertheless. And what happened? There was no one waiting for us at the airport! No one! A few of us, the players, were living in the same neighbourhood and we travelled together. It turned out there was some police presence around our flats but that was just in case somebody turned up. Yet nobody showed up to hold us accountable for our failed World Cup campaign. It all turned out to be a false rumour.

One of the most curious things I remember about our Mexico visit was the fact we got the chance to buy some typical Mexican hats, sombreros, as gifts for friends and family members. And when this stewardess told us what the public reaction to us going home might be, we decided to leave most of the sombreros on the plane! We didn't want to look as if we were coming home after a few weeks of partying in Mexico. We didn't want to make people angrier than they supposedly were. That's why we kept just a few sombreros for ourselves and then left the others behind. Later, it turned out the stewards and the pilots got all the other Mexican hats! One day we were flying in the company of that same flight crew and suddenly they started joking: 'Oh, many thanks for giving us all those Mexican sombreros the last time we met!'

	P	W	D	L	Gls	Pts
WEST GERMANY	3	3	0	0	10-4	6
PERU	3	2	0	1	7-5	4
Bulgaria	3	0	1	2	5-9	1
Morocco	3	0	1	2	2-6	1

Pele interviewed in a huge sombrero after he and the Brazil team arrive in Mexico. *Getty Images*

An exhuberant local man encourages the crowd by waving a Mexican flag and a sombero in the Estadio Azteca during the opening ceremony prior to the first match in the 1970 FIFA World Cup between Mexico and the USSR. *Getty Images*

England relax at the Hilton Hotel in Guadalajara. *Left to right*: Gordon Banks,
Keith Newton, Francis Lee, Tommy Wright and Bobby Charlton. *Getty Images*

Sandro Mazzola and Gianni Rivera were two of the best attacking players in Europe but Italian coach Ferruccio
Valcareggi's strategy to give them both game time caused a major controversy back home in Italy. *Getty Images*

Peruvian Hugo Sotil is carried off the pitch by fans after the South Americans came from behind to defeat Bulgaria 3–2 in their dramatic opening game. *Getty Images*

Gianni Rivera, Roberto Rosato, Giovanni Lodetti, Giorgio Puia and Gigi Riva walking in Chapultepec Forest, Mexico City. *Getty Images*

Captains Bobby Moore and Carlos Alberto toss the coin before the Brazil-England match. *Mirrorpix/Reach Licensing*

Geoff Hurst beats Brazilian keeper Felix but fails to hit the net. *Alamy*

Jairzinho hits the shot that beats Gordon Banks to score the crucial goal for Brazil. *Alamy*

One of the most famous images in football history: Pele and Bobby Moore swap shirts after Brazil beat England 1–0 at the Estadio Jalisco in Guadalajara. *Mirrorpix/Reach Licensing*

Bobby Moore on the attack in an unfamiliar ice blue strip against
Czechoslovakia at the Estadio Jalisco in Guadalajara. *Alamy*

West Germany easily overcame Peru 3–1 to top Group 4 on a sunny day in Leon. *Alamy*

One of the stars of the tournament, a young Teofilo Cubillas
celebrates scoring against Morocco. *Alamy*

Italy's Gianni Rivera tries to round the Israeli keeper, Itzhak Vissoker, to score during the Group Two match. *Alamy*

Peter Bonetti replaced Gordon Banks for England's quarter-final against West Germany and ended up the scapegoat for the holders' 3–2 defeat after extra time. *Getty Images*

A dejected Bobby Moore in a West Germany shirt after England had lost the quarter-final in Leon.
Alamy

West German fans celebrate in the streets of Leon following thier teams victory over England. *Getty Images*

Roberto Rivellino.
Getty Images

Agony and ecstasy as Italy break the deadlock to win their semi-final,
dubbed the 'Game of the Century', against West Germany. *Getty Images*

Pele in a familiar pose, on the ground and in pain, after being felled by Uruguayan defenders. *Mirrorpix/Reach Licensing*

Brazilians pray together after Jairzinho had given Brazil into a
2–1 lead over Uruguay in their semi-final in Guadalajara. *Mirrorpix/Reach Licensing*

Italy and Brazil line up before the final. *Alamy*

Pele looks to strike in the final. *Alamy*

Jairzinho celebrates after he scores Brazil's third goal against Italy in the final. *Alamy*

Rivellino is carried off the field after fainting at the final whistle. *Getty Images*

Tostao is mobbed and stripped of his clothes by jubilant fans at full time. *Getty Images*

Carlos Alberto holds up the Jules Rimet trophy. *Alamy*

QUARTER-FINALS

14 June	León	West Germany v England	3–2 a.e.t.
14 June	Toluca	Italy v Mexico	4–1
14 June	Guadalajara	Brazil v Peru	4–2
14 June	Mexico City	Soviet Union v Uruguay	0–1 a.e.t.

SIX

USSR v URUGUAY

The make-up of the quarter-finals was decided in the most random fashion. With Mexico and the USSR equal on points and boasting the same goal difference, FIFA's statutes ruled the group winner would be decided by a coin toss. The decision was an important one. The group winners would face the second-place side in Group 2, Uruguay. Whoever lost the toss would face Italy. The Soviets had been in this situation before. In 1968 they drew 1–1 with Italy in the semi-final of the European Championship and the Italians went through to the final after winning the toss. Wary of that reverse, the superstitious Soviets this time did what little they could to avoid a repeat result.

Anatoly Byshovets (USSR): When we had the same number of points with Mexico after the group stage, a group winner was to be decided through a coin toss. And we then had a bad precedent – when we lost the coin toss to Italy in 1968. The 'culprit' then was Shesternyov – a tall lad, a bit phlegmatic in his everyday life. So Facchetti simply beat him to it, and we lost the coin toss. So this time the coin toss was to decide who we play next – Uruguay or Brazil [Italy]. And as much as we all loved

Shesternyov, we thought he was bad luck – so we sent Valeriy Porkujan, my teammate, who was always lucky when we played cards. He always had a joker or two – so he was chosen to go for that toss. He was so nervous, because no one wanted to play Brazil [Italy].

Evgeny Lovchev (USSR): We had a day off and we went out of the city for a barbecue. Valeriy Porkujan was thought of as the 'lucky one' in the group, so was nominated for the coin toss. We were sitting in the countryside when we saw the car stop on the road some way in front of us and Valeriy jumped out, waving with joy. We were delighted as we knew that meant we were going to play Uruguay in Mexico City.

Anatoly Byshovets (USSR): When we got Uruguay, we breathed a sigh of relief – and that was our big mistake. We massively underestimated our opponent.

The game at the Estadio Jalisco was poor. Conditions were hot and sunny, which inhibited both sides and there were few chances and few moments of excitement. The USSR were missing a key component in their midfield and Uruguay's lack of recognised strikers was never more evident than here. The match ended goalless after ninety minutes and headed for extra time and although Byshovets had the ball in the net just a few minutes after the restart, it was chalked off.

Anatoly Byshovets (USSR): Well, first of all – again – we underestimated them. We were already in the semi-finals in our thoughts, even before the game, having avoided Brazil. Analysing this as a coach, one of the key reasons for our incomplete performance in that game – we missed a key player for our midfield, Victor Papaev, who missed out on the World Cup with an injury. I would compare him to Rivellino. Also left-footed, great dribbling skill, non-conventional decisions to force an attack, powerful shot – he was a key player for us and we did not have him at the World Cup. We played three at the back, but we did not have anyone in the midfield of Clodoaldo-type – to break up the attacks and to put it into the final third. That was most acutely felt against Uruguay. The defence was solid, but not much when it comes to creativeness – to go from defence into the attack. The game itself was relatively even, went into extra time, but it was ruined by bad officiating. I even scored a goal, but it was ruled out – even though there was nothing illegal there. Many later admitted that this goal should've stood. Then another mistake by the referee led to Uruguay's winning goal too.

Ildo Maneiro (Uruguay): We had Zubía who was a centre forward. He wasn't very big but he played up front and scored goals. But Hohberg decided to go with Victor Espárrago and Fontes; Fontes was a very defensive midfielder for Defensor Sporting. Victor Espárrago had never played number nine; he had played as a wide midfielder when we played with four in the middle. He played on the left for Cerro before moving to Nacional. He had extraordinary physical ability, and he would have been a fucking brilliant marathon runner. He was very disciplined.

Anatoly Byshovets (USSR): They played a very physical game – they are very similar in that respect to Argentina. They roughed us up pretty good, and the game at times looked like wrestling rather than football. Played a lot of short passes too, which was not the easiest style to play against – considering how technically gifted they were too. That was the thing with this Latin American trio of Brazil, Argentina and Uruguay – it was very tough to play against them. I was the lone striker up front – so I felt their physicality more than most. Besides, this was 1970 – and yellow cards were only just introduced, so it was all very raw. Defenders still went all in, thinking of impunity for hard tackles.

The key moment of the game was also one of the most controversial moments of the entire tournament. With three minutes of extra time left to play, Luis Cubilla tussled with a Russian defender on the goal line. The Soviet defence appeared to stop, believing the ball had gone out of play, but Cubilla played to the whistle and crossed it to Espárrago, who glanced home a header from close range. The Soviets protested furiously but the Dutch referee ruled the goal was good.

Roberto Matosas (Uruguay): The great cunning and the fight that Cubilla had to get to that ball, to win it and to be able to cross into the centre for Espárrago to score. It was never clear whether the ball was out or not. For me it did not go out, but one sees it on television and the doubt is still there. I don't think the whole ball crossed the line.

Anatoly Byshovets (USSR): If we are talking about the particular incident in the extra time, the players – particularly Kavazashvili – felt the ball was out, so they stopped. It was a clear refereeing mistake. Another one, since many football experts admitted that my goal should have stood.

Ildo Maneiro (Uruguay): It was a wonderful match, with that goal by Espárrago from Cubilla's cross. We had an incredibly good game because the Russians athletically at least were three or four times superior. But there was a teamwork in Uruguay and we deserved to win. We played very well and I remember the great game that Cascarilla had that day; it was a victory that marked my life as a footballer. I have been given great compliments in my career . . . but the most important one I ever got was that day: what Juan López [coach of Uruguay's World Cup-winning side of 1950] told me that day was impressive. Juan and I went for a walk around the field after the game and he said to me: 'There is not a blade of grass on this entire field that you did not cover,' and he gestured to the entire pitch. It was incredible to receive that praise from a world champion.

Anatoly Byshovets (USSR): I have this trait – that I want to live my life without any regrets, both as a player and as a manager. I don't care what newspapers might write, as long as I can tell myself – you have done everything you could to make it happen. In the case of that World Cup, I could not blame myself – I did everything I could. But as a team, this was a painful result to take.

Ladislao Mazurkiewicz (Uruguay): I was crying, laughing, singing. We played 120 minutes in thirty-five-degree heat, and we had feared beforehand that the European teams would be physically better than us. But that day we were even stronger than the Soviet Union.

Anatoly Byshovets (USSR): I had several games in my lifetime as a player after which I felt empty. The most painful one was against Italy in Euro 1968, when I left it all on the pitch as did the entire team – and then going out through a coin toss. Sitting in the dressing room, nervous, waiting for the coin toss – that was nerve-racking, followed by absolute emptiness inside. Uruguay felt just about the same. We were absolutely drained physically – after playing extra time in that scorching heat. And the realisation that we lost, that people expected more of us, that we ourselves expected more of us – this was extremely painful. Plus, the team's management – and the political elites back home – also expected us to go through. So we got heavily criticised at home for bowing out. FIFA named me the best player of the tournament, but back home the press gave that title to Oleg Shesternyov – the central defender who fell asleep a bit when Uruguay scored their goal.

Evgeny Lovchev (USSR): We ended up receiving just our daily allowance in Mexico, as we would only get prize money if we equalled the semi-final finish from the previous World Cup in England.

Anatoly Byshovets (USSR): We had a good chance to go far but I think we overrated ourselves a little. For me personally to lose at that stage was very disappointing. We never hit the heights as a team that I had always dreamed about and strived towards as a player.

SEVEN

ITALY v MEXICO

The host nation were one of the form teams heading into the second stage, having scored five goals and conceded none, while their rivals Italy had hit the net just once in their opening three matches. Mexico were unhappy at having to move from their base at the Azteca but the change still gave them home advantage. Toluca was the highest venue in the competition – at 2,667 metres above sea level, it was almost half a kilometre higher even than Mexico City. The Italians would have to deal not just with a small ground packed with rabid home fans but a lung-bursting atmosphere as well.

Ignacio Calderón (Mexico): We were disappointed when they told us we would be leaving the Azteca Stadium. We didn't care who we were playing because we knew whoever we got were going to be difficult because if they had got to the second round they were capable of advancing. So they told us Italy and that was fine. We had beaten Italy and Germany at the Azteca and we had beaten Argentina; we were hard to beat. So when they told us we were going to Toluca it affected us because we shouldn't have had to leave the Azteca. We had drawn with Russia on points and goal difference and we tossed a coin at the federation to decide who would leave the Azteca. But it shouldn't have been that way because Mexico were the host nation and so it was a big mistake by the federation. Maybe it would have happened anyway but I can tell you now it could have been a different story if we had played at the Azteca.

Javier Valdivia (Mexico): I don't know how that change came about, but it was a mistake by the organisers because if we were the host nation why did we have to move? I don't understand. We were very hard to beat at the Azteca, we have a tradition there, and the pitch at Toluca didn't allow you much freedom. But having said that, it didn't affect our football.

Sandro Mazzola (Italy): At the beginning there was a lot of apprehension, we were very tense. Already in the dressing rooms we could hear all the noise of the home fans. The dressing rooms in 1970 were not like those of today. You could hear and feel everything. So going onto the pitch was a real release because at least we could respond on the field to the support of the Mexicans. We wanted to prove what we could do against the host team.

At one point we looked at each other and watched the crowd as well. We looked at our opponents, who at that moment were calm. Then I remember turning to Gigi Riva and we said to ourselves, 'What do they think? That they've already won?' So in the second half we managed to score three goals in thirteen minutes and we won the game. It was beautiful. Out there on the field, there was a deafening silence. The home crowd was disappointed with Mexico's defeat. I remember how incredulous and astonished we were about that atmosphere. We were happy about how we had reacted to the initial disadvantage we were at.

Ignacio Calderón (Mexico): Lots of people said that Italy would be affected by the altitude and that we could take advantage of that. But the fact was that we had to go all the way from our training centre to Toluca. Of course, the stadium was full to bursting but that was another situation. We didn't turn up already defeated, and we tried to give it something extra and we were leading.

Tarcisio Burgnich (Italy): Playing at 2,400 metres above sea level was very difficult, very complicated. Just running put you in trouble. And it took almost a minute to recover. It was not an easy game even though we won. We were playing against the hosts and the fans were obviously all on their side. We didn't have the stadium behind us.

Angelo Domenghini (Italy): Playing at such high altitude was not easy even for Mexico. We were a little tense in the first half, and slow. They took the lead. In the second half, however, we drew level and ramped up to win the game. In the second half there was only one team on the pitch, Italy. We dominated the game.

In Sandro Mazzola and Gianni Rivera, Italy had two of the best attacking players in Europe but coach Ferruccio Valcareggi struggled to find a way to fit them both in his side. Mazzola played all three games of the opening round and Rivera was limited to one second-half appearance in the final game against Israel, replacing Angelo Domenghini at half-time. Valcareggi then decided on a novel idea for the knockout rounds – the staffetta, or relay. The move, as controversial as it was tactical, saw the AC Milan forward playing the first half before being replaced by the Internazionale player.

Enrico Albertosi (Italy): Valcareggi was a quiet coach, a father to all of us. He loved everyone the same way. For him, he played whoever was in the best form at that moment. At the start of the World Cup, Rivera had to play from the start and Mazzola had to go to the bench. But Rivera had not been well, he felt bad. So, Mazzola had played the first game against Sweden and we had won. Then, we had drawn against Uruguay and Israel. When Rivera returned, Valcareggi never changed the training simply because Italy had never lost. Then against Mexico he played first Mazzola and then Rivera and the same thing against West Germany.

Sandro Mazzola (Italy): I woke up around 1 a.m. the night before the [Mexico] game, I went to the toilet and I understood it was the famous Montezuma's revenge. Valcareggi asked me if I was fine to play one half and I said yes, I can manage one half. And so my diarrhoea played into the famous staffetta.

Gianni Rivera (Italy): The staffetta was a totally political choice; there's no way to justify it technically. It doesn't make any sense to decide what substitutions you will make before the game starts.

Angelo Domenghini (Italy): It was a choice by the coach Valcareggi and the technical staff. I don't know if the staffetta was already decided. We will never know. We do know, however, that it was our coach's choice. I don't think he had considered playing them together. This is because Gianni Rivera was more of a midfielder, while Sandro Mazzola was more of a second striker.

Enrico Albertosi (Italy): It wasn't that Rivera was inferior to Mazzola. In fact, you could see that when Rivera came on in the second half the team improved and Riva had more chances to score.

Sandro Mazzola (Italy): Riva was a very powerful player; he ran forty metres four or five times in a row and he destroyed the centre half. The rest of us when we ran forty metres we couldn't do it again.

Enrico Albertosi (Italy): They could have played together of course. But to make them play together, someone had to be taken away. And who do you take off? Boninsegna? Riva? Domenghini?

Gianni Rivera (Italy): They tried to create a rivalry between us. But that thing about our rivalry, playing one half each only lasted a few days after the World Cup but it remained in the collective memory. But there was no bad feeling between us.

Mexico had never reached the quarter-finals before but they were riding a wave of confidence and their ambitions rose even further when they took the lead through José Luis González after just thirteen minutes.

Ignacio Calderón (Mexico): We were delighted when José Luis González, 'La Calaca', scored the goal. We were winning 1–0 and we couldn't believe it, but we knew we could do more. I was really confident because of the way we were playing; they were dangerous and so when we scored I felt that we could get a victory.

Tarcisio Burgnich (Italy): We felt a little afraid of being eliminated. It was not an easy game at that altitude, and we suffered, particularly against the hosts.

Mexico's joy was short-lived. Thirteen minutes later Gigi Riva worked hard to keep a ball in play on the right and although he was closed down by a swarm of defenders the loose ball fell to Angelo Domenghini. His shot was cruelly deflected by Gustavo Peña past his own goalkeeper to draw the scores level.

Javier Valdivia (Mexico): We took the lead and we could see the Italians looked desperate, they were fighting amongst themselves. But in the second half we lost control and concentration and that was where our lack of experience in managing a lead like that in a World Cup started to tell.

Ignacio Calderón (Mexico): To be honest, we didn't have a plan. We wanted to take care at the back, go forward and try and grab a goal and be well positioned. And that's what we did at the start, and it was going well; we defended well until the own goal, which was a disaster. Riva struck the ball to my right and I was going in that direction when suddenly it was going off to my left. I tried to get back and stretch my hand out but the ball was past me and going in, I only managed to get a fingertip to it. I was so disappointed to lose my record of never having conceded a goal to an own goal like that.

Javier Valdivia (Mexico): Morally we lost it there and the defence lacked the mentality to face up to the situation and overcome it. It was like they succumbed to that very Mexican way of thinking, 'Well, we can't do anything now.' There were two things that happened: first, a mental deterioration that motivated our opponents. There are minutes in which the team that has just scored has a psychological advantage over the other team that has just conceded. For me, we lacked the mental solidity to know how to react in this kind of situation.

Ignacio Calderón (Mexico): When you concede an equaliser before half-time it's not the same as when you maintain your advantage going into the second half. You're always going to be a bit disappointed and asking yourself, 'Why now when we could have been 1–0 up at half-time?' And also, it was an own goal.

Javier Valdivia (Mexico): We never thought about playing defensively, just taking them on; there was no reason to change our style, we had to remain strong mentally. But there was an infantile error with our own goal, which was down to a lack of experience. There was no change of system and it's not the coach that matters in that case. We lacked experience at key moments in the game against Italy.

Italy brought on Gianni Rivera for the second half and he combined with Gigi Riva to turn the game around for Italy. The visitors scored three goals in twelve minutes midway through the second half, with Riva scoring twice and Rivera getting another to put paid to Mexico's hopes. The home side crumbled in the face of an attacking onslaught that was everything the Italians had failed to show up until now.

Sandro Mazzola (Italy): Gigi was a phenomenon. He was our fall back, the man we relied on. When we were in trouble, it was enough to look at Gigi. On the left you could give him the ball without problems because we knew how fast he was. Gigi was always faster than the opposing defenders. Yes, Gigi Riva was an exceptional phenomenon. He was the most modern player around. There are still few like him around today.

Tarcisio Burgnich (Italy): In the training matches it was always up to me to mark him [Riva]. I had a great friendship with Gigi: it was hard to mark him, it was hard to keep up with him, it was hard to dispossess him. Riva was physically strong and he was involved in so many goals. Gigi was a serious boy. His strength, in addition to power, was his sense of positioning and knowing where the goal was. He was always in the right position at the right time.

The Mexicans were disappointed at their own errors and fans made their displeasure known by throwing objects at the Italians, who collapsed spreadeagled on the ground when they scored, desperate to win a few seconds in which to get their breaths back. But the reality was that the wily Italians were superior to their inexperienced opponents.

Tarcisio Burgnich (Italy): The fans were against us, but we knew how to react, and we proved to be a strong team, and united as a group.

Ignacio Calderón (Mexico): In the second half we tried to attack and that was our mistake. Italy know how to play on the counter-attack; that's what the Italians are good at. We know that they later beat Germany in the Game of the Century and that they reached the final against Brazil. They were a very powerful team and they demolished us. We tried to score a second goal and they hit us on the counter-attack, and the scoreline reflected that. But it was all about their counter-attacks.

Javier Valdivia (Mexico): The Italians are masters of defence, and they were the only defensive team there. They knew how to defend an advantage and we didn't. We weren't used to it. That is the difference between Italy and Mexico. In the World Cup you can't make one mistake, or several like the ones we made.

Ignacio Calderón (Mexico): They were very lucky in the second half as well; I remember one incident [the fourth goal] when Riva ran into the penalty area and I went down to block the ball and I stopped it but it bounced and fell to him right in front of the goal. So he still had the ball at his feet and though Kalimán Guzmán closed him down he put the ball through his legs. There were fortunate moves like that. There wasn't much time left, and all we wanted was for the game to end; it was already 4–1 so there wasn't much we could do.

Javier Valdivia (Mexico): It was pure sadness; all the objectives we had, all the dreams we had, it all slipped through our hands. We lost the game, the Italians beat us; that was the problem, that was the sadness.

Ignacio Calderón (Mexico): We thought we could have gone on to the next stage, yes, but maybe not that we would win it. You have to keep your feet on the ground and you can't get carried away. Mexico went as far as they could. Period. Mexico always went as far as they could. We didn't get any further because we weren't good enough; we need to be honest. Did we want to be world champions? Everybody does, or at least reach the fifth game. So why haven't we managed to get any further than that? Because Mexico has only ever got that far, we weren't able to do more.

Tarcisio Burgnich (Italy): We wanted to get to the final to win the Jules Rimet trophy. It had been thirty-two years since we won, back in 1938. So our goal was to win again. Getting to the semi-final was the first step.

EIGHT

BRAZIL v PERU

The Brazil v Peru game threw up one of the more newsworthy encounters of the last eight, and not only because Peru were considered to be one of the few teams capable of producing the same kind of flair as the Brazilians. Rather, the intrigue came on the touchline, as Brazil came face to face with Didi, the World Cup winner in 1958 and 1962 who was now coaching Peru. Didi was a legend in Brazil and, having guided Peru to the finals for the first time since 1930, he was well on his way to achieving that status with his neighbours as well. He was also meeting Pelé and Zagallo, two of his teammates the last time Brazil won the World Cup.

Pelé (Brazil): We all knew the Peruvians. We had played them twice in 1968 in Lima. I didn't play in those games but lots of guys in our squad did. Peru had also played in Brazil and names like Cubillas, Perico León, De la Torre, Chumpitaz, Mifflin and Gallardo, especially the last of them, who played with Palmeiras, were very well known by our lads. That's why I wasn't afraid of Peru, even though they had improved a lot. I admit, there was one worry: Didi. Didi knew us and all our habits. We were more worried about Didi than we were about the Peru team. It was strange picturing Didi sitting across the field when we finally met; I wondered how he would feel seeing his old friends and teammates facing him instead of sitting beside him. I tried to put myself in his place but I couldn't.

Hector Chumpitaz (Peru): Didi always told us that Peru was the best team in the World Cup because we played lots of friendly matches before the tournament and that helped with our team development. In addition, we did an international tour playing several games and we recorded some good results, so that gave us confidence, and that is why Didi said that Brazil was not the best team, and that Peru was on a par with them. He told us about Brazil player by player. He told us such and such a player is similar to you, because he has the same quality. He compared us with the best players in Brazil, and even Pelé himself said that 'Perico' León was the best number nine in the world. I am sure that if 'Perico' León had been Brazilian, Pelé would not have been the best player in the world. So what I mean to say is that they recognised our quality, but because of the experience they had they beat us in the World Cup. We were happy for what we had done. We gave our best in each game and we were sure that in the next World Cup we were going to do even better.

Pelé (Brazil): The Peruvian forward line was good, dangerous, but their defence was weak, really weak. The Peruvians were here right after a catastrophe in their country. I am talking about the earthquakes that killed a lot of people. They had qualified for the World Cup finals for the first time. That's why in addition to their own support they had the backing of the Mexicans.

Gerson (Brazil): Didi had known us all since we were kids; he was the maestro. We wanted someone else to be coaching them, a Peruvian or a Mexican or whatever, but not him, but that is what destiny wanted and that's what happened, and fortunately we won. It was a difficult game, a little bit tight, but I think we were the better team.

Teofilo Cubillas (Peru): Didi knew that in the quarter-finals Peru would play offensively, similar to Brazil. But it was difficult to mark four number tens. Our intention was to get another team. We wanted to beat West Germany in the last game of our group so that we'd get someone else. But we lost 3–1 and we were left with Brazil.

Hector Chumpitaz (Peru): Didi told us that we had to keep hold of the ball, not give it away easily, because they [Brazil] took advantage of those opportunities. And then he [Didi] built us up by comparing us to them and he said to us, 'We have played so many games against the best teams from South America and Europe,' and that encouraged us to lose our fear. It also helped us to go out and take them on as equals.

Pelé was notorious among the Brazilian players for taking his guitar with him wherever he went and regaling his teammates with songs. He would pick up the guitar when he had a free moment or couldn't sleep, much to the chagrin of his friends and roommates. They would regularly tease him about his lack of musical talent and Pelé admitted he didn't as much play the guitar as 'bash' it. But before the Peru game, Pelé brought the Brazilians together for another reason.

Pelé (Brazil): In the evenings between our game with Romania and our coming game with Peru, as we did between all our games, we held nightly meetings at our hotel. There, led by Zagallo, we would watch the television tapes of our past games, as well as tapes of our opponents' games, and then discuss our future tactics. These discussions were completely frank and every member of the team, whether a first-string player or a reserve, was encouraged to give his opinion. Nor was criticism rare, although we made sure it was constructive. There was a feeling of 'family' that came from these meetings, and from this feeling of togetherness, another parallel activity each evening developed. And that was prayer. It started with me. I got a phone call from my wife. She said: 'We're praying for you every day. Me, my parents, my brothers and sister-in-law, my sisters, your parents and Kelly [Pelé's daughter]. Why don't you pray, too?' I didn't know whether to answer her or cry because I missed her so much. There were about forty people in our delegation and at least half of them got together to pray. We didn't pray to win the World Cup. Every day we found a reason. The poor, people with tuberculosis, lepers, Vietnam, someone's health, war, everything was a reason to pray. We asked that no one got injured and for luck. That, I think, was a very important factor in us winning our third World Cup. That unity made us stronger.

Peru were unquestionably a serious rival for Brazil and although the Brazilians knew they were up against some quality players, Zagallo, with his characteristic self-confidence, dismissed any thoughts of vulnerability and assured them they had nothing to worry about.

Mario Zagallo (Brazil coach): The presence of scouts to do detective work to study how our potential opponents Peru and Germany played, Carlos Alberto Parreira and Rogério went off on their secret mission, each one of them watching one of the teams. The reports they gave me were of considerable importance. The first observation that I read really bucked me up. 'Peru has no chance of beating our seleção.' They said that the Peruvian side, in spite of having some good ball players, had a weak defence, although the attack could sometimes be overpowering. So I admitted that it wouldn't be difficult for our seleção to score goals, although our own fortress might also be breached. The Inca side played almost in an orthodox 4-2-4 system. They didn't worry about defence, they only cared about attacking. Mistakes would be punished.

Gerson (Brazil): Peru were an excellent side: from the midfield forward they were sensational but, I'd go as far as to say, with a terrible defence and a terrible goalkeeper. So that made it a lot easier for us; it was harder in midfield. They too had been together a long time, just like the Brazilian team, under the command of maestro Didi. So he knew how we played. And we knew how they played, so they tried to stop our principal players and they managed it in spells. But our attack was superb and their defence was awful, with a terrible goalkeeper. So it was a lot easier for us. We had a certain difficulty in marking them but in compensation they weren't able to mark our forwards, right? And Tostão was the man who did the damage in that game, scoring a great goal and all that.

Hector Chumpitaz (Peru): We respected our rival, in this case Brazil, who had more experience than we did and some important players. We had played them before in a friendly match in 1969, and it ended in a battle at the Maracanã. We were winning that game 2–0, and then the situation changed because of a fight involving Enrique Casaretto and Orlando de la Torre. That hurt a little and they beat us 3–2. So we already knew how far we could go, because the same players who played in that game were also playing in the World Cup. We already had the experience of knowing how to play Brazil because we knew the characteristics of each of their players.

Rivellino and Tostão combined to put Brazil 2–0 up after just a quarter of an hour but Alberto Gallardo kept Peru in the game when he got a goal back with seventeen minutes of the first half remaining.

Pelé (Brazil): The game itself was a joy to play in. Both teams, being South American, refused to play the defensive game preferred by the European teams, and it was attack followed by attack from both sides. Zagallo, who had come to like the defensive game, at last gave in to our arguments that a defensive game against a South American team – especially a team led by Didi – was a mistake. He allowed us to play our natural game, and the results justified the decision.

Mario Zagallo (Brazil coach): Rivellino got the first after eleven minutes. After fifteen minutes Tostão made it 2–0, scoring a goal that looked impossible. But nevertheless, the Peruvian [front] line made our defence work hard.

Hector Chumpitaz (Peru): We knew we could get back in the game because we were playing well. They had scored their goals with quick counter-attacks but we had been on top and attacked more than them in the opening minutes so we were still quite sure of ourselves. But we also needed to be more careful. And so we started going forward again and we got a goal back through Alberto Gallardo and that lifted us because losing 2–0 was a difficult scoreline.

Mario Zagallo (Brazil coach): The Peru goals didn't come from rehearsed moves; we didn't let Peru get away with that much. The first was from Gallardo and came from the byline, almost without any angle at all. The first half finished 2–1 in our favour. An easy game and I didn't have any special instructions for my players in the dressing room. All we needed to do was see the game out and be a bit more aggressive.

Hector Chumpitaz (Peru): Of course, there was hope of turning the game around because we were also creating chances. We also caused them problems and that day Felix, the Brazilian goalkeeper, had a good day, better than in most of his previous matches. Brazil almost never had good goalkeepers. All that was in favour of Brazil and they took advantage of the quality they had to win the game.

It was a great match – perhaps the most entertaining of the tournament so far. Gerson was back in Brazil's starting line-up and was once again pulling the strings in midfield. The superb Tostão restored Brazil's two-goal cushion early in the second half, only for Teofilo Cubillas to cut the deficit again seventeen minutes later and leave Peru still in with a chance at 3–2.

Hector Chumpitaz (Peru): What happens is that Brazil makes a substitution, Paulo Cesar comes on for Gerson, and that confused us a little. They were already playing differently; we had played the first half one way, and in the second half they took advantage of our mistakes and got the third goal through Tostão. Then soon after we got one back through Cubillas and then Jairzinho scored the fourth and they won 4–2.

Mario Zagallo (Brazil coach): The second goal came about because Cubillas had a tremendous stroke of luck; the ball fell right at his feet after hitting the back of Marco Antônio.

Hector Chumpitaz (Peru): It was a good goal. He came through the centre. I don't remember if he played a one-two with Sotil, because the 'Cholo' [Sotil] was not a starter and came on in the second half for Julio Baylón. Then he did the one-two with Cubillas and made the second goal that brought us closer to the possibility of a draw, and we got it to 3–2. [When it was 3–2] I told my teammates that we had to keep going and get better, while at the same time making sure they didn't score again. That way we'd have a chance of equalising and getting through to the semi-final.

Pelé (Brazil): With a bit more luck we could have decided the game in the first half. But nevertheless, we were winning 2–1. At the end we won 4–2.

Mario Zagallo (Brazil coach): The final score of 4–2, given our obvious superiority, was very modest. I admit we could have made it five or even six on several occasions but we didn't have much luck with finishing.

Hector Chumpitaz (Peru): There was little left [after the fourth goal]. The problem is that when an opponent scores and there is little time left to equalise your morale fades.

Teofilo Cubillas (Peru): We had chances as well. The game was, as they say in football, end to end. And we still managed to score twice. Only ourselves and Romania scored twice against Brazil.

Hugo Sotil (Peru): They were frightened. They could relax a bit after they got their fourth goal but we were close to equalising. But they were geniuses and in the end they beat us 4–2.

Hector Chumpitaz (Peru): Many people thought that we played the same style of football as Brazil because we were not afraid of any team and weren't scared to take them on. Against Brazil, what happened to us was that they took advantage of our mistakes even though we matched them toe to toe. We had our way of playing that we did well in training, and that helped us to make it a great game. They realised that they were not facing pushovers, as everyone believed. Even they were surprised at our game.

Teofilo Cubillas (Peru): It was for me and even today, it was one of the best World Cups in football terms, one of the best. Every team had seven or eight stars. They all deserved to be there. Unfortunately, we had to face Brazil and they knocked us out. In my first World Cup when I was twenty-one years old I managed to score five goals. I was truly happy. I think that maybe if we'd played a different opponent we could have advanced a lot further.

The defeat was a sore one for Peru, but especially for Orlando de la Torre, the Sporting Cristal defender who was dropped for the game by Didi after playing in all three group matches. De la Torre was furious at the snub and had it out with his coach.

Orlando de la Torre (Peru): I went mad when I heard I wasn't going to play. I was spitting fire. Hector Chumpitaz looked at me as if to say, don't do anything, because he knew I was on the brink of hitting him [Didi].

Hector Chumpitaz (Peru): Yes, that was the intention. We could see he wanted to hit him, especially the players who played for Sporting Cristal, because they knew what he was like. After the game, we were on the bus back to the hotel, and they [the Cristal players] got off first: Ramón Mifflin, Eloy Campos, Luis Rubiños, Alberto Gallardo, José del Castillo. They went to protect Didi, because Orlando de la Torre wanted to push Didi in the swimming pool that was next to the hotel, just where the bus had parked. The players calmed him down, but he [Orlando de la Torre] said he hit him, which was a lie, because we were all there. It would have been so disrespectful if he had; it would have been like hitting your father.

Orlando de la Torre (Peru): Yes, we came to blows. After we lost to Brazil, I was indignant. And at the hotel I went looking for him [Didi] and he came at me. He was no mug, he was streetwise. We were well matched and we really went at it. He didn't take any nonsense but I was outraged by what he did.

Hector Chumpitaz (Peru): The main problem was that when we played the friendly match against Brazil in February 1969 at the Maracanã there was a scuffle, and Didi knew how Orlando was very 'combustible' and that he could get into another fight by responding to the same kind of provocations that he had faced in the friendly match. Gerson almost broke his leg in that match. Didi thought that if he played him he would get sent off in the first few minutes. So he didn't want to run that risk and so played José Fernández. He had the quality but not the match sharpness and when you don't have that continuity in a run of games it is not the same. And that is what I felt about José Fernández in the match against Brazil, having not had a run of games.

Orlando de la Torre (Peru): I had clashed with Gerson in the last Peru–Brazil game. So later they said I could get sent off, that I was going to go after Gerson. That was why they didn't play me but that bore no relation to the reality.

Another Peruvian who came out of the game with a damaged reputation was goalkeeper Luis Rubiños, who was blamed for the loss. The Peruvians truly felt they had what it took to go all the way and they looked back with chagrin on their bad luck at facing Brazil so early in the competition.

Hector Chumpitaz (Peru): Luis Rubiños made some mistakes: there was one on the left when Tostão took the ball from a corner kick, and scored. And in that sense it is very difficult when they score such a goal. But the goals came because of the quality of the players that Brazil had. Of course, we were sad because we had been eliminated, because we thought we were going to go further and as there were sixteen teams there was a chance of progressing through the rounds and getting to the final. Imagine, if we had beaten Brazil, we'd be in the semi-final against Uruguay and with a good chance of winning. I saw that Peru could be champions of the world, because the final was Brazil against Italy and we knew we could rival Brazil with the players that they had, so playing against Italy would simply be a case of grabbing the moment and winning.

It was, though, one of the best games of the tournament, played end to end with flair and passion. Not surprisingly given their line-ups, both teams opted to attack every chance they got and the game remained unforgettable to those who played in it and watched it.

Hector Chumpitaz (Peru): There was a comment from João Havelange, who later became president of FIFA. When Peruvian journalists at the 1986 World Cup in Mexico asked him what he considered the best game in the history of the World Cup, he replied: Brazil–Peru of Mexico 1970. That caused some surprise and they asked, why was it the best? And he said, 'Because football was played for almost ninety minutes.' It was a good response, because now so little football is played. That match was impeccable. If we, when we were losing 2–1, had scored a goal and tied it, the history of the game would have been different.

Hugo Sotil (Peru): The ball never went out of play. We were all on first name terms with it. And they also had a fantastic team. Rivellino, Tostão, Pelé, Gerson, Jairzinho. Pure talent.

NINE

WEST GERMANY v ENGLAND

Germany had a right to be more confident than in previous games against England. It was not just that they had matched them for so long in the final in 1966 before going down 4–2 in extra time. When the two teams met in Hannover in 1968 the Germans won 1–0 and so recorded their first win over the English since their footballing rivalry began in 1930. England were no longer invincible. Both teams retained some of those who had played in the 1966 decider and they freely admitted that game was in the backs of their minds as they prepared for another epic under the furious Mexican sun.

Uwe Seeler (West Germany): The opponent on 14 June at the León stadium is England. Memories come alive. Memories go back to London. Wembley Stadium, the referee, the controversial goal ['over the line or not over the line?!'] to make it 3–2.

Martin Peters (England): The sudden-death game with West Germany was being hailed as the day when they would make us pay for doing them at Wembley four years ago. The Mexican press had little doubt about the outcome and were heavily influenced by Germany's ten goals in their group.

Berti Vogts (West Germany): Your question [were you out for revenge?] was correct. We thought, 'We have something here that needs to be repaired, and we want to repair it, we want to send England home.' We were still disappointed with the loss from 1966. We had to do it for Germany and for our trainer. And also for the older players, like Schnellinger, Uwe Seeler or Willi Schulz, who were great personalities. They were always telling us what the English had done to us. It was a goal, it was not a goal, and all that. And the England game came at the right time. It was very tightly fought, a very hard encounter.

Sepp Maier (West Germany): We were group winners and so were allowed to stay in León for the second round. But: our first opponent was called England. And England were the reigning world champions, the most fearful opponent, or so the press wanted us to believe. We were all inflamed, especially the national coach, desperate for revenge for the defeat in Wembley in 1966. Unlike our opponents – Sir Alf Ramsey had almost all the world champions from 1966 on his side – our team was significantly rejuvenated in crucial positions. We now had Müller, Grabowski and Maier; the young Beckenbauer was in top form, Uwe Seeler fought for a proud farewell, but there were also the old fighters in the starting blocks: Willi Schulz, Helmut Haller and Stan Libuda, who sent the Scots home with his third goal in the qualifiers.

Uwe Seeler (West Germany): In the tunnel outside the dressing room, just before the whistle, I chatted with Bobby Charlton. In German. Because Bobby, this brilliant playmaker from Manchester, understood the German language. At least a couple of words. 'No chance, today is our Wembley,' I said. 'You have no chance, we will win.' Geoff Hurst, the famous 'goalscorer' from the '66 final, laughed and shouted, 'No chance, today is our Wembley, no, no, Uwe.'

Berti Vogts (West Germany): We were very aggressive towards the opponent, because we wanted to send them packing at all costs. All the players felt the same way.

As group winners the West Germans had the luxury of staying where they were, while the English were uprooted from their Guadalajara base and forced to travel to León, 220 kilometres east. León was hot and dusty and the Nou Camp stadium was the smallest of the five grounds used in the tournament with a capacity of just 23,609.

Martin Peters (England): The journey to León by road – there is no airport there – took about five hours and was something we could have done without, but it was no great hardship really. In a way it was a relief to move away from Guadalajara, and the incessant turmoil that surrounded the Hilton.

Uwe Seeler (West Germany): Because of the time difference of eight hours, the game against our 'arch enemy' England was scheduled for 12.00 noon, 8.00 p.m. in Germany. Noon, good only for someone who had a box seat: out of the sun. It radiated mercilessly on the field, whose grass was cut short. The sprinklers had made sure the pitch was quick. To tackle was extremely dangerous. The razor-sharp bristles would cut our flesh open.

Martin Peters (England): It was all or nothing now and we would soon know if nearly six weeks of killing training in all kinds of weather, thousands of miles of travelling and hours of nervous tension were all for nothing – or virtually nothing. Whatever happened against Germany, it could be argued that the trip hadn't been wasted. We had learned how to adjust to South American conditions, learned how to play their 'slow-slow-quick' football and sampled fierce local hostility.

Uwe Seeler (West Germany): As soon as I came out my tongue was hanging from my mouth. The air was thin, the temperature was fifty-five degrees. There was no shade. The team that won 3–1 against Peru at the same location four days earlier lined up to start again: Maier, Vogts, Höttges, Beckenbauer, Schnellinger, Fichtel, Libuda, Seeler, Müller, Overath and Löhr. There were only two substitutions: Jürgen Grabowski came on in the fifty-fifth for 'Stan' Libuda and Willi Schulz in the forty-sixth for Horst-Dieter Höttges.

Wolfgang Overath (West Germany): We went into the England game already full of confidence. We'd had good games against Bulgaria and Peru and we had no fear. We knew that the English had a very strong team. We had confidence but we knew that it would be very difficult.

Jürgen Grabowski (West Germany): I can say without any fear of contradiction that the English didn't have any weaknesses, they were very strong. We were on a very good run, we had no problems with the weather, we played very well after the Morocco game, we were desperate to play against England, we had no fear.

For England, perhaps the most decisive incident of the match, and indeed the tournament, came before a ball was kicked. Aware of the potential dangers posed by the local food and drink – the water was not always safe and everyone knew about the notorious Montezuma's revenge – England had taken great care to ensure everyone in the squad ate and drank from their own imported supplies. The FA had arranged for the team to take their own bottled water. Sausages, steaks, burgers and butter were destroyed before it even reached them as Mexican authorities banned dairy and meat products due to fears over foot-and-mouth disease. Instead, they had fish fingers. England's strategy offended the Mexicans but it had paid off so far and no one had suffered any adverse effects. Until the eve of the West Germany game.

Gordon Banks (England): The quarter-final against West Germany was scheduled for Sunday 14 June in León. On the preceding Friday Alf allowed us to have a beer with our evening meal. After all these years I can't remember if the bottle I was served was opened in my presence or not, but I do know that half an hour after drinking that beer I felt very ill. To this day, I am at a loss to explain what happened exactly. Alf had been meticulous about our healthcare: food, drink and even sunbathing. I passed an uncomfortable night at the hotel, most of it being spent in the loo. On Saturday morning I felt well enough to make the 150-mile trip to León. When we eventually arrived, I went straight to the room I was sharing with Alex Stepney and crawled into bed. In less than five minutes I was up again, rushing to the loo, which was where I stayed – I was glad that the washbasin was situated conveniently close to the toilet.

Alex Stepney (England): I thought I'd go back to the chalet and get my camera. Take a few pictures of the game and the lads. So I do no more than just stroll back to my room and Banksy's gone. He's in the bog and everything's coming out both ends. He just said, 'I can't do anything. I'm gone.' And he's so weak, so white, so I ran straight out and saw Dr Phillips and, of course, we got Alf.

Gordon Banks (England): The trouble was I was being sick, or worse, so often that I was getting no rest. This was no 'normal' tummy upset. I felt as weak as a kitten. My limbs ached, my stomach cramped. I continued to sweat and shiver as if I'd been pushed outside on a winter's day wearing nothing but a pair of shorts.

By the time they woke up the next day Banks' condition improved slightly and there was some hope that the worst had passed and he would be fit to play. But just hours before the game, as Sir Alf gave his team talk in the England hotel, his condition worsened again and it was soon clear he was in no state to play an important World Cup knockout match. His place went to Peter Bonetti, an experienced and able keeper but one who hadn't played a competitive match for weeks.

Gordon Banks (England): There was no lounge or conference room in the hotel available to Alf so he summoned us all to his room for a team meeting. We all crammed in and I sat down on the floor by the door. As Alf began speaking, I began groaning. The stomach cramps had returned and with a vengeance. I'd hardly eaten a thing and there can't have been anything more to come. As Alf talked to the squad he kept glancing over in my direction. Eventually he addressed me in person. 'Well?' Alf enquired. I shook my head. 'Not well,' I replied. Alex Stepney and Nobby Stiles helped me to my feet. I heard Alf tell Peter Bonetti that he was playing in place of me and I walked out of the team meeting and out of the World Cup.

Alex Stepney (England): Alf got Peter Bonetti and he said, 'Right, Peter, you'll be playing and Alex, you'll be substitute,' and that was it. So Peter had no time to think about it. We were going across straight into the game, the dressing rooms. I don't think there was any doubt in anybody's mind. Peter had always been a good goalkeeper. There were no worries about that.

Bobby Charlton (England): We could always fall back on the fact that we were not exactly stripped of goalkeeping strength. If we feared the loss of the best, the rest was far from dire. However, in our bones we had come to believe that Banks was irreplaceable. He was unique, everyone knew that, and not least

Pelé. He was our rock and our talisman, someone upon whom we had come to rely at our most critical moments.

Francis Lee (England): The German game. Everybody thought Banksy might have diarrhoea, he might have been sick, he might have an upset stomach but he can still play because he was such a calming influence on the defence. But he didn't.

Martin Peters (England): When Peter, or the Cat as we call him, was given the news that he was in, he took it calmly, but I could guess that he was nervous, a perfectly natural reaction. After all he had hardly played for six weeks and to be thrust into a match of this importance at such short notice must have been an ordeal. Banksy was sure to be missed – he had justified his label as the world's number one goalkeeper on this tour – but we were fortunate in having the Cat to come in. In almost any other side in Mexico he would have been first choice, as anybody who saw Chelsea's Cup final games with Leeds in April would testify.

Bobby Charlton (England): Alf Ramsey retained his composure when he announced that Bonetti, who had been warned the night before that he might have to play, would be in goal, but it was no great task to guess what was going through his mind. It was going through all our minds. 'Not Banks down, anybody but Banks.'

Allan Clarke (England): I was sharing a room with Banksy and the day before the quarter-finals he went downhill. Peter Bonetti was the other goalkeeper in the squad and he was a fabulous goalkeeper. But you want your best players out there.

Francis Lee (England): There was another alternative. In big games you need big temperaments and experience in big matches. Of which Peter really hadn't got. Chelsea weren't winning everything. The other goalkeeper was Alex Stepney, who played for Manchester United. He had just won the European Cup. Alex Stepney was a big-time keeper. He had a good temperament, and nothing seemed to bother him. I think he should have played Alex Stepney. But you see in those days, and to some extent it is still around, the England manager listens to the London press. The London press have their say in picking the team and I think that was the case, the London press picked the goalkeeper. This cannot be blamed on Peter Bonetti. Because Peter Bonetti probably hadn't played for six, eight weeks. I just thought it was a game for a man with a big temperament.

It was another boiling hot day in León, where West Germany had played all three of their group games and where they were treated like the home side. Even without Banks, England started well and were far the better team for at least the first hour of the match. And after thirty-two minutes they got the goal their superiority merited.

Jürgen Grabowski (West Germany): In León it was almost like playing in Germany. The Mexicans were very 'pro-German'; they showed such enthusiasm.

Wolfgang Overath (West Germany): Before the game against our arch enemy England, we were by no means tense or nervous. We knew that losing to the world champion was no shame. And we had already achieved our target by topping our group. Maybe we were a bit too carefree, because it was 1–0 to the English before we really got going. Our defence fell asleep for a moment and Mullery nipped in between them and shot the ball home. That happened in the thirty-second minute.

Alan Ball (England): León had been the Germans' 'home'

ground during their Group 4 exploits and the critics were quick to point out that in progressing to the quarter-final stage they had scored ten goals to our two. We had conceded only one, Jairzinho's goal for Brazil, and Banksy rightly deserved praise for the two clean sheets out of three, but soon we had a problem.

Martin Peters (England): Almost immediately after the game began I thought that this was going to be the easiest of the lot. Though it was hot, like in Guadalajara, the León ground was open and a refreshing breeze took the edge off the heat. There were also many England supporters present and I cannot pay them tribute enough – they let us know they were there and were marvellous. After the tightness of the marking and the unbearable heat of the group matches, this was altogether different. The Germans gave us much more room and I knew this was going to be my best game yet. I had not been too pleased with my form in Guadalajara because I was not getting involved up front as much as I should have done, but I knew only too well that such was the heat that had I gone up in support of Geoff Hurst and Francis Lee I would have been struggling to get back. Here in León, I buzzed around like I was in England.

Bobby Charlton (England): It seemed inevitable that we would score, and we did after thirty-two minutes. In view of his impact, and his show of self-belief, it was fitting that the goal was scored by Mullery. He started and finished the move, which confirmed our clear edge, finding Newton on the right, and then bearing down on Sepp Maier's goal with a perfectly judged run to meet the return pass and send the ball high into the net.

Martin Peters (England): We were playing so well that I wasn't surprised when we scored in the first half. Geoff Hurst had been brilliant, but it was Alan Mullery who made the vital breakthrough when he brushed past the German defence and had a great shot on the turn.

It was Mullery's first goal in thirty internationals and fully deserved. England were on top and five minutes into the second half Martin Peters doubled their lead. It looked like they were cruising towards the semi-finals.

Martin Peters (England): At half-time it looked good for us and a good deal less so for the Germans. As we came off, those of them who did not have puzzled looks on their faces were arguing amongst themselves. Alf said in the dressing room that he couldn't see them scoring and he was right, I thought. I just couldn't visualise a goal from them the way they were going and I would have bet then the final score would be 1–0. I was wrong – and mighty pleased to be for a while! Keith Newton, another of our successes, made the running for Alan's goal, and he played a big part in our second with a first-time cross after Geoff had pushed a ball inside their full back. I steamed in from the left and after Francis Lee had just failed to connect, I got a touch at the same time as a defender and the ball spun past Maier.

British TV commentary: Newton is overlapping like blazes down the right side. He's chased all the way back there by Löhr. A good cross ball, on the far side is Hurst. And it is in the net. No, Martin Peters, sorry. Martin Peters makes it two-nothing. And there's the man who made the goal, Keith Newton. Hurst and Peters going in together on the far post and it was Peters who gets the touch and puts it past Sepp Maier . . . Peters going in hard and fast, into the back of the net. Martin Peters, two-nothing England. Now that is the sort of thing that really should smack these Germans right back on their heels.

Bobby Charlton (England): Martin Peters had not been as influential in Mexico as he was at Wembley, but five minutes into the second half he demonstrated again the most precious of his qualities. After Newton crossed to the far post and Maier failed to gather the ball, the 'Ghost' was there to force it home. We were 2–0 up and cruising, and at that moment I could not have been persuaded that I was in the last minutes of my international career.

Martin Peters (England): It wasn't one of my most spectacular goals, but I have never been so glad to see one go in. I couldn't see how they could possibly catch us now and for a spell we played 'keep-ball', playing possession football with a series of short, precise passes that emphasised our superiority in midfield. As far as I was concerned the Germans were dead, and all but buried. No team had ever scored three against us when we were two in front, not in Alf's reign anyway, and it must have been 100/1 against it happening in this game.

Uwe Seeler (West Germany): Four minutes after the break, Martin Peters increased the lead to 2–0. My head was super-red. The legs grew heavier. But I ran and screamed, screamed and ran. The tenor of my calls: 'Come on, we will beat them!'

Bobby Charlton (England): The rhythm of our game was everything Ramsey had hoped for in the team meeting that had been overshadowed by our anxiety over Banks. The job was being done entirely to his satisfaction. Franz Beckenbauer was chasing me this day, and without the tight reciprocal responsibilities that had previously been placed on me. As long as I was having an influential effect, Beckenbauer's attacking ability was left in the margins as we restated our right to be world champions.

Bobby Moore (England): I will never forget the feeling when the ball hit the back of the net. I have never been so sure that a goal had sealed victory than that one. It all seemed over. The Germans looked completely demoralised and beaten. The flag-waving, horn-sounding German supporters were silent. They as much as anyone had accepted defeat.

Nobby Stiles (England): We were looking like world champions. Bobby Charlton, with Frank Beckenbauer again in attendance, was running the show from midfield.

Wolfgang Overath (West Germany): We continued to believe in a win against England until the fiftieth minute, when the defence made a stupid mistake a second time. Martin Peters was right on hand and dashed our hopes with his goal.

The introduction of Jürgen Grabowski after fifty-seven minutes boosted the Germans, as it had done in previous games. Grabowski would become a key player for West Germany in the years to come – he played in every match of their triumphant 1974 campaign – but even though he was twenty-five years old, the Eintracht Frankfurt winger was not an established first team player in Mexico. He had made just seven appearances in four years for the Mannschaft but here in Mexico he had a devastating effect when he came on and with twenty-one minutes remaining West Germany got a goal back, when Beckenbauer drove past Mullery to the edge of the box and hit a low right-foot shot that squirmed under Bonetti's body. But even then, England, who had been so dominant until now, remained confident.

German TV commentary: *Goal. It's a goal, Franz Beckenbauer with a lovely solo run and a wonderful shot into the far corner. It's only 2–1 but the English were feeling too confident. And with* *twenty-two minutes left, ladies and gentlemen, one can still have hope. Bravo, Franz Beckenbauer.*

Jürgen Grabowski (West Germany): Every player wants to play from the start, but I was not in the starting line-up against Morocco. We were losing 1–0. I came on in the second half and we won 2–1. So it was already positive for me. I thought the next game I would be in the starting line-up and I was disappointed again and it continued like this against England, and it would go well every time. And Helmut Schön sincerely said to me, 'I have someone that I can throw into the fire whenever I need to,' and that worked out wonderfully. In fact, for me it was a fatal situation, because I hadn't known this situation in my club; to be a substitute player was something foreign, and I benefited from it in Mexico. It was a positive story for me, but I can't say I was really happy about it.

Berti Vogts (West Germany): We had two very good wingers. We had Libuda from Schalke 04 and Jürgen Grabowski, who was our strength. Changing these players around was practically our secret weapon.

Bobby Charlton (England): Grabowski came out running hard and quickly proved that his coach had been right. For the first time, the Germans looked capable of hurting us.

Alan Ball (England): Franz Beckenbauer, who had started moving forward fluently, tried a shot that slipped under the Cat and into the net. It should have been a simple, everyday save, but he missed it: 2–1.

Wolfgang Overath (West Germany): Franz didn't let us deteriorate. At just the right time, he did a wonderful dribble and hit a beautiful shot that goalkeeper Bonetti did not see coming.

Martin Peters (England): We were all over them and not even when Beckenbauer pulled one back did I feel any less confident, though it was a goal that could have been avoided and provided Germany with a glimmer of hope. It all started when one of our attacks broke down and the ball was pumped quickly to Beckenbauer, who still had a lot to do. He fought his way past Mullery and with the coverers racing across, shot past the Cat, the ball appearing to pass under his body. I must be honest here and say that I thought Peter should have had it, and indeed nine times out of ten he would have. I am not blaming him, merely voicing my opinion, and I'm pretty certain that Banksy, had he been there, would have stopped it.

Alan Mullery (England): It is a difficult thing to say, but yes he made a boo-boo for the first goal, there was no doubt about that; he dived over the top of the ball. But goalkeepers make mistakes and when they make mistakes normally the ball ends up in the back of the net and literally when that one went in he lost a little bit of confidence.

Bobby Charlton (England): The unavoidable truth was that Banks would not have conceded the Beckenbauer goal. It was a soft goal. Bonetti mistimed his dive and that brought the usual consequences when the last line of resistance is perceived to be vulnerable – a degree of panic in a defence that had previously looked so serene. There, so eloquent in its absence, was the value of a goalkeeper such as Banks. He made the difference between victory and defeat, reinforced confidence and warded off doubts, because you knew that if the worst happened and you broke down there was every chance you would be rescued. So sadly for a man who had enjoyed such a fine career, it was now clear that no one was more in need of rescue than Peter Bonetti.

Francis Lee (England): The decisive moment was the goal they scored because it should never have been a goal. It's very easy to blame anybody for anything in a game because that's what football is all about. But he [Bonetti] won't be pleased about that no matter how many times he sees it. But still, that's the game, play on.

Overath and Beckenbauer were coming into the game more and more and there was concern that England appeared too content to defend their lead. The big talking point, however, came just seconds after Beckenbauer's goal, when Sir Alf Ramsey removed Bobby Charlton and replaced him with Colin Bell.

Uwe Seeler (West Germany): Then in the sixty-eighth minute, Franz Beckenbauer succeeds with a long shot at goal. Only 1–2. Then [a minute] later: the English are so confident of a victory that they replace Bobby Charlton with Colin Bell.

Bobby Charlton (England): It was then I saw some activity on the touchline that told me Ramsey was about to make what some will always say was the most controversial and damaging decision of his England career. Colin Bell was warming up on the touchline and this, I knew right away, meant that the manager was about to continue his practice of protecting me from the worst effect of the conditions. I didn't want to leave the field, I was part of the game and I was not suffering, but I did recognise the manager had to look at the wider picture. I was thirty-two, I had done a lot of running, and in three days' time we had to play a semi-final at an altitude 1,500 feet higher than we were at present in the Estadio Jalisco in Mexico City. So I prepared to leave, hoping that Grabowski would not be allowed to do any significant damage and our momentum would be maintained. I saw no big reason why this should not be so. Colin

Bell, like Norman Hunter, who would come on for Peters in the eightieth minute, was a strong, good player who would grant the Germans few, if any, liberties. Yet I did feel a certain unease, partly because my legs felt so good and also we had achieved such a good balance in our performance. Sickeningly, this worry was compounded before I left the field. Beckenbauer went forward, and for some reason I will never know, but maybe it was because I was momentarily distracted by what was happening on the bench, I left him to do so, and he scored. As I left the pitch I recalled one of Ramsey's more insistent instructions before the game. 'If Beckenbauer gets to the box,' he said, 'don't let him work the ball on to his right foot.'

Uwe Seeler (West Germany): They already imagined themselves in the semi-finals. We kept on working. Got five corner kicks in three minutes.

Alan Ball (England): Sir Alf made two substitutions, with Colin Bell and Norman Hunter, two strong boys full of running, replacing Bobby Charlton and Martin Peters. Bobby had played three hard games in a week covering acres, as had Martin, another long-distance runner. The plan was for the two substitutes and me to shore up the middle of the park. With Colin Bell running all over the place and Norman in his 'none shall pass' mood I looked at them as two wise substitutions with a semi-final only three days away. Then things started to go wrong. They put on a flying winger, Grabowski, and he began to cause us problems, although with twenty-two minutes left we looked home, if not comfortably.

Bobby Charlton (England): Looking back it is easy to see when the process began. It was seven minutes after Peters had, in all our minds, put us into the semi-final against Italy, who at the time were slaughtering Mexico 4–1 in Toluca. That was the moment

Schön played his last card. He sent on his quick and aggressive right winger Jürgen Grabowski against Cooper, who, he might have guessed, was tiring after a super performance.

Alan Mullery (England): When I played against Brazil I lost a stone in weight running around in the Mexican sunshine. Bobby Charlton was quite a few years older than me, and he was tired in the games like everybody else was tired. Alf tried to nurse him. And taking him off against Brazil. Alf did the same thing [in this game] but it didn't come off.

Allan Clarke (England): Alf Ramsey very rarely pulled a lad off. The only way he would make a change during ninety minutes, whether it's a friendly or a World Cup qualifying match, the only time he would make a substitution was if someone was injured or if someone was having a really bad game. Alf was very loyal to his players. So I could understand it from that point of view.

Bobby Charlton (England): He took me off in all the other games early. Because I was the oldest player and I didn't have any hair, I think that everybody thinks you are affected by the heat and the sun. And if there was a game that was safe then he would save me for the next match so he used to bring me off regularly. And he had done in the previous matches. But that match I felt really good, I felt as though I could run all day. And we got into a 2–0 lead. And I was on the pitch but I had been told that I was ready to come off when Beckenbauer picked the ball up and he went through and scored. But then I came off and I had to sit back and watch them coming at us. And we lost our concentration a little bit.

Francis Lee (England): Nobody was surprised he took him off, he was thirty-three, thirty-four and the fact that the sun was that hot, it just didn't stack up. He could have played the full amount but at no time was it felt that he needed to play. Don't forget you're not talking about a team that is scraping to get into the tournament, you're talking about the favourites along with Brazil before the tournament.

Bobby Charlton (England): The substitution remains controversial but England were still a goal up and still in charge. If there were certain fears, there was still at that stage an overall sense that we were the stronger team, and that the stirrings of concern would in the end remain no more than that. But as I watched the drama begin to unfold, these stirrings grew in force and as the Germans threw themselves forward with Beckenbauer at the heart of it all, I began to worry that our fears over the absence of Banks were about to be confirmed.

Wolfgang Overath (West Germany): If Beckenbauer's shot had come a few minutes later, the goal might have been in vain. We threw all our strength into the match and it all paid off.

The departure of Charlton turned the game in West Germany's favour. Fourteen minutes after Beckenbauer made it 2–1, they got an equaliser. It was the most peculiar of goals, Seeler jumping to head the ball with the back of his head and send it looping slowly into the net over a stranded Bonetti. The English couldn't believe it. There was still almost ten minutes to go.

British TV commentary: *Schnellinger number three. Here's Seeler. Seeler has done it! Uwe Seeler has equalised. And the crowd goes mad! With just nine minutes of this game left, Uwe Seeler has equalised for Germany. The entire stadium erupts. Germans, Mexicans alike. All for this little man, Uwe Seeler. Five foot six and a half and once again using his head to do it. This is how they did it. There's Seeler,* *his back to goal. And Seeler in now with the flick, Bonetti on the near post as the ball sails away across the face of his goal into the right side.*

Uwe Seeler (West Germany): Schnellinger crosses from the left into the box. I stand on the edge of the box with my back to the goal. I can vaguely see how goalkeeper Peter Bonetti remains in the corner of his goal. I jump towards the approaching ball. It lands where I have relatively little hair. On the back of my head. I let myself easily fall into the cross and push my head under the ball, quickly upwards. And this wonderful thing happens: the ball lands where it belongs. In the upper left corner of the net.

Alan Mullery (England): And then they scored a second one with a Uwe Seeler header and it just bounced over the top of him and they are back in the game again. And Peter probably at that stage is wondering why he is not sitting on the bench and Banks should have been playing. But to blame him is completely ridiculous. He was part of a side that had Peter Bonetti and another ten players. And at that time he was a very good goalkeeper.

Martin Peters (England): I didn't see the ball enter the net because my view was obscured, but I did see the hasty wallop out of defence that put Schnellinger in possession. It was unlike us to do that and practically any other time it would have gone unpunished, yet the fact remains it was a bloomer. That was two clangers and they both cost goals.

Bobby Charlton (England): And they got an equaliser, I'm watching it, and I can't believe this is happening from the touchline.

Wolfgang Overath (West Germany): Uwe Seeler, a model of commitment and diligence, scored a fabulous header in the eighty-first minute, with a real 'Uwe goal'. A cross came in and he glanced the ball towards the goal. After completing a high arc it sank into the far corner. Bonetti was caught out on the goal line. We hugged each other joyously.

Sepp Maier (West Germany): And again I have to talk about Uwe Seeler. I will never forget what he did in this game. The kick-off was at noon. The sun was high in the sky right above the stadium; we had our own shadow at our feet. Uwe left alone up front and fell back slightly to do the work of five men. My God, how he ran! From one penalty area to another. From the left to the right wing. His skull glowed like a light bulb, he was so red from heat and exertion: the veins were so far out of his forehead that I thought in the first half that his vessels would burst at any moment. And then his headed goal. He hit it with the back of his head and didn't give the goalkeeper a chance. What a struggle, a sensation that we created there. And the crowd? The Mexicans stood behind our team like another player.

Bobby Charlton (England): The rest was a complete reversal of more than two-thirds of the match – it was their attack against our defence, and twice more our defence cracked.

Nobby Stiles (England): It was terrible to see the game, and the World Cup, sliding away from England and big Jack couldn't bear it. As Beckenbauer took control of the game, Jack walked away, cursing. He couldn't accept that Alf's World Cup was going to end this way and he went into the shade beneath the big stand, listening to the roar of the crowd and fearing the worst. I stayed in my seat, watching with the gut certainty that the moment had been lost, and, also, reflecting all over again on the greatness of Bobby Charlton. When he left the field, Beckenbauer was suddenly huge and it made you consider the extent of the talent that had, over most of two massive games – the World Cup final of '66 and this one – forced the Kaiser into such a subdued role.

Bobby Moore (England): Geoff Hurst so nearly put the issue beyond doubt soon afterwards. He flung himself through a ruck of players, scorning the danger of flying boots, to get his head to a cross from Colin Bell at the near post. But the ball tantalisingly swerved inches wide. Such is the margin between World Cup success and failure.

Wolfgang Overath (West Germany): Just as had happened four years ago, we took the game into extra time. Just like then, it was 2–2.

Uwe Seeler (West Germany): 2–2: extra time again. Another drama? Not this time. This time luck is on our side.

Francis Lee (England): Then it gets to 2–2 and extra time and we are all over them. They brought on Colin Bell, who played with me at Manchester City, who was a very good runner, a good athlete and I just said to him when he came on, 'Belly, this could be your day. You've got more stamina than anybody on this pitch at this moment in time. Get at the ball, follow the ball, pressurise the ball, get involved with it all the time.' I said, 'You win the bloody game for us.' And he played all right but he just played his own game.

The match went into extra time and although both sides were exhausted they kept looking for the goal that would get them into the semis. The match ebbed and flowed, from end to end, and both sides had chances to score. The decider, when it came three minutes into the second period of extra time, was again the result of slack defending from England and this time it was Gerd Müller who did the damage. The England defenders were outjumped once more as Hannes Löhr headed a cross from the right flank back across goal and Müller volleyed home from close range to score his eighth goal of the competition.

German TV commentary: *Pass from Löhr. And it's Müller! 3–2! 3–2! Pass from Löhr. It's 3–2 for Germany. After being 2–0 down. And now ladies and gentlemen, all hell has broken loose around me. I'm sorry if my voice got a little carried away but what a goal, what a move. And there's still twelve minutes to go.*

Wolfgang Overath (West Germany): Even though we had adjusted very well to the heat during the tournament, we were worried about the additional thirty minutes of extra time. All players knew: whoever got the third goal would win. And this third goal was scored by Germany's king scorer. Gerd Müller, whose goals – as a newspaper called it – had 'Müllerised' us into Mexico managed to score as spectacular a goal as Uwe Seeler did before. A header from Hannes Löhr reached him at chest level. It was too high to shoot. But not for Gerd Müller, who could score his goals from all positions. Bonetti stayed rooted on the line again, and the game was decided for us in the 108th minute. The English goalkeeper stared at the goalscorer as if he had come from another planet.

Bobby Charlton (England): And it goes into extra time and Müller got a third goal and I couldn't believe it. Because we played so well in that match and we were deservedly in front 2–0. And yet at the end of the day we were out.

Uwe Seeler (West Germany): Our 'never give up' mindset is rewarded. Wolfgang Overath, who played another great game, passes the ball to teammate Hannes Löhr. The Cologne player passes to Jürgen Grabowski. The 'Frankfurter' crosses the ball in front of the box. And who is there? The man who scores every time, of course: Gerd Müller. 108th minute: 3–2 for us.

Bobby Moore (England): No matter how hard we tried we were unable to retrieve the situation. We came close to equalising several times but somehow it appeared the script for this 120-minute drama had been written before a ball had been kicked.

Alan Ball (England): Some of our lads were wilting in the intense heat and with eleven minutes to go Gerd Müller, unhindered, was hooking the ball past a transfixed England goalkeeper. We tried to get it back. We worked ourselves to a sweat-soaked standstill, but we could not get the goal. It has to be admitted that they were better than us in extra time. We could not raise ourselves to the pitch that we had before. I never thought we would lose. We lost 3–2 in extra time after squandering a 2–0 lead.

Bobby Moore (England): I have rarely been so sure of victory than after we scored our second goal against the Germans. Defeat seemed out of the question. It did not appear possible that we could lose such a lead. Yet the impossible happened. The way in which we bowed out was so completely frustrating. No team proved they were our betters, no team humbled or overpowered us. It was hard to escape the feeling that fate had not intended us to win, as though we were powerless to prevent our own destruction. I don't think any of the players or English supporters who were at León will ever be able to relive that game without shaking their heads in disbelief. So much planning, dedication, skill and effort count for nothing in the face of the unpredictable whims of football. I for one will not be able to remember those 120 minutes without wanting to thump my fist on the table and ask, 'Why? Why? Why?' And no one will ever be able to give me a satisfactory answer.

Martin Peters (England): For my part, I was convinced it would end 2–2. I imagined lots would have to be drawn and I could see in my mind one team jumping up and down with delight and the other slinking away unable to grasp they were out of the World Cup in such a ham-fisted manner. But it didn't come to that, and once again I misread the situation. I could not believe that they could get a third against us – surely, they must have used up all their good fortune for years to come. But the goal that finished us was not really luck – it was another clanger if you judge our defence by its own standards . . . we were not decisive in the air, and Müller, who had hardly been allowed a kick by Brian Labone, was unmarked as he hooked in the ball on the six-yard line.

The memory of those three German goals will always be with me. When I am out of the game in the years to come I know I will be haunted by them. The scar will be permanent. You can be as tough as old rope, but there are some things that can never be erased.

Bobby Moore (England): I kept remembering the sight of Alan Ball tearing around the pitch in his usual style when we were two-nil up and saying to passing Germans 'Auf Wiedersehen'. It was how we had all felt. The game was won yet here we were preparing to make a premature trip home.

Alan Ball (England): It was disbelief. A bizarre, bizarre game. All my time – I played seventy-two times for England – I never ever witnessed again going through the emotions and how it was towards the end of that game. It was like a dream. This can't possibly have happened. Their goals were freak goals. Seeler off the back of his head. Things happened in that game that don't normally happen.

Wolfgang Overath (West Germany): I think we had a lot of luck against the English. We were the best team, yes, but they handled us very well until 2–0 when they substituted Bob Charlton, to save him for the next game. And that was when the game changed. All of a sudden it started to fall together for us and we played really well, and deserved to win. But the English were far better until 2–0.

Bobby Moore (England): To be two goals in front with twenty minutes remaining and then lose was to us bordering on fantasy. Never before since Sir Alf had taken over the helm had such a thing occurred, with what was generally recognised as the most efficient and well-organised defence in the world.

Uwe Seeler (West Germany): I no longer remember the remaining twelve minutes. Only the final whistle. I think we lay flat on the grass in the stadium for at least half an hour. But what impressed me a lot is that the English turned out to be good losers. Just like us in London four years earlier.

Sepp Maier (West Germany): The game against the English has long gone down in football history. We recovered from a 2–0 deficit and won 3–2 in the extra time. We defeated England. Revenge for Wembley. What a sensation.

Bobby Charlton (England): There is nothing so bleak as losing a game you know you should have won.

Martin Peters (England): I could hear the pandemonium, the klaxon horns and delirious chants of 'Alemania, Alemania!' and I was waiting for the lads as they trooped in. If you ever hear that footballers are mercenary types whose minds are stuffed with thoughts of how much they can squeeze out of the game and nothing else, tell them about the scene in our dressing room. It hurts now to be reminded of it and I was far from the worst affected, because in a curious way I felt detached, not being on the field to the end.

Alan Ball (England): Back in the dressing room, it seemed like twenty minutes before anyone spoke. Everyone was just bewildered by the turn of events. How could it happen? How could we lose after being 2–0 up? It hurt because we felt we could win the World Cup and become immortalised in English sporting history.

Martin Peters (England): The place was like a disaster area. Some were crying, others sat about like mummies staring into space and it was worse than ever when Alf came in. 'You gave everything. Try not to feel too badly. I feel proud of you,' he managed to say. We, in turn, felt desperately sorry for him, for there is a fantastically strong bond between us.

Alan Mullery (England): After extra time they were better than we were and that was game, set and match, and it was probably the most disappointed I've ever felt after a game of football. You can lose games but losing in World Cups makes you feel differently.

Alex Stepney (England): I've never been in a dressing room like it in my life. No one spoke. We didn't know what to say. And Alf, the man he was, made a fantastic speech. He said, 'You've done me proud, you've done yourselves proud, you didn't deserve that.' And he went round and shook every player by the hand and said, 'Thank you very much for everything you've done.'

The result stunned England, who were distraught at having to relinquish their world crown. There was a long and sometimes bitter post-mortem that was largely focused on Bonetti's performance in goal.

Martin Peters (England): Inevitably, inquests were started almost immediately, not by us, I hasten to add. Players and systems were damned, heads were called for and excuses were made, but we kept silent. We knew what we thought – that it was errors by a team who are usually so miserly with handouts that killed us. Just that.

Allan Clarke (England): Peter just had one of those games; he made one or two mistakes that he was punished for. He wasn't too happy but these things happen.

Nobby Stiles (England): The reality of it had to include a harsh judgement on the fine goalkeeper Peter Bonetti. He was at fault in all of the goals, and if that hadn't been so, if Gordon Banks hadn't woken up as a victim of Montezuma's revenge, if a brilliant header by Geoff Hurst hadn't missed a post by a fraction instead of bouncing out to the lurking Francis Lee, the chances are that Alf would have returned to England as, once again, a confirmed hero.

Bobby Charlton (England): [For both goals], in the eighty-second minute and the nineteenth of extra time, there was good reason to believe that Banks would have seen us through the crisis, first when Uwe Seeler's back-header drifted over Bonetti and then when Gerd Müller got behind Brian Labone and volleyed home the winner.

Martin Peters (England): I don't know what Peter thought. We never talked about it, not even when we were in Acapulco for a few days on holiday; but I suspect he had gone over the incident many times in his mind.

Peter Bonetti (England): I have great memories of my playing career – except for that one day in León; it was a nightmare.

Gordon Banks (England): Everyone was devastated after the Germany game, no one more so than Peter Bonetti. Peter believed he had let everyone down, though we all tried to persuade him otherwise.

Allan Clarke (England): I remember after the West Germany game, Beckenbauer and the Germans came back to our hotel and we had a drink with them. I went up to Peter and said thanks for getting us home early, Pete. And he didn't like that at all. He just looked at me. He was as sick as a parrot.

Francis Lee (England): I felt sorry for him because I think he should have played the other fellow. Alex could have done the same thing, or Alex could have played a blinder. It's all ifs and buts. I definitely, definitely, definitely think that if Gordon Banks had played . . .

Martin Peters (England): For seventy minutes . . . I have never been so certain in all my life that we were going to win a game of football; and I don't care what has since been written about that hideous day in León. I know how close the Germans were to total collapse. I was next to them, I saw the despair on their faces, the gestures to each other that indicated they were resigned to the worst; and the frantic arm-waving and shouting from their trainers' bench could do nothing to help them. So nobody has to tell me that we threw away a place in the semi-finals – and a probable place in the final, because I say without hesitation that Brazil and England were the only teams of real quality in Mexico.

As if Banks hadn't suffered enough, he was dealt another cruel blow by the delayed TV broadcast. In order to boost ticket sales, the local broadcast of some matches went out as live, an hour or so after kick-off. In his hotel room, Banks was watching the game when his teammates trooped in.

Gordon Banks (England): I was feeling dreadful but my spirits soared as I watched Alan Mullery, with his first goal for England, give us a 1–0 lead at half-time. Five minutes into my televised broadcast of the second half, my joy turned into euphoria as I watched a low cross from Keith Newton converted at the far post by Martin Peters. I rubbed my hands with glee: 2–0! The lads were doing England proud. About twenty-five minutes from time the door of my room opened and in shuffled Bobby Moore, Brian Labone, Alan Mullery and Alan Ball. Their faces were grim, but I wasn't falling for another of their practical jokes. After all, on the telly we were still two up. 'How'd we get on,' I asked. 'Lost 3–2, after extra time,' Bobby said glumly. 'You're having me on, how'd we really do?' I asked. 'We're out, Banksy. We're going home,' said Bally. 'Pack it in, lads,' I said. 'I'm not in the mood.' Then Bobby Charlton came into my room and I froze. Tears were streaming down his face – and at last the penny dropped. This was no wind-up. That's how I remember our game against West Germany. We are still leading 2–0. I didn't watch the remainder of the broadcast, nor the edited highlights that were shown later in the day. I just couldn't bring myself to sit and watch it and endure the pain. To this day I still haven't seen the match in its entirety.

The other big talking point was Ramsey's decision to remove Bobby Charlton right after Beckenbauer had pulled a goal back for the

Germans. Charlton was thirty-two years old and Ramsey had used him sparingly throughout the tournament, concerned the heat and altitude might affect him more than his younger teammates. In each of the last two games, Charlton was hauled off with the second half not even halfway over. The decision to preserve his most experienced player for the next match looked good early on but Ramsey's judgement was now called into question.

Bobby Charlton (England): The great debate ever since has been whether Ramsey was right to replace me and I know that it haunted the manager until the end of his days, but the most important factor of our defeat, I will always believe, was that when the Germans made what appeared likely to be their last change in that World Cup, Gordon Banks was journeying between his bed and his bathroom. The Germans needed to score three goals in the last quarter of the match and the fact was that even the best teams did not score three goals against Banks in the course of a whole game.

Wolfgang Overath (West Germany): After this game, many blamed the defeat on the man who had to stand in for the sick Gordon Banks. I don't think Bonetti was the big scapegoat. He certainly made mistakes, but who says Banks might not have made also mistakes in the same occasion? If there were reasons for the defeat alongside the way we grew as the game went on it was this: Ramsey should never have taken Bobby Charlton out of the game after 2–0. Without him, the brain of the team was missing, the man who holds the ball in difficult situations. And not just that. The English played slightly arrogantly. It backfired.

Bobby Charlton (England): People criticise Alf for actually pulling me off but he had done it before and he did it for a reason. And he told me afterwards, he said I wanted to make sure that you were all right for the semi-final. And he said I am sorry for the way it worked out. And that was my last game; I never played again after that. But it was perfectly understandable. I wasn't complaining when Alf pulled me off. If there was one thing I was really regretful about it was that I felt so good. When you've got a hostile environment like Mexico. Mexico City is 8,000 feet, I think León was at 6,000 feet, and it is wearing and you can't breathe properly unless you are ready for it and you are fit. But we had done the right training. I felt really good. I felt like I could run all day. But when he said it was time to come off, I said all right and off I went. And at the end of the day it wasn't a mistake. That's fate I suppose. Had we gone through we could well have won the World Cup.

Alan Ball (England): Looking back I believe we subconsciously took our feet off the pedals. We also hit the wall physically.

Francis Lee (England): The thing is as well, you have to remember that England have got a very strong defence. If somebody had told you that the biggest problem England would have in this World Cup is that they would concede too many goals, you'd have said don't be silly. They might get beat 1–0, and it would be a big loss if they'd got beat 2–0, you know, but they scored three. The only reason we are sat here now talking about this bloody game is that it is a game we should have won but we didn't win. You can talk about it till the cows come home. We didn't win, we should have won, we didn't win. That's it.

Martin Peters (England): We played badly in only one match, against the Czechs in Guadalajara, and they hardly even suggested a goal against us. Leaving aside the merits of our system, we played according to plan and until we allowed Germany to creep back into that nightmare quarter-final in the last ten minutes of normal time, the means were going to be justified by the end. It was as inevitable as anything could be in football.

Bobby Moore (England): I heard the players held a wake at the hotel, trying desperately to hide their bitter disappointment. They were joined by a group of English supporters and sang and danced while Germans looked on bewildered, wondering if they had really won that day. It was a night to drown our sorrows, to try and forget. Sir Alf had asked, 'When does the Tommy Wright show start?' although he was not present when the Everton full back sang, repeatedly, the 'Everton Song' in the hotel bar-cum-nightclub. Jeff Astle also went up to the microphone in answer to many requests and a group of the lads sang 'Back Home'. One person who did miss the match was Sir Alf Ramsey's wife, though it was through no fault of her own. When she went to her seat, it was occupied by Mexicans who refused to budge. Despite approaches to several officials, she was still unable to find a seat and in the end gave up and returned to Sir Alf's room at the hotel to watch the match on television.

Uwe Seeler (West Germany): So, we made the impossible possible. But we had no idea that the drama would continue.

Alan Ball (England): There was an amusing moment the following morning on the long coach trip from León to Mexico City. Tommy Wright lapsed into tears, and as he was crying Sir Alf came up to him and put a sympathetic, fatherly arm around him, saying, 'Don't be too upset, young man. You've got plenty of time. There's another World Cup coming up in four years' time and you're young enough to be in that.' There was a pause, and then Tommy delivered his reply and his reason for being upset. 'There's no beer left on the bus,' he said.

SEMI-FINALS

| 17 June | Mexico City | Italy v West Germany | 4–3 a.e.t. |
| 17 June | Guadalajara | Brazil v Uruguay | 3–1 |

TEN

ITALY v WEST GERMANY

The Italy v West Germany semi-final was seen in some quarters as the lesser of the two semis, or certainly the least exotic. Italy had failed to shine so far and West Germany were clear favourites. Bobby Moore, who had stayed on in Mexico to perform a pundit's duties at Brazil v Uruguay, would wryly admit he picked the wrong game to watch. The spectacular end-to-end encounter turned out to be one of the most exciting football matches ever played and became known as 'The Game of the Century'.

Sandro Mazzola (Italy): Before the kick-off, we knew that there were all the prerequisites for an exceptional match. It was a big game. All the features were there: technique, speed, compactness.

Berti Vogts (West Germany): For me as a younger player, you always looked enviously at Italy. And at that time all the best German players, like Helmut Haller or Karl Schnellinger [went to Italy] and after that so many others went there, to big clubs like Inter Milan, AC Milan, or at that time Juventus. So we only had eyes for Italy, like nowadays you look at the teams from the Premier League.

Tarcisio Burgnich (Italy): West Germany were one of the favourites; they had an excellent squad, an excellent team. Even when I played with Inter, it was not easy facing the German teams. Against the Germans and against West Germany it was always a tough battle.

Berti Vogts (West Germany): We were tired because of the extra time from the England game. And add to that the celebration. We had sent the World Cup winners home, etc., etc. And then we had to play against another big team like Italy, and the games against Italy are always very tight, even today. If you beat England, you always have to celebrate. This is important. [Laughs]. At that time, we had been in Mexico for two months, so I think you are allowed to celebrate. [Laughs]. In the motel and the sport school where we were based, there was nothing much to do. Schön even counted the number of beers we had there. He was a strict trainer, but after the England game he looked the other way. He celebrated with us for a while. Then he went to sleep and he said, 'Leave the boys alone.'

Uwe Seeler (West Germany): Italy had shown only basic football to win in the group stages. They scored just one goal against Sweden, played two 0–0 draws against Uruguay and Israel, and then defeated the Mexicans in the quarter-finals.

Sandro Mazzola (Italy): A few newspapers came to our training camp. Everyone thought we would be defeated. West Germany was an exceptional team, but we also knew we were strong, that we had excellent individuals just like the Germans. So, the fact that the predictions were against us, that was an incentive to us; it brought out our pride and made us aware just how important it would be to get to the World Cup final. They were not in the semi-finals by accident. So we prepared for that game against

West Germany by studying their weaknesses, trying to figure out how to attack them. We encouraged each other and our group was very united. Furthermore, that semi-final against West Germany was played at a lower altitude [than the quarter-final against Mexico]. Therefore, we were confident.

Uwe Seeler (West Germany): 102,000 spectators created a crazy atmosphere. Every scream, every song would be screamed back a dozen times. Ourselves and Italy, it was two top European teams who were facing each other. The Italians came as European champions in 1968. We were there as World Cup runners-up in 1966.

The game began with a bang as Italy took the lead after just seven minutes thanks to a goal from Roberto Boninsegna, who scored with a left-foot drive from around twenty-five yards out.

Uwe Seeler (West Germany): The sun beamed again. This time, however, it was fighting a yellow-grey smog. Breathing at an altitude of 2,000 metres was extremely difficult. How could you play soccer under these conditions? We cursed the time difference again. The support of the Mexican fans was with us.

Sepp Maier (West Germany): The Mexicans loved us. How people cheered for us when they realised we were in trouble! A unique atmosphere in the stands. I can still hear it today: 'Ala bio - Ala bao - Ala bi ba ba - Alemania - ra - ra - ra!'

Uwe Seeler (West Germany): After seven minutes, all support from the public was gone. Italy led 1–0 through Boninsegna. But much worse was that we noticed that the referee Yamasaki – a Peruvian with a Japanese passport – was entirely on the side of the Italians.

Wolfgang Overath (West Germany): It was as if we were cursed. We also started against Italy by losing a goal. For a split second the two strikers Riva and Boninsegna spotted a small gap in our defence and they scored to make it 1–0 and with that all our good intentions went out of the window. From that moment on only one team attacked and it was us. Helped on by the cheers of the Mexican fans, we made one chance after another. But luck was on Italy's side.

Sepp Maier (West Germany): In terms of team strength, we were actually equally well served in all positions. The game seemed completely open. But Berti Vogts made a mistake in the eighth minute. Boninsegna caught the ball . . . goal. A shot that Willi Schulz, our former 'sweeper', should have chased away from his attacker. The way Boninsegna had a free shot, it gave me no chance.

Wolfgang Overath (West Germany): Applause accompanied us into the dressing room and we got applause when we came back for the second half. Straight away the Italians were pinned down in their own half again, but we couldn't score.

The Italians were masters at shutting up shop and they set out to defend their lead. That handed the initiative to the Germans, for whom Grabowski started for the first time, and they poured forward in search of an equaliser. Overath was inspiring, Beckenbauer his usual commanding self, Seeler tireless as always.

Sepp Maier (West Germany): In the second half, the Italians set up their catenaccio. It drives us almost to despair. We just can't get through. Time is running out. And from the stands the chants continued: Ala bio - Ala bao - Ala bi ba ba - Alemania - ra - ra - ra!

Angelo Domenghini (Italy): During the regulation ninety minutes, after scoring and making it 1–0, we only defended. Then, at the end of the game, we conceded the equaliser and collapsed. I repeat, during regulation time all we did was defend. West Germany pushed us until the end and got the draw.

Wolfgang Overath (West Germany): The Italians, no angels in the first half, were completely lost. The only way they could stop us was with fouls. We should have been awarded a penalty in the sixty-fifth minute, as the noisy protests of the fans confirmed, when Franz Beckenbauer was felled in the penalty area. But referee Yamasaki ruled it was a free kick instead of a penalty. And just like that the Italians escaped one more time. Beckenbauer, on the other hand, had to pay. He suffered a serious shoulder injury when he was brought down. With a grim face, he got up and carried on.

Uwe Seeler (West Germany): The pace was getting harder, and we threw everything forward [into attack] after the break. But the Italian defence stood like a wall. In the sixty-seventh minute, Beckenbauer was fouled by Pierluigi Cera. A clear penalty, the crowd all agreed! But referee Arturo Yamasaki saw the foul outside the box. We surrounded the referee and protested while Beckenbauer lay there on the ground: he had dislocated his right shoulder. Since we had already made two substitutions, the Kaiser had to grit his teeth and keep playing. The tension rose with every second. Siegfried Held circled a volley past goalkeeper Albertosi in goal, but Roberto Rosato was able to clear the ball on the line in an acrobatic manner. Müller and I had a number of good chances.

Sepp Maier (West Germany): Beckenbauer with a solo run through the Azzurri defence line. Foul in the penalty area. But Mr. Yamasaki doesn't whistle. Every time our strikers or midfielders get through, they are sacked, held, kicked. No whistle from Mr

Yamasaki. How would the game have ended if we had had a normal referee and not this Mr. Yamasaki, a Peruvian of Japanese descent, whose Mexican boss had Italian parents? But I don't want to go into the referee any further.

Wolfgang Overath (West Germany): Franz Beckenbauer had to be treated before the extra time. With his shoulder in a bandage, and his arm tied to his body, he ran with us onto the field.

The dressing rooms at the Azteca were at one end of the ground. In later years, FIFA would insist that World Cup stadiums have dressing rooms under the main stand so the teams could walk out together onto the middle of the field. But in Mexico, with the game seemingly over, some West Germany players, dispirited and exhausted and almost out of hope, headed towards the tunnel behind the goals.

Uwe Seeler (West Germany): We were running out of time. Only a few more minutes, the Italians would have the victory. But just as against England in the quarter-final, we hadn't given up yet. In added time there was a blaze in the Italian penalty area, and finally the tireless Grabowski sent in a cross into which defender Karl-Heinz Schnellinger, a few metres from goal, prodded forward – the ball was in the net. The heroic Albertosi had been overcome and the Italians couldn't believe it. Especially with Schnellinger being an AC Milan player.

British TV commentary: A tremendous amount of injury and stoppage time has been soaked up by the referee. Grabowski still fighting for it. The cross ball. Schnellinger! Schnellinger has done it! Karl-Heinz Schnellinger has scored the equaliser, deep, deep into injury time. There may not be time for this game to restart. It's definite now we're going into extra time. Karl-Heinz Schnellinger of AC Milan, he plays for an Italian club. There's no time on the clock.

There's been no time on the clock for a long time . . . The stadium is pandemonium . . . This one is very alive, absolutely alive.

Sandro Mazzola (Italy): It was a dramatic moment, we were all so tired. I went up to Schnellinger and said, 'You play in Italy and then you score that goal against us,' and he replied, 'I was on my way to the dressing room, I thought the game was over and I was going to the dressing room when they gave the corner.' We dropped our guard because we thought we had won.

Wolfgang Overath (West Germany): When the regular time was almost over and it was still 1–0 for Italy, we switched off. We continued to attack, but what should happen? Almost a miracle. And this miracle happened. In the ninety-first minute Karl-Heinz Schnellinger, who played his club football in Italy, pushed forward and forced the ball over the line to equalise. The stadium went wild. It was not for nothing that 100,000 Mexicans cheered for us.

Enrico Albertosi (Italy): The stadium clock was right in front of me, I looked at it and ninety minutes were up and I thought we've done it. But the referee added a little time on. Schnellinger was there and we went up to him, because he played at Milan, and said, 'What are you doing up here?' And he said, 'The game is over so I was on my way to the dressing room and I was there and scored a goal.'

Karl-Heinz Schnellinger (West Germany): I've always said that goal, that was a gift from God, that people will always remember and no one will forget me. It was a gift from above. For me it was just the proof that I was a good professional; without that goal I would have been forgotten.

Angelo Domenghini (Italy): West Germany scored from a corner kick in the ninety-third minute. We were intimidated, we thought that our World Cup ended there and then when they made it 1–1. We thought we would be knocked out. It would have been a shame because in a World Cup all the games are exciting, from the first to the last. This is the World Cup. If you go ahead, you will experience a series of unforgettable emotions, otherwise you pack your bags and go home.

Sepp Maier (West Germany): We want it so bad, but how? We are waiting for the final whistle when the unbelievable happens. Grabowski dribbled past his opponent with a nice feint. He crosses. Schnellinger is there. Schnellinger, of all people, who earns his caviar at AC Milan. A step forward. And goal! 1–1 in the ninetieth minute. Extra time. Extra time in Mexico. At fifty degrees out there on the turf. Dear God!

Berti Vogts (West Germany): It was an enormously important goal for us, right before the end of the game, that enabled us to take the game into extra time.

Siegfried Held (West Germany): He was a German international and it was clear that he was trying everything to help his team. It's not hard to imagine that his reputation among the Italians increased because he did the best possible for his team.

Tarcisio Burgnich (Italy): It was an incredible game, but our biggest failing was conceding a goal in the last few minutes. We were upset by an opponent like that. We wanted to avoid the extra time. We knew we had played a good game and we showed how strong a squad we had. Instead, fate mocked us. And West Germany believed in themselves right until the end and got the equaliser.

Wolfgang Overath (West Germany): It was lucky for us that Yamasaki let the game go into injury time. That was our salvation, at least for the time being.

The game moved into extra time and exhaustion, both mental and physical, soon became as much a factor as skill or determination. West Germany had played extra time against England just three days previously, while Italy had played their quarter-final on the same day at the highest ground in the tournament. The conditions were taking their toll. The upshot of that was a see-saw thirty minutes of football that had the fans on their feet, breathless and astonished.

Uwe Seeler (West Germany): And then the most dramatic extra time in football history began.

Enrico Albertosi (Italy): Everything changes in extra time, it's a whole new game because you have thirty minutes and not ninety and you are playing a final, the most important game ever for a footballer's career.

British TV commentary: *Libuda with a corner. Müller in the box, Seeler's there, so is Held. Seeler is challenging, gets a touch and Müller is in there and it goes over the line. It's there! Gerdie Müller has done it, 2–1. Gerdie Müller. The Germans go wild on the bench, on the field, in the stands. What an incredible series this has been for Gerdie Müller. For the fourth time Germany have come from behind to take the lead. Against Peru they did it. Against Bulgaria they did it. Against England they did it. And now they've done it in the semi-final against Italy.*

Uwe Seeler (West Germany): Müller was able to nip ahead of Poletti and push the ball into the net in front of the surprised Albertosi. The spectators were completely thrilled. 2–1!

Siegfried Held (West Germany): That was certainly a strange goal. But it counted and that's what matters.

Wolfgang Overath (West Germany): The final victory, desired by Mexico's soccer fans as well as by the 10,000 German football tourists, seemed certain when Gerd Müller scored the strangest goal of the tournament in the ninety-fifth minute. As always on hand when he sensed a chance, he jumped between goalkeeper Albertosi and a defender, I think it was Rosato. The ball bounced off Müller's body and rolled leisurely across the line.

Sandro Mazzola (Italy): They were strong of course, but we were too. There was a tremendous disappointment and the fear of being eliminated. Because then West Germany went ahead in extra time and made it 2–1. At that moment we felt the weariness of the World Cup. We had always played at over 2,000 metres and it wasn't easy at all. We had played far from Italy, far from our families; there was a moment of discomfort in all of us.

Tarcisio Burgnich (Italy): That was really a difficult moment, I remember it well. We risked being knocked out but with a massive reaction, with heart, passion, determination, we managed to turn the match around. We gave it everything, we really believed we could do it. For Italy, it is still a memory that remains indelible, it was a beautiful match.

Uwe Seeler (West Germany): Our joy did not last long. In the ninth minute of extra time, AC Milan's Gianni Rivera played a free kick into the box, which Held could only clear in the direction of approaching Tarcisio Burgnich. He had no difficulty in overcoming goalkeeper Maier. The reigning European champions had equalised.

British TV commentary: *Oh my godfathers! It's all tied up again. Burgnich the scorer. So we got a whole new ball game going. Six minutes of the first period of extra time still remain. And it's 2–2. A terrible mistake by Siggi Held. And Burgnich keeps calm. The thirty-one-year-old right back puts Italy back in the game. The two most dramatic goals of the game have been scored by defenders, Schnellinger for Germany and Burgnich for Italy. And this game is becoming more alive and more fiery as every second ticks by.*

Wolfgang Overath (West Germany): With their reserves depleted, the highly strung Italians sank to the ground. They had already given up when Siggi Held suffered a mishap: he couldn't clear the ball from the box and defender Burgnich was on hand and shot sharply to make it 2–2. I could have screamed from anger.

Siegfried Held (West Germany): There was a cross, and one of the Italians jumped up in front of me. I stood behind it and instead of reacting at lightning speed, the ball bounces off my chest right and fell right at the Italian's feet. It was just a stupid coincidence. I thought, 'Damn! You are very unfortunate.'

Tarcisio Burgnich (Italy): I didn't score many goals in my career but I have to say that when I did they were good goals. Very few, but very good. I would go up front only on rare occasions, usually at set pieces. I scored with my left foot, which was not my good foot. That equaliser gave us a huge boost and then Gigi Riva made it 3–2.

British TV commentary: *Boninsegna is in the middle and so is Riva. Here's Riva now. And there he is! Luigi Riva! Luigi Riva makes it 3–2 to Italy! Watch Riva now, the man with the golden boot; at the far post Sepp Maier can't get a touch. Forty-five seconds of this first period of extra time still to play. The Italians, who looked as if they were beaten right out of sight when Schnellinger equalised, are now ahead again . . . This game which has swayed consistently from the very kick-off, sways back into the favour of the Italians again . . . There are still fifteen minutes left, fifteen minutes of tension, fifteen minutes of excitement, fifteen minutes of what could become pandemonium . . . Italian players are stretched out all over the field.*

Wolfgang Overath (West Germany): The 2–2, however, had a doping-like effect on the Azzurri, and they were in the lead again three minutes later. Riva eliminated the German defence in a confined space and gave Maier little chance with a clever shot.

Uwe Seeler (West Germany): Italy took the lead again shortly before the change of sides. Angelo Domenghini passed from the left flank into the path of Luigi Riva, who did not miss the chance. Incredible, but true – this was Gigi's twenty-second goal in his twenty-first international!

If Riva's goalscoring record was good, Müller's was, remarkably, even better. The Bayern Munich striker would end his career with sixty-eight goals in sixty-two internationals, including getting the winner against the Netherlands in the final at home in 1974. His performance in Mexico was astonishing. His hat-tricks against Bulgaria and Peru lifted him into an elite group of three players who have scored two hat-tricks in one World Cup, alongside Hungarian Sándor Kocsis in 1954 and France's Just Fontaine in 1958. The stocky little dynamo scored ten goals in six games; it was the last time anyone reached double figures in one World Cup tournament.

German TV commentary: *Another corner, the seventeenth for Germany, this time from the right side. From Grabowski, Libuda has the ball, it's going in, Uwe Seeler . . . Goal! Goal Germany! Goal Germany! Headed on by Uwe Seeler, then a header from Müller,* *past two Italians into the net. It's tied 3–3! I don't believe it! A drama like this can only happen once! I don't believe it. And what the players are going through on the field, my vocal cords are going through the same thing. 3–3, what a goal, what a goal.*

Uwe Seeler (West Germany): The second half of the extra time brought even more drama. The game remained incredibly fast, and both teams could have scored in almost every attack. Germany managed to equalise again. Once more I got to a header and Müller was again on hand to accommodate the ball in a classic manner in the Italian box. Rivera, who was guarding the back post, was stunned.

Wolfgang Overath (West Germany): Now the Italians felt like they were the winners, but Gerd Müller made sure in the 110th minute: 3–3; we could hope again.

Enrico Albertosi (Italy): Seeler headed it, Müller nodded it on but Rivera was a metre off the post and it went in between him and the post. I said things to him that I can't repeat here. And he said, 'The only thing I can do to make up for it is to score.'

German TV commentary: The Italians attack. And it's a goal for Italy! They left Boninsegna all alone, Rivera runs forward, and shoots the ball in the net. Boninsegna was alone. A moment ago, the mood was still high, the nerves cannot put up with it any more. It can hardly be described what is going on here. A goal for the Italians, the Germans were sleeping. A defensive error the likes of which I've never seen before, certainly not by the German team. But they just can't manage it any more, they just can't.

Uwe Seeler (West Germany): But the Italians were not to be deterred by our equaliser. Immediately after the restart,

Boninsegna pushed through to the goal line on the left and then cleverly played the ball back to Rivera. The European Footballer of the Year in 1969 sent Maier the wrong way and scored the fifth and decisive goal of extra time. The striker, who had come into the game after the break, had proven why the tifosi had wanted him on from the start of the tournament. The game wasn't over yet. After two hours of soccer under the brooding Mexican sun, both teams were physically exhausted and the last few minutes seemed like a slow motion.

Tarcisio Burgnich (Italy): It was an incredible game, but our biggest failing was conceding a goal in the last few minutes [of regulation time]. We were upset by an opponent like that. We wanted to avoid the extra time. We knew we had played a good game and we showed how strong a squad we had. Instead, fate mocked us. And West Germany believed in themselves right until the end. West Germany equalised, 3–3 and Rivera 4–3.

Italian TV commentary: What a magnificent game, Italian viewers. We will never be able to thank our players enough for the excitement they have given us today.

Gianni Rivera (Italy): When I scored to make it 4–3 against Germany it was a weight off my shoulders. I knew I was at fault when they scored because I wasn't close enough to the post.

Sepp Maier (West Germany): I can't really remember the extra time. We were leading, then the Italians equalised. Then 3–2 for the Azzurri. Seeler heads to Müller . . . Goal! 3–3. Kick-off, Boninsegna fools Willi Schulz . . . Goal, 4–3.

Sandro Mazzola (Italy): There really was a collapse, but Burgnich's goal and Rivera's 4–3 were liberations.

And that was that. After a dramatic thirty minutes of extra time, Italy had done just enough to drag themselves into the final. The game was so amazing a plaque was later erected at the Azteca celebrating its happening.

Italian TV commentary: *And there goes the referee's whistle. Italian viewers, after two hours of suffering and joy we can announce that Italy are in the final for the Jules Rimet trophy. This Sunday, at 8.00 p.m. Italian time, the final is Italy-Brazil. Italy have eliminated West Germany. It was an incredibly exciting game, a game in which Italy began with a goal from Boninsegna in the eighth minute and it was only due to the incredible time added on by referee Yamasaki and a goal from Schnellinger that condemned, if we can call it that, the Azzurri to thirty minutes of extra time. Thirty dramatic minutes.*

Sandro Mazzola (Italy): At the end of the game we did not believe what we had done, it was truly a great feat. West Germany did not want to leave the field, they were distraught; they did not want to go back to their dressing room.

Tarcisio Burgnich (Italy): For them it was a defeat, a match lost in a truly incredible way. It's a victory that is still talked about today. Italy's victory against West Germany is part of football history.

Uwe Seeler (West Germany): The Italians lived up to their reputation as time-wasters and stayed on the ground after every duel, kicked the ball up in the stands and arguing long and hard about every refereeing decision. We were irritated as the redeeming final whistle blew, and some of them collapsed with exhaustion. Suddenly it didn't seem to matter who won and who was defeated. The crowd was completely overwhelmed and knew they had seen a truly unforgettable game.

Wolfgang Overath (West Germany): Unfortunately, it ended badly for us. Willi Schulz, with his strength at the back, could not stop Boninsegna. His pass into the box came to Rivera, who quickly understood the situation and completely unmarked wrong-footed the ball past Maier for 4–3. That was the death blow for us. The Italians did not let this lead slip away nine minutes before the final whistle.

Berti Vogts (West Germany): I think Italy just had a bit more luck than we did. We had the extra time [from the England game] and then three days later we had the altitude. We had to fly [to Mexico City], and the Italians were already 'home'. They had played there before. We had to travel, and that was a disadvantage for us. But it was a 50–50 game, and the luck was with Italy to advance into the final against Brazil.

Sandro Mazzola (Italy): Watching today's football, I have never seen any matches like Italy 4, West Germany 3. It was an epic encounter. It was so exceptional that in Italy our fans had celebrated as if that was the final and we had won the 1970 World Cup.

Sepp Maier (West Germany): What a great time. My most beautiful World Cup ever, even if we were eliminated against the Italians in the semi-finals. In the Estadio Jalisco in Mexico City, in front of a hundred thousand people. The football thriller par excellence. One thing is certain: the game Germany–Italy in Mexico in 1970 will be remembered as long as football is played on this planet.

Wolfgang Overath (West Germany): As exciting as the extra time was, maybe we could have been spared if Rosato's foul on Franz Beckenbauer hadn't happened. Without the shoulder injury, Franz would have played very differently. In addition, the fourth goal should not have happened because without Franz in his usual place nobody had looked after Rivera.

Sepp Maier (West Germany): I didn't even know what the score was any more. It went by so quickly. The game had a very fast pace, despite the murderous heat, despite the difficulty in breathing due to the altitude, and despite the extra time. The spectators were no longer sitting. They stood on the benches, screaming at the top of their lungs 'Alemania, Alemania' until we got the equaliser. Then: 'Ra, ra, ra, Italia' – until the Italians were again up front. A cauldron. And then it was all over. We were grieving to death.

Tarcisio Burgnich (Italy): Mistakes were made in that match but the game of the century was born out of the defensive mistakes by both teams. West Germany was a strong team. Winning in that way gave us a lot of enthusiasm just because of how tough they were.

Sandro Mazzola (Italy): Were the defences terrible? It was an intense game that defied all the patterns.

Wolfgang Overath (West Germany): Despite the defeat, we had no reason to hang our heads in shame. This semi-final game was, in my opinion, even better and more dramatic than the game against England. Once again, we got better as the game went on but we ran out of luck in the end. When a newspaper wrote: 'Watch this game and then die (happily)', that probably says enough about the 120 minutes of that 17 June in the Estadio Jalisco in Mexico City.

Siegfried Held (West Germany): The game was certainly exciting and dramatic but it was shaped by many mistakes, especially mine. When you make a mistake, you are the one to blame. But it would certainly have been possible to win the game. That makes it all the more annoying.

Enrico Albertosi (Italy): When we qualified for the final, we celebrated in the evening. That's only right after a victory like that. Then, the next day we started to prepare for the final with Brazil.

Sepp Maier (West Germany): Should I be superstitious now? [Reserve goalkeeper] Horst "Bread" Wolter and I shared the room in the training camp. I had a cassette recorder with me and Bread was crazy about the song 'El Condor Pasa', which was a big hit at the time. Every time I got ready for the game, he let the tape run. 'Close your eyes, listen. That calms you down.' I sat down obediently like a little boy. A really good relaxation exercise. As I said, the semi-final took place in Mexico City. We had moved into a new quarter in Puebla and were driving with the bus over the mountains to the stadium. 'I forgot the tape,' Bread said to me. He looked contrite and thoughtful. 'Hopefully everything will go well.' That was before the Italy game. He didn't say anything afterwards, he just sat sadly in his corner. I almost believe that he blamed his forgetfulness on our defeat.

Gerd Müller (West Germany): No one has forgotten that match. It still drives me crazy thinking about it and I haven't recovered from it to this day.

Uwe Seeler (West Germany): Later, a plaque was placed in front of the stadium in Mexico City so that the Germany–Italy game, this grandiose chapter in World Cup history, will never be forgotten. Sixty thousand people welcomed us returning home in Frankfurt as if we and not the Brazilians had become world champions. Politicians crowded next to the players in the photo and told us what they always say on such occasions. The footballers were the 'best ambassadors of our country'. They weren't wrong.

ELEVEN

BRAZIL v URUGUAY

The original match schedule had both semi-finals in Mexico City, which was an advantage for Uruguay because it was only a two-hour bus ride from their base near Puebla. Brazil, meanwhile, would be uprooted from their home away from home in Guadalajara and forced to fly the 350 miles east to the Mexican capital. However, the Brazilians, no strangers to back-room shenanigans, immediately got to work on the organisers and lobbied for a change. Their success would give Brazil an added advantage when the teams took to the field on 17 June.

Mario Zagallo (Brazil coach): We left the Estadio Jalisco and began the preliminary study of [what was going to be] a fierce battle. It would be wonderful if the semi-final was played right there in Guadalajara and not in the Mexican capital as was scheduled. That same afternoon, right after we beat the Peruvians and the Uruguayans beat the Russians, the CBD [the forerunner to the CBF] officials went to work on the luminaries of FIFA. The skill we applied led us to the successful conclusion that we wanted. The next day, it would all be resolved: the Uruguayans would come to us. We'd have our fans behind us.

Pelé (Brazil): We weren't worried about whom we'd face. We were only concerned about possibly having to leave Guadalajara. According to the schedule we'd be leaving. Happily, that night it was all set: Brazil would face Uruguay at the Estadio Jalisco in Guadalajara.

Ildo Maneiro (Uruguay): Brazil had made that move to change the venue because they were supposed to come to the capital, to Mexico City, but they made us travel to Guadalajara, which was where the Brazilians were. The temperature and climate and the altitude were totally different from Mexico City.

Atilio Ancheta (Uruguay): We had played 120 minutes against USSR and we were tired and when we went to play Brazil the Uruguayan officials were taking a break in Acapulco. We should have played in Mexico City. We were in Puebla, which is 100 kilometres from Mexico City, and Brazil were far away in Guadalajara. The Uruguayan officials were not aware . . . when they changed the venue to Guadalajara. The officials didn't even go to the meeting and when we discovered it was 11.00 p.m. at night.

Ildo Maneiro (Uruguay): After qualifying for the semi-finals we celebrated with a drink which was customary after each game; it was football from another era. And at night they warned us that 'at 15.00 hours' we would fly, that we had to get up at six in the morning to travel to Mexico City. It was hugely exhausting. At that time, we weren't very interested in the political side of affairs, but obviously the Uruguayan delegates disappeared, and it wasn't even from them that we found out the venue of the game had changed. Besides, it was unimaginable that FIFA would schedule a game to be played in one place and then change it; they did the dirty on us.

Atilio Ancheta (Uruguay): We were in Puebla until the day before the game. We left Puebla at 5 a.m. We had a cold breakfast because the organisation was not great. We took a bus to Mexico City and then we flew to Guadalajara and got there at around 5.00 p.m. Then we went to the hotel and there was a fiesta there. At night there was another party, with music all night. Everyone in Guadalajara was supporting Brazil so there were all these fireworks going off.

Ariel Sandoval (Uruguay): We had to go to Guadalajara while Brazil were already there from the previous game. From Puebla it was about two hours to Mexico City by bus, then we had to wait for the plane and fly to Guadalajara. From Guadalajara airport we went to the hotel. When we arrived at the hotel at about ten o'clock in the morning of the day before the game we found that all the air conditioners were broken. I didn't play but I sat there sweating on the subs' bench. Even after all that and without Rocha we came close.

Roberto Matosas (Uruguay): The game that I suffered the most from physically in Mexico was against Brazil in Guadalajara. That day I suffered. Because we had played extra time against Russia to get to the semi-finals, it was exhausting and we also went from the height of Mexico City, where it had been cool, to the heat of Guadalajara.

The Uruguayan players knew what they had to do and there was no special preparation, even though it was a semi-final against one of their biggest rivals. Just the sight of Brazil's famous yellow jerseys was enough to scare some nations but Uruguay was definitely not one of them. Uruguay may have been smaller than many Brazilian states but they were never overawed by their bigger neighbours.

Roberto Matosas (Uruguay): I think that a characteristic of the Uruguayan footballer has always been to respect the rival but not fear him; one always believes in his strength and that he can beat anyone. Especially since there is a great tradition that still continues to this day and that is that beating Uruguay is never easy. So we have become imbibed with that spirit over many, many years and you can see that out on the pitch. Sometimes it is a football that isn't great to watch, but it is a hard football to beat because we never give up. Coaches used to be people who would talk for eight or ten minutes, but nowadays a practice before a game takes forty minutes or an hour. But before, there was much more belief in the players themselves, that they could play both their individual role and fulfil the collective part to benefit the team; there was much more confidence in them. That is why the coaches, especially Hohberg and Langlade, what helped the most was the great emotional stability they showed. There were never screams or misplaced actions, they were always very balanced people and that was what they passed on to us.

Ildo Maneiro (Uruguay): We had a good World Cup because we worked very well, we had the best goalkeeper in the world, Ladislao Mazurkiewicz, and in defence was Roberto Matosas who had class and experience, and Atilio Ancheta who was a young man with a lot of ability and a physical presence. We were a team that worked hard, but based on the historical strengths of Uruguayan soccer: the team was well balanced but we were not an attacking side, we were always conservative.

Although the injury-hit Uruguayans hadn't exactly set the heather alight – they scored just three goals in their opening four games, including extra time against the USSR – Brazil coach Mario Zagallo knew exactly how difficult an opponent they could be. The

Uruguayans were tough and had no qualms about mixing it with their more talented rivals. Zagallo told his players to prepare for the worst.

Mario Zagallo (Brazil coach): I never stopped warning my players about the unsporting means they might resort to. We couldn't be spellbound by their tricks and time-wasting. Our players had been immunised against spitting, against irritating provocations, against improper tricks and against vile abuse. They knew what it was like to be fingered from behind in order to get us riled and force us to lose our temper and react and get sent off. It was a World Cup semi-final and that demanded cold blood.

Pelé (Brazil): I saw some of Uruguay's games on tape and I followed the results in their group and concluded that they couldn't beat us. They were a frightened team, they didn't want to attack, they held back. Against Brazil they put only one man up front. Knowing all that I never believed we would lose. But I did think that we had a better team in 1950 and we still lost.

Mario Zagallo (Brazil coach): The Uruguayan shirt was light blue and similar to that worn by the English. Just like them the Uruguayans played with two men up front. So I would have to use the same tactical scheme that I used against England, even though we were facing a South American team, and for that reason, one with more skill.

Atilio Ancheta (Uruguay): We had confidence that we could get better; we were very united but we lacked someone to score goals. We had Cubilla on the right but not many others. The hardest game was against Brazil; there is a lot of rivalry and we beat them in 1950 and so that history was always present. Even with friendlies there was a big rivalry. I think because of the common border, we know each other quite well. We are always together. We know their players and they know our players.

Pelé (Brazil): Uruguay have been a nightmare for Brazilian football since 1950.

The fans knew little about the machinations over the venue and were instead caught up by history. Twenty years previously, Uruguay had beaten Brazil 2–1 at a packed Maracanã Stadium in Rio to win the World Cup and end Brazil's hopes of winning the competition for the first time. The defeat was a crushing one for Brazil and scarred the national psyche for years to come. The semi-final in Guadalajara would be the first time the two teams had met in a World Cup game since that fateful encounter and both sides were aware of the significance of the rematch. Uruguay, or their fans, wanted to use 1950 to inspire their players, while some in the Brazil camp knew that if they did not deal with the psychological issue in the run-up to the game they could suffer.

Mario Zagallo (Brazil coach): The Uruguayans and the Russians played extra time in the Mexican capital and the Brazilians were cheering for the Russians. But the Uruguayans won and that left us with a dilemma. They would come after us with all they had, like a ghost in a light-blue shirt. The victory myth was a constant with those boys. With all their hearts and all their determination, just like in 1950. That's what they said. I was on my guard. I always had worries in my head, despite the background of the Uruguayan team in that World Cup. Up until then, they had not demonstrated their true merits to the best of their ability. Their results had not been extraordinary. But anything could happen, just like in Rio de Janeiro, in the year 1950.

Piazza (Brazil): Some elements in the press, in that week before the Uruguay game, they came up to me and said, 'Look, Piazza, aren't you worried that Jalisco turns into the Maracanã of 1950?' I was seven years old in 1950. I didn't even have a transistor radio. We didn't have electricity in my house. I only found out later that Brazil lost the World Cup. So the fears of those journalists, principally those that saw that World Cup, those that lived through that disappointment, the frustration of not being able to celebrate the title in Brazil, they were all expectant. And sometimes restless and worried that Brazil wouldn't get past Uruguay.

Gerson (Brazil): The press created it all. We knew about it but we had people there who weren't even born in 1950 and I was one of the oldest and I was nine years old in 1950. I saw one game here in the World Cup, Brazil against Spain, and Ademir scored a barrowload of goals but I had only vague memories.

Mario Zagallo (Brazil coach): The vultures in some of the press had the bad taste to entertain themselves for four days by preparing depressing front-page headlines with prophecies such as 'the ghost of 1950 is haunting the Estadio Jalisco'. I was eighteen in 1950 and on duty at the Maracanã in my olive-green uniform and my helmet. If I was eighteen and older than the players in our seleção how old must they have been in 1950. They had no memory of that late afternoon when we stopped short of winning the title that was within our grasp. They were all boys; they were hardly even aware the World Cup existed.

Pelé (Brazil): It was impressive what happened on 16 June, the eve of the game. Everyone who came to our hotel said: 'You can lose the World Cup but you can't lose to Uruguay. They've been stuck in our throats for twenty years. We need to get them out of there. We need to beat the gringos to show them that we're not cowards as they sometimes make us out to be. They say they only need to put on the sky-blue shirt for the Brazilians to tremble. We have to beat them.'

Roberto Matosas (Uruguay): We were talking about it among us Uruguay players, but the coaches never made any reference to it.

Pelé (Brazil): Brazil didn't play Uruguay in the '54, '58, '62 or '66 World Cups. That was why the 1970 game, twenty years after the defeat at the Maracanã, continued to have a special significance. It was the first time 1950 had been mentioned at our concentração. The funny thing was that most of our players hadn't even been born when Brazil lost the title to Uruguay. The thing was just to keep training and prepare our spirits for the match ahead.

Carlos Alberto (Brazil): The majority of the players who were there in 1970 didn't even remember. Maybe Pelé remembered something but Pelé was nine years old at the time. The thing was in 1970 it was the first time that fans had really started to travel with the team. It's not like today but several Brazilians had gone there to support us and all that. And as the concentração was on a street, there was an avenue there in front of the entrance; it wasn't like today where it's a closed hotel and no one can get near. Several Brazilians went there and were talking about 1950: 'Shit, do you think the same thing will happen like in 1950?' And as people were talking about 1950 it's going to get into your head. Into everybody's head, right? And I think that hampered us a bit until we scored that goal through Clodoaldo.

Brazil began the game with an uncommon sluggishness. Whether they were worried by the ghosts of 1950 or not, the seleção's opening half hour was their worst of the tournament so far.

Mario Zagallo (Brazil coach): I am not fooling myself by saying the first thirty minutes of the game against the Uruguayans were a disappointment thanks to the psychological influence of those sordid campaigns run by part of the Brazilian press and certain unworthy journalists. Our team was unrecognisable. I had the impression that we had swapped shirts. As if some Mexican joker had wanted to create confusion and have the big stars of Brazil playing in Uruguayan shirts. I confess that I was astonished. I didn't know what to do about such apathy. Suddenly we lost that silly goal to Cubilla. But that was the least of it. Worst was that moment of bewildered incomprehension, just like in the game against Czechoslovakia. They scored the goal and I couldn't get out of my seat, I was inert. But at that moment against Uruguay I could tell that things were serious. Our seleção couldn't complete a simple pass; we didn't create anything from the back. The Uruguayans could have won the game in those opening thirty minutes. They were bossing it.

Pelé (Brazil): Even though the majority didn't understand the profoundness of the drama at the Maracanã [in 1950], it was still difficult to ease our nervousness. Our early passes were all misplaced, our defensive line wasn't right and we could not break down their blockade at the back.

The first half was not even halfway complete when Uruguay took the lead with the most unusual of goals. Brito gave the ball straight to Morales barely thirty-five yards from goal and his pass found Cubilla on the right wing. His mishit shot bounced past the hapless Felix, who crumpled in a heap on the goal line.

British TV commentary: *Brito, that's a dreadful one to Morales. Cubilla has a great chance. He's scored. Cubilla has scored. What an incredible goal. Cubilla has scored. Seventeen minutes. And Felix thought it was going wide and makes no attempt to stop it and as he watches it, too late he realises it is going in the net.*

Gerson (Brazil): No one understood what happened at the Uruguay goal; the ball went this way, then that way. The ball can't get through like that and we knew it, it went here and there and Clodoaldo tried to cut it out, but Clodoaldo wasn't to blame, he tried to stop the back and forth and he didn't. And so this guy nips in, Brito went with him, the ball was free, there was a big confusion . . . Cubilla hit it with his shin, Felix was expecting a shot and it bounced and got past him.

Felix (Brazil): That goal against Uruguay I only let in because of Zagallo. In the previous game against Peru, Gallardo scored the goal from a very tight angle. Zagallo gave me a dressing-down because he thought that I hadn't positioned myself correctly, that I should have been closer to the post. I said that wasn't possible, but he insisted that was what he wanted me to do and if I did that and there was a problem he'd take the flak. That's what was said, and that's what happened. Against Uruguay, Cubilla miskicked his shot and I was tight on the post, where Zagallo wanted me to be. In addition to that, the pitch had been lengthened, and the mark of the old goal line was almost at the edge of the six-yard box. When I ran out I slipped on the line. The ball went in and I went in after it. It was my mistake.

Atilio Ancheta (Uruguay): When Brazil lost the goal the Brazilians went white. He [Felix] just fell down, they were terrified, I could see it in their faces. I think they started to think of 1950. They froze a bit. Brazil were worried about losing another goal. But they came out a different team in the second half and they were used to the heat and altitude.

Edu (Brazil): When Uruguay scored, everyone was going, 'See, there you go.' But it was a goal, I don't know where they got it from. We knew that Uruguay were never going to be able to handle us because we had been spectacular against England, Peru, so they were never going to be able to live with us and they didn't. But the press kept saying, we can't forget 1950, remember what happened in 1950, etc.

Pelé (Brazil): We were at fault for the Cubilla goal. Felix was expecting a rocket. The bigger mistake came earlier when Clodoaldo, who was in control of the ball, gave it away for free.

Mario Zagallo (Brazil coach): The Uruguayans' goal had no merit: the goal they scored was a result of general silliness. It wasn't the result of care or competence.

Roberto Matosas (Uruguay): I think that Pelé was very important in that match because of how he was addressing his teammates when they were losing 1–0. They had lost their bearings a little bit and the only one who was calm and collected was Pelé; he was fundamental for the Brazil comeback. We conceded an equaliser at a time in the match when we were dominating them, right at the end of the first half.

Ado (Brazil): Pelé was incredible; at team meetings he said what he had to say. But the real big leaders on the pitch were Gerson and Carlos Alberto. One time, he said to me, in the Uruguay game if I remember correctly, Carlos Alberto said: 'Come on you sons of bitches, keep it tight up front,' and he looked at Pelé and the respect he had to speak like that to Pelé. Pelé looked at him and just made his sign with his hands. Keep calm. He didn't say much. But when he did have to speak, he would come up to you and say, 'Right, let's do this.' And Gerson was impressive.

The goal prompted the Brazilian players to take action. Zagallo had given his team a significant amount of autonomy and told them if they needed to change things around to go ahead and do what they had to do. Midfield general Gerson had been marked out of the game and realised there was little way to free himself from his opponent's tight marking. So he decided to sit back and take up Clodoaldo's position in front of the defence and let Clodoaldo push forward and join the attack.

Carlos Alberto (Brazil): Right there things got a bit complicated, and the team wasn't playing well. Then at some point in the game, Jairzinho was down and being treated by Mário Américo and Gerson called me over and said, 'Shit, Carlos Alberto, I'm struggling because this guy is tight on me.' If you see your teammate is heavily marked then you don't risk passing the ball to him, especially against a team like Uruguay that plays it as hard as they do. The guy will suddenly be right on top of him. And he'll ignore the ball and commit the foul. So Gerson said to me, 'I think I am going to swap positions with Clodoaldo, what do you think? So instead of standing here being marked, I'll drop deep and if he keeps close to me, I'll end up marking him. And we free up Clodoaldo.' Clodoaldo hardly ever went over the halfway line. He stayed back to cover for me, or for a possible move forward by Everaldo, but he always stayed back. So I called Clodoaldo over and told him Gerson's idea. 'Gerson's suggesting this, let's try it. We need to try something to change the game. Gerson is going to take your position and you take his and take the game to them.' A few minutes later he went up and scored, so I mean it's luck as well, Gerson having noticed the situation and Clodoaldo being there to take the pass and score. But when you try something like that during the game, generally things happen. Now, when you wait for the first half to end so you can get back to the dressing room and hear what the coach is going to say, sometimes nothing happens. So it's all luck: when the team is going well then things happen. We call it luck but things normally happen.

Ado (Brazil): Gerson was terrible; he wanted to take bites out of people. They called him the Papagaio [the Parrot] because he talked all the time. [Laughs]. There was one game, against Uruguay, or Chile, or who knows, that was a difficult game, and he came into the dressing room and Gerson started smoking. Man, we had come off at half-time, angry, all that running about under a boiling sun, the heat, everyone walks into the dressing room, the subs and all that, and Gerson went to smoke. And Claudio Coutinho said to him, 'Fuck, Gerson, you're smoking?' And he went, 'Go and fuck yourself, I'm the one playing out there.' And I thought, 'God Almighty! These guys were really wound up.'

Felix (Brazil): Against Uruguay, what happened? Who was in charge? You saw Gerson against Czechoslovakia, him and Jairzinho, what did they do? They put two men on Gerson and Clodoaldo was free; they put two men on Tostão and Pelé was free. So what did Gerson do? Zé, that was Zagallo's nickname, Zé. He made these signals and he understood. Because he felt the two guys there and Clodoaldo was on his own, so what did he do? Go on. I'll keep these two boys occupied and you're free.

Carlos Alberto (Brazil): Gerson and Pelé were the players that made the difference. Every team that wins the World Cup always had, always have, a player that makes a difference. Pelé was that man for us, although Gerson was the brains of the team. All the moves that started at the back, the first player was Gerson. When I got the ball: Gerson. Sometimes he'd give it back to me, but the first ball I got: Gerson. The Uruguay coach was watching, like we watched them, and they could see that Gerson . . . 'Man, we can't give this guy so much freedom. Get someone close to him at the very least.' They didn't mark man to man, but if they had someone close on him it would be a bit more difficult for him. They could see that our team would not be quite so free-flowing.

Brazilian radio commentary: *Everaldo. Clodoaldo. Brazil are on the attack. Tostão. Let's go, my people! What a pass to Clodoaldo. Look at that! Look at that! Look at that! Look at that! A new score. Clodoaldo! Look at that! Look at that! Look at that! My lovely Brazil! On the scoresheet, Clodoaldo. On the scoresheet, Clodoaldo is on the scoresheet! Brazil! Brazil! Brazil! Brazil! Brazil!*

Clodoaldo's goal, his first ever in a Brazil shirt, came at a crucial moment for the seleção. The equaliser, scored just seconds before half-time when he charged forward and got on the end of a pass into the box from Tostão, allowed Brazil to go into the dressing room all square. Brazil had not been behind for more than twelve minutes and this goal saved them from any corrosive self-doubt.

Carlos Alberto (Brazil): It was crucial for the team psychologically and for stopping Uruguay. It was all square again and when we're drawing they know how difficult it is to beat us. Do you know what I mean? So when we came off at half-time I remember when I got to the tunnel that led to the dressing room and Zagallo came up to me: 'Man, what a brilliant idea. Whose idea was it?' I said, 'Gerson told me and I called . . .' Because we had the coach's permission to change something if we had to, 'to not wait'. Zagallo was very intelligent in that respect. He gave the players freedom.

Felix (Brazil): They made that change and Clodoaldo scored the equaliser, right away. So we had that freedom. If Rivellino had any difficulties, he had that freedom. What it meant was, even though as a coach I am tough, I give you freedom to resolve problems. We were the ones that saw the problems out on the field.

Mario Zagallo (Brazil coach): We needed that equalising goal. It was the starting point of our reaction. It came at the right time, just before the break.

Dario (Brazil): If Clodoaldo hadn't scored that goal in the first half then with all respect Brazil wouldn't have come back against Uruguay. We came back because Brazil scored at the right time. And that bit of skill from Tostão was fantastic, extraordinary. No engineer can do what he did with that pass; no mathematician can do what he did with that pass. It was the most divine move I've ever seen in my entire life.

Piazza (Brazil): Sometimes, against Uruguay for example, we were terrible in the first half. We weren't great in that first half. But we managed, truly, to always play better in the second half.

Pelé (Brazil): We were lucky that we got a goal through Clodoaldo, one of the kids who didn't even hear about the final of 1950. We equalised at the end of the first half and that goal was important in giving us encouragement and a new impetus.

Clodoaldo (Brazil): The goal against Uruguay was historic for me, my first goal in my first World Cup. I equalised after forty-five minutes of the first half. There's no way I will ever forget it.

Zagallo rarely shouted or screamed at half-time and he rarely needed to. But the poor showing in the first forty-five minutes against Uruguay forced him to read his players the riot act. There was little talk of tactics; instead the thirty-eight-year-old fumed at his charges' feeble and uncharacteristically nervous performance.

Mario Zagallo (Brazil coach): Having equalised at the end of the first half I was able to give my team talk in an atmosphere of confidence. In fact, I didn't so much give a team talk, as much as deliver a reprimand in the severest terms. 'What's going on? You think you're going to lose to that team? The Uruguayans are useless! It's embarrassing seeing you walk off the pitch with your heads bowed. They should be trembling, not you! We have to start playing this game like we did in our previous matches. You are better than they are. This Uruguayan team doesn't have what it takes to score again. They really aren't good enough! We'll win; they just played 120 minutes against Russia and they won't be able to keep up with us. Let's step up the pace and we'll beat these guys easily!'

Gerson (Brazil): The Uruguayan team was a weak side, in every way; we could have played them fifty times and we'd have beaten them easily fifty games. The only thing was that our team, as Zagallo put it so well at half-time, Zagallo said, 'When are we going to start playing? Is this Brazil? Is this our seleção? You lot are having me on, what is there for me to say?' And really, there was nothing he needed to tell us, the problem was all down to us.

Carlos Alberto (Brazil): We got to the dressing room and Zagallo said to us all, 'Let's get on with it. Let's go.' And that was such that the team was settled when we went out for the second half and we played. That goal came at the right moment but I think that because of the presence of the Brazilians at the concentração talking about 1950, there was a fear that everyone shared: 'Hmmm, could the same thing happen again?' That, in a way, was psychologically prejudicial for us.

The second half was always going to be difficult for Uruguay, who had played an extra thirty minutes at altitude just three days before. Without a recognised striker they still lacked a cutting edge up front and taken together those factors meant the second period was only going one way.

Atilio Ancheta (Uruguay): We could see that the second half would be very different because they were another team. We were very tired because of the 120 minutes in the mud against the Soviet Union. That tired us out a lot. We were up for it because of the rivalry but we lacked stamina; that was what we missed. That and the fact we didn't have a striker. We had been playing at sixteen or seventeen degrees and suddenly we went to almost forty degrees. So it was 120 minutes against the Soviet Union and then with the change of temperature, that was our biggest problem. We were tired.

Ildo Maneiro (Uruguay): The game went exactly as Professor Alberto Langlade (our physical trainer) had told us it would. Langlade said that we would hold up well for the first half and we did. The first half we did well, with Montero Castillo marking Pelé very tightly and trying to control Rivellino and Gerson, who was the brain of the team. Then we had the fatal blow of Clodoaldo's equaliser. When we reached the dressing room at half-time there was a deflation; everyone could see we had just taken one of those blows that knock you out. We were exhausted at the end of the first half and we played a heroic second half. We almost made it 2–2 with a header from Cubilla.

Atilio Ancheta (Uruguay): Brazil had the best team so far and they were full of confidence. We played well in the first half but we lost it in the second half. We scored through Cubilla but Clodoaldo equalised before half-time and that meant they went in with a whole different outlook. We had a chance to make it 2–1 when Felix saved a header from Cubilla and if that had gone in it might have made a difference.

Pelé (Brazil): The second half saw Brazil constantly on the attack, despite a roughness of play that even exceeded the first half – and in the first half the Uruguayans, always noted for their rough play, played as if there were no referee on the field.

Another key moment for Brazil came almost midway through the second period, when Jairzinho picked up a loose pass just outside his own penalty box. The Botafogo winger put his head down and started motoring.

Brazilian TV commentary: *That's the lightest of touches, Tostão to Jair. And this is a nice move, pay attention viewers. A goal for Jairzinho! Sensational! We've scored! We've scored, viewers! A goal for Brazil! Sensational! A great goal. A great goal and a deserved goal, one for the football of patience, talent and brilliance and above all for the way it was created.*

Jairzinho (Brazil): It was an eighty-metre goal. Because I anticipated what was going to happen. I passed to Pelé, I kept moving forward over the halfway line, Pelé was in midfield and gave it to Tostão. Tostão passed it forward, Matosas the defender was there. I did a dummy without the ball and then I pushed it past Matosas and then kept going forward, forward, forward. Mazurkiewicz came out and then I hit an angled shot and it was 2–1 to Brazil.

Ariel Sandoval (Uruguay): We wondered what might have happened if Matosas had fouled Jairzinho at Brazil's second goal. Maybe it would have gone to penalties. Or maybe we'd have lost anyway.

That second goal, midway through the second half, was a killer for Uruguay. The Charruas were better at preserving a lead than chasing a game and as the second half wore on the Brazilians' superior fitness began to tell. In the last minute, Pelé powered forward and teed the ball up for Rivellino to put the result beyond doubt.

British TV commentary: *Twenty seconds left on my watch. Tostão to Pelé, Jairzinho away down the right. Pelé knows he's there but he might have a go himself. Trying to get it on his right foot. Setting it up. And there it is, Rivellino has scored! Three-one! The game absolutely sewn up!*

The match ended 3–1 and Jairzinho kept up his record of scoring in every match. But curiously, the game is remembered as much not for the goals that went in but for the one that didn't. With just seconds remaining, Pelé tried the most audacious dummy that left Mazurkiewicz chasing shadows. The ball never went in but the attempt is even today one of the most iconic moments in World Cup history.

British TV commentary: Pelé streaking away, that's a beautiful pass for him and he goes round the goalkeeper, he just let it run on and he scores, Noooooo! The most magnificent dummy. He didn't touch the ball at all, it goes past the goalkeeper.

Ladislao Mazurkiewicz (Uruguay): Pelé was on his own. If I hadn't come out he would have scored. I was outside the area and he did something exceptional, but he didn't score. Obviously, that is what I wanted, to stop Brazil scoring. I retired from football in 1982 and people still remember me. It's not just past glories that are rewarding to me; it is so nice to know that people still remember me even in my old age.

Pelé (Brazil): I think I was hasty. I was through, I sold Mazurkiewicz a dummy. I saw that Ubiña was getting back to cover and I wanted to shoot before he got into position. If I had stopped, I could have dribbled it round him or placed a shot into the corner. The ball went out after I hit it first time. Nevertheless, I know the ball hit Ubiña and that if it hadn't it would have gone in.

Ladislao Mazurkiewicz (Uruguay): It is always important to remember he didn't score. I did enough to put him off. [Laughs].

Ildo Maneiro (Uruguay): I remember that great move he made with Mazurkiewicz; he made a couple of plays that were from another planet at that time. That move where he feints and lets the ball run past him, I watched that from the substitutes' bench because I had been taken off with cramp. The class of both was impressive because Mazurkiewicz manoeuvred Pelé into a position where he couldn't score. Any other goalkeeper would have collided with the player and conceded a penalty or Pelé would have been so quick as to score. But Mazurkiewicz had enough skill to get back and cover the goal. Pelé feinted and let the ball run on, then he goes to get it and hits an angled shot. The defender Ancheta is the one who tried to clear it but ultimately it was not a goal.

Mario Zagallo (Brazil coach): It would have been our fourth goal if we had a gram of luck. A long ball went to the feet of Pelé. Mazurkiewicz came out from where he should have stayed. Pelé dummied him with a shimmy of his hips and the goalkeeper was left grabbing at wind. Pelé went to the right of the keeper and let the ball run past him on the left. Pelé ran around his adversary, picked up the ball and realised a Uruguayan defender was getting back to cover. Nevertheless, he hit the ball past the defender who is probably still chasing. But the ball was stubborn and went past, just skimming the post. It would have been a historic goal if Uruguay's luck hadn't been in.

There were other memorable moments, and not all for the right reasons. The Brazilians thought the Uruguayans were dirty. Pelé was so incensed that when the final whistle went he ran to the referee to give him his shirt. He was stopped by fans. One Uruguayan stamped on Pelé but the wily number ten was harder than most people gave him credit for and he waited patiently to get his revenge. At one point in the second half, he led his marker down the left flank and threw a perfectly timed elbow into his face. It was nasty but cunning – and done seemingly out of the referee's direct line of sight. Remarkably, the referee awarded a foul to Brazil.

Dagoberto Fontes (Uruguay): When we were on the wing, he was running and I chased him and went to slide in for a tackle and he jumped and swung his elbow into my face and caught me right in the eye. I didn't roll around on the ground because

I didn't want him to see how much it hurt. But the truth is my eye ended up somewhere halfway down my neck.

Pelé (Brazil): I knew he was coming in to make a nasty tackle, so I caught him hard with my elbow. It was a violent blow. The referee gave a foul – in my favour. He could see that the Uruguayan had approached me with bad intentions. I was glad that I only hit him in the forehead because if I'd caught his nose or jaw I would certainly have broken it. I remember thinking, 'God! My elbow hurts!' Imagine what his forehead felt like . . .

Carlos Alberto (Brazil): The problem with Uruguay is that they deliberately try to hurt you. They confused playing hard with playing dirty. So we had difficulty at the start of the match with Uruguay.

Jairzinho (Brazil): The Uruguayans were dirty, very dirty. Gerson had gone down and they stamped on him and they did the same thing with Pelé.

Ado (Brazil): Pelé, there was one game, I don't know who it was that got hit, Pelé went and gave him a fucking almighty elbow in the face. Against Uruguay it was, he hunted him down and then let him have it. He'd be sent off for it today; I don't know if he wasn't sent off because he's Pelé but I remember clearly in that game thinking, these guys are really going to make somebody suffer.

Felix (Brazil): You remember that incident against Uruguay, when he went . . . the guy was at him, at him and at the right time he just went . . . bang! As he was running. No one saw it, but the cameras caught it. And we got the foul.

Atilio Ancheta (Uruguay): Uruguay were always strong; that is the way we play football, because we don't have the technical quality that Brazil has. We were normal, tough, hard, but never violent. We went in hard and strong but we never broke anybody's leg.

It was five wins out of five for Brazil and they were now ready to play for the biggest prize. Before the tournament began they had set themselves the task of reaching the final. Once there, they believed, they could focus on winning the Jules Rimet for a third time but until then they had worried just about getting that far. For Brazil, that was the least their fans would expect.

Pelé (Brazil): Just like in 1950 we were superior to the Uruguayans. But this time, twenty years later, the best team won. The beats we played after the game were louder than ever. We left the stadium with our instruments and we didn't stop singing until we got back to the hotel. Then we kept going on the terrace.

A defeat in the semi-finals was no disgrace for Uruguay, a country of less than 3 million. But there was no hiding the feeling that with a bit more luck – and a striker – they could have done so much more.

Luis Ubiña (Uruguay): We had bad luck: Rocha was shredded, Morales was out for fifteen days because he had an operation on his knee; they had to put Fontes and Espárrago up front because we didn't have anyone else. No one really gave us any credit for what we achieved.

Ildo Maneiro (Uruguay): Brazil had a team that made history; they had extraordinary characters and in the final they toyed with Italy. We faced the best team in the world and got as far as we could, deservedly so.

Juan Hohberg (Uruguay coach): We reached an honourable fourth place when no one believed in us and if we had had a goalscorer there is no telling what might have happened.

THE FINAL

TWELVE

BRAZIL v ITALY

The Brazilians were confident of victory but they were not immune to nerves. Pelé, who already had two World Cup winner's medals in his drawer at home, admitted he felt tense and Tostão, who had come through more than most to get to his first final, was particularly worried.

Tostão (Brazil): I was very tense, very worried, as was everybody. The game kicked off at midday, I think because the tradition in Mexico was that the bullfights started later in the afternoon. We got up for breakfast and there was this enormous tension; no one said a word until Dario – Dario is the funniest, most talkative person the world has ever seen – asked to address the group. He went to the head of the table and said: 'I want to let you all know something important. Last night I dreamt that I scored three goals, so pick me to play and I guarantee you won't regret it.' [Laughs]. Everybody started laughing and the atmosphere lightened. He didn't even make the subs' bench. But the tension was massive.

Ado (Brazil): The coach going to the game that day was tense. We had this habit of singing, Jairzinho always led the way, beating away on his drum, everyone else joining in and singing along.

Pelé (Brazil): When we were on our way to the Estadio Azteca Stadium, on that rainy morning of 21 June, we were playing our samba when without knowing why I had a crying fit. I had a rattle in my hand and I pretended that I had dropped it under the seat of the bus. I stayed bent down until it was over. I didn't want them to see me. I was, after all, the most experienced guy there and I needed to transmit calm. It would have been dangerous to transfer that to the rest of the squad. Those tears got it out of my system and I was all good by the time I ran out.

Ado (Brazil): Once we got to the ground we were all a bit relieved. We felt, well, we've got this far, there's no way we're losing now. And I thought, 'We're going to be champions, because Italy are dead on their feet, they played 120 minutes.' We could see that they were dragging themselves onto the pitch while we were quite spritely, having had a relatively easy game before, winning 3–1. We were all fit and ready to go.

Pelé (Brazil): I was the most established of all our players. So I tried to put the players who were playing their first final at ease. I only gave interviews to say that we were going to win, that we were the best. That could affect the spirit of the squad. 'If Pelé says it then it must be true,' the younger guys said. In private, I was sure that was the case.

Mario Zagallo (Brazil coach): The Mexican newspapers said we should hammer the Italians. But luckily those papers didn't find a way into our concentração. We were confident that we would win a third World Cup but we respected the Italian team. Our optimism didn't extend beyond 2–0 or 2–1. I myself didn't believe we'd win by much more than 2–1 and I wouldn't have been surprised if it had been a draw. The way the Italians played and the results that they had secured this far, in addition to the individuals they had in their side, identified them as a natural candidate to win a third title.

Pelé (Brazil): The final can be seen as the third revenge for Brazil. The first was against England, champions in 1966. The second came against Uruguay, for the 1950 defeat, and now, some people remembered that we had lost to Italy in the 1938 World Cup. That fact meant nothing to any of the Brazilian players. We just wanted to win the Jules Rimet trophy definitively. We wanted to win the title.

Over at the Italian camp, Ferruccio Valcareggi told his team they had nothing to fear from the Brazilians but his players were not naïve; they knew the enormity of the task ahead of them.

Sandro Mazzola (Italy): Our coach planned well for our games. He was very close to us, and he told us how strong we were and how Brazil could be beaten. He told us several times that the seleção was not so strong, but we obviously had doubts about this. But it was his way of encouraging us. After all, you don't play a World Cup final every day. And we also wanted to get a kind of revenge on the [Italian] federation because we had found out that they had booked us a return journey on the day after the group stages ended. When we found that out we were angry. We were in the final.

Tarcisio Burgnich (Italy): Italy–Brazil was the most important match of the time. Both of us had already won two Jules Rimet trophies. Us in 1934 and 1938; them in 1958 and 1962. However, the Brazil we played against was on another level, from another planet. They had incredible players, scary individuals.

In addition to form – Brazil had scored fifteen goals in five games, the Italians just nine, and three of those came in the extra time against

West Germany – there was fitness and organisation to consider. The Italians had played an additional thirty minutes in the semi-final and they knew that both teams who had played extra time in the tournament so far had gone on to lose their next game, no doubt hindered by their extra exertions. There was also some discontent in the Italian ranks over their final preparations.

Enrico Albertosi (Italy): In my opinion, logistical errors were made in that World Cup. First: the game was played at noon local time, an unusual time. We weren't used to playing at that time. At breakfast we ate spaghetti. Second: we returned to Italy immediately after the end of the match against Brazil. So the night before we had our minds on something else: packing and other things because we would leave direct from the stadium to go to the airport and not return to the hotel first. We only started thinking about the game when we got on the coach. It was only at that moment that we were psyched for the final.

Pelé (Brazil): On the 17th, to get to the final, they had played 120 minutes against the Germans in that really tough game that ended 4–3. Before that they had played against Mexico in Toluca, the highest city in the country. I thought that would affect their performance.

Sandro Mazzola (Italy): The tunnel is always a bit special. We were waiting for the arrival of the referee and the linesmen. It was a surreal situation and we said to ourselves, 'Now let's show them.' I remember going up the tunnel steps, to enter the field; it was really terrible. The image I can't forget is when we were lined up for the national anthems. We wanted Brazil to think we weren't afraid, but yes, we were afraid. The Brazilian national anthem played and they belted it out. Then the Italian anthem came on and we were petrified looking at the Brazilians. So I said to my teammate, the captain Facchetti, if we don't sing they are going to think we're scared of them. And so we sang but it was a disaster because we were so emotional at being in our first final that the words didn't come out properly.

Pelé (Brazil): The Mexicans transformed the Estadio Azteca into the Maracanã, with the same atmosphere. I think that 30 per cent of our victory should be credited to the Mexicans.

Brazil started the better of the two sides as they both tried to feel their way into a game played under heavy and humid skies over Mexico City. Italy soon took control of the match, however, with Felix forced into two good saves as the Italians, hoping to catch out a keeper they knew was shaky, tried their luck from long range. However, it was the South Americans, slightly against the run of play, who opened the scoring as Pelé got Brazil's 100th goal in World Cup competition.

Pelé (Brazil): The game had been in progress only seventeen minutes when we scored the first goal. Rivellino crossed a high ball over the heads of the Italian defence and I jumped as high as I could, higher than the defender and headed the goal over the fingertips of Albertosi.

British TV commentary by Bobby Moore: *It was a very simple goal there by Brazil but marvellously taken by Pelé. It all just started from a simple throw-in; here we can see Tostão take it. Rivellino just crosses a simple volleyed ball but Pelé is up there like an eagle and a tremendous header. A wonderful goal by Brazil and a wonderful time to go into the lead. And I must say it's the first bit of freedom that Pelé has had but he made full use of it.*

Pelé (Brazil): I timed my jump to perfection. I leapt in the air, striking it with my fist screaming

GOOOOOOAAAAAALLLLLL!!!!!! until I was almost hoarse, while the others smothered me under them in congratulation.

Sandro Mazzola (Italy): We began the match by getting our marking wrong. We put a great midfielder like Bertini to mark Pelé and a defender, Burgnich, to mark Rivellino, who played in midfield. So that left us short-handed in the centre of the park and we had to do an awful lot of running.

Pelé (Brazil): They tried to provoke me. Bertini gave me a kick when we had one tussle and then he punched me in the stomach. He was always poking me trying to get me to react. When I went down he ran up to me shouting, 'Cinema! Cinema!' I think the Italians forgot that this was my fourth World Cup. I had a little bit of experience, right?

Sandro Mazzola (Italy): We asked the coach several times to change [the marking] and he eventually agreed once the ball had gone out on the left-hand side of the field. And the Brazilians, who were very intelligent, when they saw that Bertini had left Pelé and Burgnich had left Rivellino, Rivellino crossed it and Pelé was on his own as Burgnich was still going over to cover him. Pelé rose towards the heavens but he was practically unmarked. If he had had someone on him then it might have been much harder for him to get up.

Giacinto Facchetti (Italy): We jumped up together, out of synch, to head the ball. I was taller than him and could jump higher. When I hit the ground, I looked up perplexed. Pelé was still there, heading the ball. It seemed as though he could hang in the air for as long as he wanted.

Pelé (Brazil): It was our first goal of the game, but it convinced me that between the accuracy of our attack and the defensive nature of the Italian game, only a gift from us would ever earn them a goal. And at thirty-seven minutes into the period, that's exactly what they got!

The Italians were slightly the more dominant side in the first half and they got the goal their pressure deserved eight minutes before the break. Brazil had looked suspect in defence and on this occasion they far too casual. Brito's slack header went to Clodoaldo, who gave the ball away as he nonchalantly tried to back-heel a pass midway through his own half. Boninsegna nipped in and although Brito dashed back and Felix ran out of his goal they couldn't stop the Italians drawing level.

Brazilian TV commentary: *Mistake by Clodoaldo and the Italian Boninsegna is through and danger, it's Boninsegna. Gooooal de Italia! Boninsegna. That was a costly mistake by Clodoaldo. A mistake by the Brazilian defence. The clock says thirty-seven minutes gone in the first half. The scoreboard at the Azteca reads Brazil 1, Italy 1.*

Pelé (Brazil): Clodoaldo, without thinking, back-heeled the ball, intending it for Brito, but he missed entirely. Boninsegna swept in instantly! Felix dashed out to save, [but he] had no chance and Boninsegna was on his way. He went past our goalkeeper and put the ball into the unguarded net with no effort. And the score was tied!

Mario Zagallo (Brazil coach): There's a time and place for joking around; that back-heel was madness. What a dressing-down I had to give that great player! But it's also good that I put my arm around him. I've always been sure of one thing; you only make mistakes if you're out there playing. Aside from that error, there were no others that could be blamed on Clodoaldo. His performance against the Italians corresponded splendidly with our expectations.

Pelé (Brazil): I wasn't worried. It was unfortunate by Clodoaldo. He tried to back-heel the ball and gave the goal away. If the goal had come from a normal move, created by the Italians, things might have been different. But it wasn't. So we all knew it was a mistake. Of Clodoaldo, of Brito and of Felix, but we knew we had time to correct the mistake.

Enrico Albertosi (Italy): We always think we can win. Because when you take the field, you always want to win. Especially if you are playing a World Cup final. Then, of course, there is also the other team. So you have to play, you have to respond blow by blow. They went ahead through Pelé, who remained suspended in the sky, just like basketball players do. We levelled the scores through Boninsegna.

Pelé (Brazil): The Italian team made no effort to attack but retreated to their normal defensive game, and it gave us the chance we needed to recover our spirits and our morale.

Tarcisio Burgnich (Italy): After Brazil took the lead we matched them. It was a wonderful thing. We went all out to equalise and we succeeded. We really wanted to win the Jules Rimet. We wanted to win it for our fans, for public opinion. Italians are always demanding when the national team plays.

The first half was finely balanced and ended 1–1, although not before a moment of controversy.

Pelé (Brazil): Then – at what at the time I was sure was forty-four minutes, thirty seconds of the first half, with what I was positive was a full half minute yet to play – I was in possession of the ball and was prepared to kick what seemed to me to be an almost sure goal – when the whistle suddenly blew and the first half was over. The official time is never what the clock says but is kept by the referee in a major game of football – but for a moment I had that old, cold feeling. Were we going to be victimised by a referee from Europe in favour of a European team, as had happened in the past? I went into the locker room at half-time nursing this fear: but the second half proved it to be unfounded.

Tarcisio Burgnich (Italy): Throughout the first half we played a good game, even though our opponents were superior. It's just a shame that we had not recovered physically from the semi-final. Brazil came to the final in better condition than we were.

Mario Zagallo (Brazil coach): The first half went as I had predicted. When we crossed the halfway line the Italian midfielders would meet us to defend themselves against Gerson and Clodoaldo. Jairzinho would drag Facchetti into the penalty area, giving Carlos Alberto the opportunity to advance up the open right flank. A gap the likes of which you've never seen before would open up before him. It would be so big that everyone would notice it. It was hard for me to believe that the Italians wouldn't cotton on to this at some point of the match. But they were looking the other way. The gap opened up several times and Carlos Alberto took advantage of it.

Pelé (Brazil): We were in great condition. We were more rested. The way the Italians wore themselves out in the game against the Germans was fatal for them.

Mario Zagallo (Brazil coach): I feared the Italians would change their tactics in the second half. So at half-time I told my players to tighten up in the sector where the hole had opened up, in the thinking that the Italians would put another plan into action. I tried to second-guess the Italian coach and drew up a scheme on the other side of the pitch from that where we had operated in the first half, over on the left with Rivellino and Everaldo. But it wasn't necessary.

Pelé was inches away from connecting with a Carlos Alberto cross right at the start of the second period and then Rivellino hit the bar after an hour as the game broke down into a series of scrappy fouls. But Brazil only had to wait until the sixty-sixth minute to take the lead again.

Ado (Brazil): Gerson didn't have a strong shot. He was much more of a passer, and he could fire off these long balls with a real precision. At training, they would line up twenty balls and Gerson would hit them, bang, bang, bang. And I said, 'If you score against me, I'll buy you dinner, I'll buy you whatever you want.' Man, it drove him crazy. And so in the game against Italy, when he scored the second goal, he caught it perfectly, and he ran to the bench and screamed, 'There you go, you son of a bitch. I told you I'd score and there it is.' [Laughs]. I gave him a big hug and said, 'Congratulations.' It was funny.

Angelo Domenghini (Italy): We played the game with Brazil until sixty-five minutes, or rather, until then we had been better than Brazil. Then they were lucky to make the score 2–1 and then three minutes later they made the third. After that they gave us the runaround.

Sandro Mazzola (Italy): One of our biggest mistakes was leaving Gerson free in midfield and he organised the play. When it went to 2–1 we realised we didn't have the strength to mount a fightback. Playing an extra half hour at 2,000 metres above sea level requires an enormous effort. Some players were peeing blood [after the game] because of the strain. Against Brazil we matched them for an hour. It would have been nice to play them without that extra time in the match before.

Ado (Brazil): When we were going to the stadium we believed that we were going to be champions no matter what because Italy were down and out. With all due respect to them, we went 1–0 up, Italy equalised, and all of a sudden we found our form. Clodoaldo had a great game, Rivellino, Pelé, Jairzinho, I could see that we were getting into a groove and I felt that Italy fell away after half an hour or so because they had had such a difficult game in the semi-final. They felt it, plus there was the altitude of Mexico City; the heat was something terrible, and they couldn't handle it. We were used to playing in forty-degree heat. In Rio the sun is very strong. Even in Guadalajara the sun was strong, and we joked that each of us had our own individual sun beating down on our heads, it was terrible.

The game was not yet over, but the goal deflated the Italians and it wasn't long before Brazil got the third that essentially sealed the match. Once again it was Jairzinho, who never seemed to tire for a second throughout the entire tournament, who did the damage. Alcides Ghiggia scored in all four Uruguay games in 1950 and Just Fontaine scored in all six of France's matches in 1958, including the third-place play-off. But Jairzinho's seventy-first-minute strike meant he became the first man to score in all six games and in every round, including the final.

Brazilian TV commentary: *Everaldo gives it to Gerson, Gerson gets into the box, he lifts it up for Pelé and it's a goal! Gooooooooooal* *for Brazil, Jair, Jair, Jairzinho with a third goal for Brazil. Brazil for a third World Cup. It's a win for guts and determination and heart and for 90 million people in Brazil.*

Enrico Albertosi (Italy): I know for certain that when I faced Brazil, I thought I would never face a stronger team than that in my life. They were stratospheric, and we had the feeling that they could score at any time. We held out for almost seventy minutes, then we collapsed. Part of the reason was because of the extra time played against West Germany, and part was because we had always played at over 2,000 metres.

Pelé (Brazil): From that point on there was no doubt as to what the final result would be.

Tarcisio Burgnich (Italy): They were strong, creative ball players. It was beautiful to watch. But what made the difference in that game was our physical condition. I remember that after Italy–West Germany we had cramps, and physically we were in bad shape. It was not at all easy to recover after that 4–3.

Enrico Albertosi (Italy): The psycho-physical collapse happened . . . when Jairzinho scored. It was then that we realised that there was nothing we could do.

Mario Zagallo (Brazil coach): In the second half no one could have missed how our players drew on their reserves of stamina. The Italians, by contrast, were terribly tired; inside, they must have been desperate to hear the referee's final whistle.

And then came Brazil's crowning moment, when Carlos Alberto crashed home a spectacular fourth with just four minutes remaining. Eight Brazilian players touched the ball in the build-up to what is still considered one of the great team goals of all time. The goal is often described as an example of the spontaneity that seemingly characterises Brazilian football. But the Brazilians knew that was only half the story. The fourth goal, they said, was as much about planning and organisation as creativity.

Pelé (Brazil): The Italians had a special marking for me and Jairzinho. So we came up with a plan. Because they man-marked and followed their players wherever they went, Jair and I decided that when Gerson or Clodoaldo got the ball we would move out to the left. Facchetti would go with Jair, leaving a space for Carlos Alberto, who took advantage of it all the time, including for our fourth goal. The guy who was marking me, Bertini, also followed me wherever I went, even when the match was all but over. By following me and Jair they left space for our other players coming from the back.

Tostão (Brazil): Parreira travelled to see Italy play and passed the information on to us. Italy played Germany in the semi-final. He gave us a team talk on the eve of the game. He took millions of photographs, put them all in a sequence, about fifty of them, showing, for example, how the full back Facchetti marked. They marked man to man. He pointed out that if Jairzinho went to the other side of the pitch the player would accompany Jairzinho. He showed us the Germany game; where each player positioned himself, their movements on the pitch, all with sequential photographs. It's almost absurd to imagine how it would be possible to do that today with all the technological resources we have. [Laughs].

Carlos Alberto (Brazil): We knew it was a move that could happen. Look, forty-one minutes gone in the second half, we're winning 3–1 and victory is guaranteed, more than guaranteed, we already thought we were world champions. Absolutely. Forty-one minutes, two minutes to go and I was at the back catching my breath because of the pace of the game and the altitude because no matter how well prepared we were, and we were well prepared, going from Guadalajara you're always going to feel it a bit, right? I could have stayed at the back taking it easy, waiting for the clock to tick away. The mentality of that team was so attacking, so when Tostão won the ball, when he got the ball in midfield, and he knocked it back to Everaldo, what could Everaldo do? Give it back to the goalkeeper and kill three minutes, but as our mentality was to go forward, we got the ball and came forward. So I looked around and there was no one on my side and I remembered the instructions that Zagallo gave me. So I had a look and thought, 'Right, there's no one on my side of the pitch,' that's what Zagallo had said. So I waited to see what would happen when the ball was fired over to the left to Jairzinho, to Rivellino. And I said, 'All right, I'm going to edge up slowly. If the ball goes to Pelé, I know it'll come to me,' because we had that understanding together at Santos. And that was what happened. And maybe because Pelé also remembered the instructions that Zagallo gave us, 'Man, could Carlos Alberto be remembering what Zagallo said?' Happily I remembered. So I set off: the moment that Jairzinho touched the ball for Pelé, I sprinted forward. And my timing was just right – that was why the shot was so powerful, because I didn't need to adjust my steps before hitting it.

Brazilian TV commentary: *Clodoaldo dribbles round one, dribbles round two. That is the green-and-yellow style! Ball to Rivellino, Rivellino to Jair. He gives it to Pelé, Carlos Alberto is free. He's running. Goooal! Gooooooooooooooooal! Caaaaaarlos Albeeeeerto, in the number four shirt! Maaaaaaaaaaaaarvellous! What a pass, from Pelé to Carlos Alberto. The photographers have invaded* *the pitch! The Brazilian players are ecstatic with Carlos Alberto's goal! It's the third World Cup for Brazil; you can celebrate. Cry with us. Forty-one minutes have gone. Long live the three times World Cup winners! Congratulations to Brazil! Congratulations to the seleção! The pride of our people! It's carnival time!*

Carlos Alberto (Brazil): So you see, it was all planned; there wasn't a lot that was improvised in that team. Because Brazil's strength is improvisation, isn't it? The creativity. But some of the important details of that campaign were all planned. We weren't robots, or machines, as many people call the European players, but we knew what could happen.

Gerson (Brazil): We knew how Italy played, their tactical set-up: they marked man to man and so we had a variation for that scheme. If they marked man to man, and the whole Italian marking system went this way, then there was space for Carlos Alberto to move in to alone. They played with two men in the middle of the park; we played with three and sometimes even four and the goal we conceded was our silliness. After the World Cup we sat down, after it had all sunk in, to analyse what we did and see what we could have done better.

Carlos Alberto (Brazil): More than my shot, it was a beautiful move that represented what that team was all about. The majority of the players touched the ball, and it went all over, without the Italians, who were also a great team, being able to do anything.

Enrico Albertosi (Italy): We continued to attack, but we lost our balance and Carlos Alberto arrived to make it 4–1.

Tarcisio Burgnich (Italy): Facing a team like the seleção was not easy. Throughout the first half we played a good game, even though our opponents were superior. It's just a shame that we had not recovered physically from the semi-final. Brazil came to the final in better condition than we were. Even today I still regret our physical condition. We could have played on a par with Brazil if we had recovered from the semi-final against West Germany.

Bobby Moore (England): I felt a little sorry for the Italians trying hard to disillusion and embitter so many would-be revellers. But try they did and for two-thirds of the game they rebelled against destiny. They too had men of flair, men of character, and perhaps even a more established, if cautious, playing system. They fell, like all before them, to the attacking genius of a side which often seems so inadequate in defence.

There was almost no time left on the clock and everyone knew the game was over as a contest. Photographers ran onto the field to get pictures of the joyous champions and some fans joined them. Just seconds after the restart the final whistle went.

British TV commentary: There is no time left on the clock up here now. Brazilian fans are waving their flags. Photographers tearing down to get pictures of the final celebrations. The band ready to march on . . . Now the crowd has just got into complete pandemonium. Referee Rudi Glöckner will have to get well on top of this now . . . There are hundreds of photographers down there, spectators and there are people being chased all over the field. There are players on the park, there are spectators on the park, there are now police on the park, everybody's on the park. The game is over. Brazil have won it. Pelé is being mobbed.

The scenes when the final whistle went were unforgettable. The Mexican fans who had so enthusiastically embraced the Brazilians poured onto the field with delirious abandon. Some of them wanted to touch their heroes and lift them shoulder-high and parade them around the ground. Others attacked them like vultures, stripping them of shirts, shorts, socks and boots. It looked joyous but the players were terrified.

Carlos Alberto (Brazil): At the end of the game when the referee blew his whistle, there was pandemonium. All our players got their kits stripped off! Everybody was delirious, but the Mexicans loved football and we had a Latin relationship. If Italy had won, you wouldn't have seen such scenes.

Pelé (Brazil): What happened when the referee blew his whistle to end the game is indescribable. The pitch was invaded. I was stripped of my clothes. I only had my underpants. When I saw the fans run on, knowing that they would do anything to get a hold of souvenirs I took my shirts and shorts off. I am scared by all that grabbing. When that happens someone might get hurt. They took my boots, hauled them off me. Happily, as I had always said I wanted to keep the boots from my last game, I was able to keep the ones I used in the first half. Noting that the pitch was heavy and slippery, I had worn longer studs. I changed them at half-time after realising that I didn't need such high studs. They are my only souvenir of the World Cup.

Carlos Alberto (Brazil): We couldn't get away. There was no way to escape because they had enclosed the pitch. Rivellino fainted. It really was a show by the Mexicans that impressed a lot of people. The way they received us, the joy they showed the Brazilian team for winning; man, it was so cool, it was really fantastic. It's something that sticks with you; it was unforgettable. Truly. Truly.

Tostão (Brazil): In the dressing room after the game, I gave Dr Roberto Abdalla Moura my winner's medal and the shirt I'd played the first half in. I had put it aside because I knew the one I wore in the second half would be ripped from my body after we won the title, and that was exactly what happened. Dr Roberto was the doctor who operated on my eye in the United States, eight months before the World Cup. He had been invited by the backroom staff and he came from Houston to Mexico, where he slept in the team hotel with the players and he came to the stadium to watch our games.

Edu (Brazil): When we scored the fourth we left the stands and went down to the dressing room because we knew we'd not get down afterwards. We were in our uniforms, and they'd have taken everything from us. We were wearing Brazil jackets, all the official gear. So when the fourth goal went in we said, 'We need to get down there because it's going to be madness.' The Mexican fans were all over the Brazilians, right? They loved us. Brazil had beaten Italy 4–1 and Italy had knocked out Mexico. So the Mexicans said we'd got revenge for them. It was wonderful. And when we got down to the pitch you couldn't get on, as so many people had invaded the pitch. And they were trying to strip us. Even the reserves. They wanted everything. Tostão left the field in his underpants. They never got anything from us because we never made it onto the pitch; we only got as far as the tunnel and when we saw what was going on we headed back to the dressing room. And there it was a party.

Piazza (Brazil): There, on the actual day, when we thought that 70 per cent of them, who knows how many, were Mexicans who were celebrating, as excited about the victory as it if was them that had won, it was, well, what can you say? I still can't not get emotional when I think about it. That's why when people ask me, 'What was your biggest moment of the World Cup?' I say, 'Man! I think principally it's that I recognise the sweetness and the support that the Mexicans gave us and that humility and the beauty of that sportsmanship.' That's what we want, that connection between peoples, that serve as an instrument of peace and beauty. So I always say that and I was so happy to see the joy on the faces of those Mexicans after we beat Italy. It was almost total, the joy they showed as they enjoyed the title as if it was theirs. So look, that for me was one of the most unforgettable moments. It's still alive. Even today.

After making it back to the dressing rooms for a temporary respite, the Brazilians had to return to receive the trophy. They were the first team to win the Jules Rimet trophy three times and that meant they were given the trophy to keep forever.

Carlos Alberto (Brazil): We knew that if we won that World Cup the trophy would be ours to keep. In fact, I think FIFA could review their decision to rotate the trophy so that if someone wins it three times they get to keep it and they make another one. Because that motivates players. I'll see the trophy, and so what? Then I have to give it back. No, the sentiment is different. It's different playing for something that will be yours forever after you win it two or three times.

Pelé (Brazil): We had to go back out on the field to pick up the Jules Rimet which was now ours to keep. It was crazy, because we didn't have spare shirts or shorts or socks. Everybody was crying, players were hugging fans and journalists.

Piazza (Brazil): When the match against Italy ended, when they asked me, 'How are you feeling?' When the final whistle went we felt, 'We're champions! It's real!' and the euphoria was enormous.

We were like, 'Wow, what's happening?' All these things went through our head. 'How is my mum? How is my fiancée? How is my brother? How is my pal? How is Brazil?'

Carlos Alberto (Brazil): Getting handed the cup is such a happy moment, so emotional, trying to tell you how I feel, it's just not possible to say how I felt. And to know that at that moment you are representing a country, receiving the trophy, because at that moment it's not an individual, you're receiving it in the name of a nation, in the name of a squad of players, not just those that were there, but all of them. Winning the World Cup isn't just for the players; everyone in the country is a world champion, right? So that thing of getting the trophy and kissing it, because I thought it was beautiful, and I had never seen it before. So when the Mexican president handed me the cup, I thought it was pretty and that was why I wanted to kiss it, and that was a first as well. Bellini was the first to lift it and he said that it was heavy, and it was heavy. So he lifted it up. And so that desire to kiss it has become the fashion. Now you see everyone kiss the cup before they lift it up.

The celebrations continued when they left the Azteca. The players sang their hearts out on the coach back to the hotel and after changing clothes they went from one event to the next, some of them more official than others.

Pelé (Brazil): We did a lap of honour under a shower of ticker tape and a spectacular ovation. It was a long day, and the party at the Azteca never seemed to end. And it kept going on the coach; we were all happy and everyone was singing. I managed to get out of it. I got my rosary beads and went to pray. If you look at all the photos and films of the celebrations I am not there. Not that I didn't want to be there. But I had a commitment to God. I asked him to get us all home safely to see our loved ones. When we got back to the hotel, I disappeared without excusing myself, and went to my room to pray. Photographs of the festivities upon our return to the hotel will show that I was not present. It was not that I didn't want to be there, or that I thought myself different from the others. It was that I felt a more important responsibility, and that was my duty towards God. I thanked him for our health; I thanked him for the health of our opponents. I asked for a safe journey home for all who had participated in the tournament. And then I had to stop, because my room was being invaded. It was time to leave for the banquet which would mark the close of the 1970 games. The banquet was held at the Hotel Maria Isabel on the Reforma, in the centre of Mexico City. There was a show starring our own Brazilian star, [musician] Wilson Simonal, and everyone was very happy with the entire evening. The show went on until one o'clock in the morning but the party in the streets went on all night, despite the rain that had returned. One would have thought it was Carnival in Rio, as the streets along the Reforma were jammed with people singing, dancing, drinking – a mixture of Mexicans and Brazilians showing their pleasure that we had won.

Carlos Alberto (Brazil): There was a reception at the embassy before we travelled back to Brazil and the cup had pride of place. It had a seat all to itself, a seat on the plane.

Tostão (Brazil): Hours after the final there was a dinner and a party laid on by FIFA for the winners. After dessert I slipped away. I grabbed a lift from a Mexican and I went back to the hotel where I met my parents. We hugged and cried.

Pelé (Brazil): Before we went back to Brazil we wanted to visit the Mexico City cathedral. We wanted to go to a Mass and thank

God for the title and for everybody's health. We couldn't. There were too many people at the doors of the cathedral. We were on the coach but we couldn't get off, it was impossible.

Dario (Brazil): That party. And after that in Brasilia, the parade . . . But at that point the penny hadn't dropped. We were saying, 'Is this all a dream?' The first thing we thought was that it was all a dream. We didn't believe it. It was too good to be true.

In Italy, meanwhile, few people could argue the Azzurri were not beaten by the better team. The Italians matched Brazil for much of the game and it was only in the last half hour that they succumbed to what was one of history's all-time greatest sides. But the tifosi did not get over the staffetta, or rather, the lack of it. The system had appeared to work, with Rivera a key player as Italy scored three second-half goals to beat Mexico in the quarter-final and again in the semi-final when he got the winner in Italy's epic 4–3 victory. But Valcareggi abandoned the idea in the final, throwing Rivera on when the game was already lost, with just six minutes of the match remaining. For many fans, his decision, or more accurately the belatedness of it, was baffling and inexplicable.

Tarcisio Burgnich (Italy): That's all people talked about [the staffetta], but we Italians are famous for criticising. We are like that; we have lots of flaws.

Enrico Albertosi (Italy): It stayed a long time at 1–1 and so Valcareggi didn't want to change things immediately. Then when we went 2–1 behind we made the first change. We had players who did not play well; the effects of the semi-final and the altitude made themselves felt. Then at 3–1 Valcareggi told Rivera to go on. Maybe Gianni didn't expect to play at the end.

Tarcisio Burgnich (Italy): In my opinion, Valcareggi hadn't noticed that there were so few minutes remaining. This is because, in short, it was a hectic match.

Enrico Albertosi (Italy): The thing was that Rivera in the second half against Mexico made assists to Riva and also scored a goal and against West Germany he got the decisive goal. For this reason, the Italian fans were convinced that Rivera would come on in the second half against Brazil.

Angelo Domenghini (Italy): We were very disappointed that the reporters had so emphasised Rivera's six minutes in the World Cup final. When we returned to Italy, to Rome, some officials had even been attacked, there had been injuries. Furthermore, we players had been taken to a shed and tried by journalists. Too bad; it was important for us to play the World Cup final.

Enrico Albertosi (Italy): The staffetta wasn't put into operation after the first half because there were two players on the pitch who weren't in great shape. And Valcareggi said if I make the change, I only have one more change to make.

Angelo Domenghini (Italy): Rivera had come off the bench against Mexico and we had won. Valcareggi hadn't changed this and the staffetta was born there. The staffetta had also worked against West Germany in the semi-finals. It was Rivera who scored the decisive goal. [Rivera] said absolutely nothing [to me]. He accepted the idea that he had only played six minutes against Brazil. He was a serious professional. After all, you're wearing the national team shirt. In playing only six minutes, you still collect a presence with Italy. Of course, I don't think he enjoyed playing only six minutes, but he always accepted it. I would not have accepted being told to go on the field just six minutes from the end, in the final with the result 4–1 for Brazil. The thing I don't like is that when we talk about the 1970 World Cup we only talk about these six minutes. Because of these six minutes, there was pandemonium.

The decision not to include an in-form player who had been so vital in the previous two matches baffled Italian fans, who took their anger out on Valcareggi and his backroom staff. There was also indignation about the organisation.

Enrico Albertosi (Italy): We have never understood the fans' resentment of Valcareggi. We players knew why he [Rivera] had not come on. Rivera had great class and could have helped us but taking it out on the coach was not right. Valcareggi led Italy to the final, after eliminating West Germany in the semi-finals in the match still considered the most beautiful game of the century, in football history, from every era. When it came to Valcareggi there was just no gratitude. In 1968 Valcareggi led us to the European Championship. Our national team had talent, had great champions. And two years after that victory, we managed to eliminate West Germany and reach the World Cup final to play against the strongest Brazil team of all time. Moreover, Italy came from a disastrous World Cup. In 1958 Italy did not qualify, in 1962 in Chile we had not done well and in 1966 we had been eliminated by North Korea, which was a big defeat for us. In 1970, we finally reached the final.

Angelo Domenghini (Italy): In Italy only the first place counts. They should have congratulated us for the World Cup we had played. Instead, it was as if it hadn't happened. Unfortunately, only those who finish first count.

After the party the Brazilians headed to the airport for the long flight home to Brazil. They didn't know what to expect when they got there but their expectations were put on temporary hold by an unscheduled stop in Acapulco.

Mario Zagallo (Brazil coach): The flight to Acapulco was great. When we touched down there we got an unpleasant surprise: one of the plane's engines had a problem. The landing was a forced one, done so they could repair it. I realised something that had never entered my head before: when you don't have a propeller to keep an eye on when you're in the air, the passengers don't know if the engines are working properly. We had to wait two hours for the repairs to be completed. I was petrified when I found out that the problem had arisen when we were in the air, not long after we took off from the main airport in Mexico City. My fear crept up on me and only came when we were on solid ground in Acapulco. It wouldn't be funny if death caught up with us far from Brazil, right at the moment when we were missing home so much. The delay in Acapulco made us hungrier. We hadn't had any dinner. The only thing there was plenty of was nerves. But maybe it was the hunger that kept our fear at bay. The lads got together at the back of the plane, tuned up their improvised instruments and went for it, with their whistles and beats. We really put on a show, with the best music in the parish. The leaders of the samba, as always, were Brito, Paulo Cesar, Pelé and Jairzinho. Half of them were Botafogo [players].

Pelé (Brazil): I like to sleep but I wasn't able to sleep on the flight home. First because of my natural nervousness and second because my teammates wouldn't let me. Some were singing and others, still overcome, were crying with happiness. It was like that all the way to Brazil. I hadn't slept the night before either. I only managed to sleep two days later once I got home to my house in Santos.

Mario Zagallo (Brazil coach): We only got to eat around two in the morning. We were dead tired and so people slept until we approached Brasilia. As we headed in to land, Pelé and myself had to wake everyone else up. I didn't stop repeating, 'Listen people, it's going to be crazy! You're going to get a knot in your throat that won't be easy to undo! Let's see if you can handle it!'

The seleção's arrival in Brasilia has gone down in history. Brazilians were forbidden from congregating under draconian laws passed by the right-wing military regime. Freedom of association, expression and movement were all curtailed in a bid to prevent any opposition. So for many Brazilians, this was a chance to do what they loved to do; get out on the streets and party, dance, sing and drink. It was like Carnival, but for a football team.

Ado (Brazil): We didn't know the fans had been so into it, that they had participated so much. It was as if it was a release. It was as if it was a relief. The people were oppressed. Brazilians are very emotional. There were no protests in 1970, but there had never been such a celebration for a football team. It was amazing, wonderful, but we never had any inkling it would be like that. People were free, and they went out onto the streets to celebrate. It was madness; I didn't really understand it. I thought, does football really mean that much to us? I played with small teams, like Londrina, and a very big team, like Corinthians, where our average crowd was 40,000, 50,000 and it was crazy. But 80 million people on the streets celebrating. There were kids, old people, youngsters, it was madness.

Mario Zagallo (Brazil coach): What happened when we arrived in Brasilia resonated more greatly than I could have ever imagined. There weren't many people at the airport. But on the road to the presidential palace the world that was there to grab our emotions was enormous. I had never seen so many people. The entire population of Brasilia were on the streets. The people there, shoulder to shoulder, clapped us, shouted, sang, broke through the barriers. Everyone wanted to get close to us and on top of the open-top trucks that were taking us to the presidential palace. Everything that we saw and felt was unprecedented, surprising, singular and amazing. That spectacle in Brasilia will live in my memory forever.

Dario (Brazil): Because we were in a dictatorship and Brazil won, that was a great balm for the Brazilian soul, for those that had lived under pressure or threat. We lived like kings, and when we walked along the street the only thing that didn't happen was them laying down the red carpet for us to walk on. I'll honestly never forget it. It was wonderful. [Laughs].

Ado (Brazil): When we got to the airport in Brasilia the way people greeted us was impressive. Everyone was out on the streets, the Planalto [the presidential palace] was mental, the president received us, and we started to realise what we meant to Brazil at that time.

Pelé (Brazil): The reception in Brasilia was spectacular. President Medici turned into the humblest of football fans like all the rest.

Mario Zagallo (Brazil coach): It's delicious to feel that the president of the republic is as human as everyone else.

Pelé (Brazil): The first telephone call [while still in the dressing room] we got was from President Medici. He spoke to me, Carlos Alberto, Rivellino, Gerson and others. The call . . . wasn't great. There was a lot of noise because there were lots of reporters speaking at the same time. The line came and went. It was a great honour for us to speak with the president, and we could tell how excited he was, no less so than we were. I think the main reason people identified with him was because of that support he gave the seleção. He brought everyone together. He cheered every goal and the people's happiness enveloped him as well. He went from being a president to being a fan . . . and he was respected and admired for being both.

Carlos Alberto (Brazil): Everything came together; it was such a moment of huge joy and we are all conscious of it, all the players, of the joy we were giving to the Brazilian people at a difficult time. So I think we contributed in some way, we contributed in a positive way, let's put it like that, because a defeat at that point, I don't know what that would have been like. But thank God it all worked out and people were able to forget politics and the hardness of the regime for a little while.

From Brasilia, the team flew to Rio de Janeiro, where, after they had paraded the twenty kilometres from the Galeão international airport to the city centre on the back of a fire truck, another celebration was planned.

Mario Zagallo (Brazil coach): We arrived very late at Galeão. And how it was raining! There were no stars in the sky, but there were star watchers on the ground; the seleção's players. People were there waiting on us, in spite of the torrential rain. It was as if it was raining alcohol to get the crowd hyped up. We couldn't believe we were worthy of such a reception. When we saw that all those people were still standing there three hours later, in the pouring rain just to catch a quick glimpse of us as we went by, and even then half hidden on the fire truck, I wanted to start crying again. But I didn't cry as the people's deliriousness forced me to hold back the tears. None of us will ever forget that reception.

Ado (Brazil): When we left Brasilia we went to Rio de Janeiro, and that was mental – they invaded our hotel. They came in, got into our rooms, they wanted our shirts, whatever stuff you had they took. I was left with just the clothes on my back.

Mario Zagallo (Brazil coach): There was one particularly emotional moment. It came when we were in the Novo Tunnel [a well-known tunnel connecting two neighbourhoods in Rio], which was all lit up. There, a lady dressed in long black trousers and a red blouse took a run and jumped up on the truck. She came with her arms spread open and with a huge smile on her face. And then suddenly she fainted.

The players hoped that once they arrived at the hotel they would get rooms and showers and a chance to relax a bit before they were forced to appear at yet another official celebration. However, their hopes were soon dashed . . .

Mario Zagallo (Brazil coach): We were totally exhausted. We hoped that we would get a rest and a chance to freshen up. But there were no beds in the Hotel Plaza. Quite the contrary; there was a small vestibule full of people, so full you couldn't breathe properly. I suddenly felt anxious, and I had difficulty breathing. I came out in a cold sweat and I couldn't stop myself. I opened my jacket and shouted: 'I can't take it any longer, I need to get out of here!' A detective came up to me and whispered in my ear, 'Hold on to my belt and come with me.' He cut a path through the crowd. We kept going, with a dribble worthy of some of the seleção's own players. When I realised what was going on I was in the Hotel Plaza's kitchen. Eventually I found a stairwell and I went up. I got to the fourth floor and I saw all our luggage. I sat on one of them and was able to rest a little. Some of the players stayed in the hotel and slept but Gerson, Roberto and myself, we got out around 1.00 in the morning, sneaking out of the back door. Outside there were more people waiting and more autographs to be signed. By a stroke of luck, our VW Kombi appeared and the police motorcycle escort led us away. In all the confusion I hadn't been able to tell my family that I was coming home to sleep. When midnight came and went all the people who had been waiting for me in front of the building that had been done up with flags and banners had started to drift away. When the taxi left me at the door I went up to my floor and I met with my folks and a few residents of the building who I was closest to. What really surprised me, though, was that when the taxi dropped me off there was a really loud siren, the same one, people told me, that went off every time they celebrated a goal for Brazil during the World Cup. There was another surprise when I got to my flat: close friends and old neighbours had come to give me a hug in my home sweet home. My flat had turned into a small version of that vestibule in the Hotel Plaza. So there was another impromptu party, with champagne and everything. I only got to bed around three in the morning. I couldn't have been happier!

Rio was the last official stop but cities and states had planned celebrations for their own local heroes. Ado, Rivellino and Emerson Leão, for example, came to São Paulo, and Tostão and Piazza headed for Belo Horizonte. Pelé, who was keenly awaited in Santos, left Rio to rush home to his pregnant wife, in the process disappointing many fans who were desperate to see him.

Pelé (Brazil): According to the bosses, Rio was the last stage of the journey. We paraded through the streets on the back of a fire engine. When we got to the Hotel Plaza I received a message from João Havelange and Antônio do Passo saying that my wife wanted to speak to me. Until that point I hadn't managed to get a line through to Santos. My wife was expecting our second child and

I was worried. I kept trying until I eventually got through with the help of a telephone operator. This was three o'clock in the morning. She was quite het up and said she needed me. So of course it's natural that I needed to be with my wife at a time like that. I wanted to see my family. So in the middle of the night I hired an air taxi and flew home. When I saw the repercussions of my decision I was sorry for the people who wanted to see their heroes and who had supported us all along to our victory. We had spent six months training, far from home, and I had given everything I had to the national team, without thinking of my family or anyone else. Wasn't it fair, I ask you, that I went home? I was sorry for the people who had gone to the airport and who had come onto the streets but I thought that they would understand my situation. We had fought so hard and won the cup, which was a real dream come true. Would people really think bad of me because of this absence? I did the right thing and I have a clean conscience. One thing is for sure, if, before the final against Italy, someone in my family had died, my wife, my children, my father, my mother, my uncle, whoever, I wouldn't come back to Brazil. I would have stayed and played. I don't think it is fair that once I was home, with my wife needing me, I shouldn't go to her. People understood what I did, of that I am certain.

Ado (Brazil): And then we came to São Paulo. And that was mental as well. Some of the players didn't come as they couldn't handle any more of it. Here [in São Paulo], we paraded on the back of an open-topped fire truck, we went to the mayor's office, and we each got given a Volkswagen Beetle that people are still discussing today.

Emerson Leão (Brazil): I got a car, and I didn't even know how to drive and I never had a licence. They took me to Ibirapuera Park, which is close to where I live now. 'Look, the cars are there and each car had a [player's] name on it.' I got a green Volkswagen that I had to drive home. Can you believe it? So I got in and drove home. I had had some – in inverted commas – 'lessons' from the Volkswagen Kombi van my dad had. I drove home, parked the car in the garage and locked it up. My dad said, 'How did it go?' 'It went well. The car's there.' 'Who drove it home for you?' 'Me.' 'I don't believe it.' I said, 'Neither did I.' [Laughs]. So I gave him the keys and I only got them back once I got my driving licence. So the World Cup gave me some very different things. I was just a kid, right?

Baldocchi (Brazil): It took me three days to get home. We were a day in Rio de Janeiro, then the next day we went to Brasilia, they paid tribute to us there, then we went to São Paulo. In São Paulo it was downhill from the airport. Everything was jam-packed. And the street I lived on they decked the whole street out in tribute. So it took me three days to get home. And just when the dust started to settle, folk arrived from Batatais – my cousin was the mayor there at the time – and said, Batatais is going to honour you at the City Chambers, it's nothing too grand, a simple thing. That was on the fourth day. So I got my wife, who was pregnant, and said to her, 'Let's get out of here.' So we jumped in the car but when we arrived at the entrance to the city the whole place had ground to a halt. They had laid on a party, and it was amazing. So I took four or five days to sit down and say, 'Right, now I am at home with my family.' But it was worth it, well worth it.

Piazza (Brazil): It wasn't easy for us to see the footage that they show today. We didn't have that ease of communications. So when we got to Brazil, when we saw everyone there, celebrating, welcoming us, man, it was so emotional.

THIRTEEN

THE LEGACY OF BRAZIL 1970

The tributes showered on the Brazil team were massive, with several players singled out for special praise. Gerson was heralded as the brains of the team; Clodoaldo the surprise package. Tostão was the selfless technician whose sacrifice allowed his attacking teammates space in which to operate and Rivellino provided firepower with one of the most powerful and deceptive shots on the planet. Captain Carlos Alberto led with assurance and Jairzinho set records. No man has ever beaten his run of scoring in all six games of the tournament including the final and his string of forty-seven dribbles has been beaten only once since, by Diego Maradona in 1986.

Bobby Moore (England): Pelé may have been top of the bill but we must not underestimate the enormous ability which surrounded him and made Brazil's hat-trick possible. Winger Jairzinho scored in every game and illustrated superb control and shooting power all along the line; Tostão, with the hardness and aggression of his European counterparts and the ball wizardry of his South American teammates, was the ideal spearhead; Rivellino menaced and threatened whenever in possession and was able almost to bend the ball around corners; and, in Gerson,

Brazil had one of the most astute, effective and talented midfield players of recent years. I know he was the one man who impressed the English players more than any other in Guadalajara.

Ildo Maneiro (Uruguay): Playing against Pelé was impressive, and Jairzinho just flew. The quality of the players that Brazil had was impressive. They say it was a selection of five number tens: Jairzinho started as ten in his career, Gerson, Tostão, Pelé and Rivellino or Paulo Cesar were all ten, all class players.

Angelo Domenghini (Italy): We saw a great Brazil in the 1970 World Cup. So, I would say that with the names Brazil had, it was the best team ever. Especially in attack. In defence and in midfield, however, they were a normal team. But in front they had Tostão, Rivellino, Pelé and Gerson. No team in football history has ever had such a strong attack. Never. This is the strongest attack ever, while in defence they had gaps.

Ronnie Hellström (Sweden): I don't think they ever had a better team than then, with Pelé at his prime. I only saw Brazil play after getting back home. They played technical, attacking football. Pelé was incredible. Their individual qualities were on a different level compared to European football. Also, they had speed and combinations. In the final the Italians were left scrambling. The Brazilians were outstanding.

Tostão (Brazil): It was a team that had the greatest [player] of all time, along with several others that are up there among the best in history. There was also an exceptional understanding, and we played a football that was revolutionary for the time.

Berti Vogts (West Germany): They had the best players you can offer. Their personalities, what they could do with the ball, and also in the altitude they still could play with a good rhythm, lots of ball possession. [Was it the best] that ever existed? I don't know. I don't know the Brazilian teams from the 1950s and the beginning of the 1960s. But this team from 1970, it was such an experience; they had Pelé and more.

Tommy Svensson (Sweden): Brazil absolutely deserved to win; they were the best team in the tournament by a margin. It's tricky to compare different teams through the years but that Brazil side must have been one of the best teams ever.

Inevitably, there was special love for Pelé, the man who had silenced the naysayers and become the first player ever to win three World Cup winner's medals. Pelé's goal against Italy was his twelfth in World Cup finals and with it he became only the second player to score in two finals, along with his compatriot Vavá. His six assists have also not been bettered in a finals since.

Clodoaldo (Brazil): It was a dream, a real privilege to play with guys like that. So much creativity and ability to start attacks. I won't mention Pelé, because he's not on quite the same level as he was from a different planet.

Tostão (Brazil): Pelé really prepared for that World Cup. He wanted to end his international career with a major victory, both individually and collectively, so nobody would harbour any doubts that he was the greatest of all time.

Rivellino (Brazil): Pelé was a huge star. The best player in the world. Ever. To me there is no equal. He always led by example on and off the pitch. And, even though he was a huge star, Pelé never shouted that you had to play the ball to him. Never. He always had a positive attitude and always made others play better.

Bobby Moore (England): What is there left to say about Pelé, aptly titled 'the King of Soccer?' No player can surely have gripped the imagination, thrilled the senses or prompted a greater adoration on a football field than this man. In an age when individuality bends in the case of greater teamwork and a higher work rate, he has remained the supreme one-man act. In the end it was almost as though the World Cup in Mexico had been staged for his benefit. Football is a game of emotion and I doubt if any one man has stirred more hearts than Pelé.

Tostáo (Brazil): I tried to keep up with him. Before he even received the ball, he was on the move, and with his expressive eyes he was telling me what he wanted to do. Analogue communication, through the movement of the body or the eyes, is imprecise but it is much richer than the digital, through words. The body speaks and it doesn't lie.

Mario Zagallo (Brazil coach): He prepared as never before to play a good World Cup in 1970 [for this] to be his high point. He'd been injured at the start of 1958. And at seventeen, he wasn't quite the Pelé he went on to be. In '62 he was injured in the second game, and he was injured again in '66. So 1970 was his chance to show his genius. He therefore really prepared to show his football. His influence was collective, and he made things easier for the others, because he attracted the marking. So his desire to show his talent was something completely natural. And he was always a good teammate; he was always concerned with things he thought were not correct from the collective point of view. I'll give you an example from 1970: we were in our base in Mexico, and our base was behind bars, and the public were on the other side of the bars. And the players kept going over to sign autographs, until he called the meeting with all the players and coaching staff and said, 'Look, we're here to win the World Cup, and I'm feeling that our attention is not properly focused because all the time we are going over to sign autographs and have our photos taken and this is not good and we have to change our way of thinking on this.' So both on the field and off it he was exceptional.

Roberto Matosas (Uruguay): Pelé was undoubtedly one of the greatest I faced in every way: for the technical part, for the mental part. [He was] a player who you could cancel out for eighty-nine minutes but you always knew that in the very last second he could come up with some genius. He was not one of those footballers who disappear for twenty minutes. If you could anticipate him, then all the better. If not, then you were already a little screwed. He invented the one-two with his rivals; Pelé came driving at you and played the ball off your leg and then kept running forward to pick up the ball. [They called it] 'Pelé's wall' with the rival; he was the only one who ever did that.

Edu (Brazil): Pelé was the one who was concerned about preparations. He told us, I am prepared for this World Cup and the world is going to know all about Pelé. He was really upset because people had compared Eusebio to him in 1966. There was a huge difference between Pelé and Eusebio. He was hurt, really bothered by it and in the 1970 World Cup he did it all. He wanted to show to the world the real Pelé; he wanted the world to know who Pelé really was. The dressing room was happy, the same as usual. We had a few players who liked to pass the ball around, put one guy in the middle, all that horsing around and shouting. And there was that thing that Pelé did: he got his kit and there was a bench and he lay down on the bench and wrapped his kit around his boots, using that as a pillow and took a nap. That was his way of focusing, and he did that at Santos as well. We'd be shouting and he'd sleep through it. He did it before every game; he always did it.

Martin Peters (England): In Mexico, it was like playing against a god. Though I had seen him on television scores of times, it wasn't until last year [1969] when we met Brazil on our tour of South America that I saw him in the flesh and to be honest I was not particularly taken with him. He was a bit flash and did not want to get too involved where it mattered, in our penalty area. But as the World Cup unfolded it was clear that I had underestimated Pelé's competitiveness, his ability to take up damaging positions and the sheer magic of his control in tight situations. Mooro, who played him brilliantly on the occasions they came face to face in Guadalajara when Pelé was trying to 'lose' Alan Mullery, told me that the subtlety is still there, but that electrifying turn of speed has faded.

Angelo Domenghini (Italy): The best player of all time was Pelé. He scored over 1,000 goals. In addition, he had overwhelming physical power. Without a doubt, Pelé was the strongest ever. In general, I think everyone makes mistakes, but Pelé made fewer mistakes.

Javier Valdivia (Mexico): He is a superstar, full stop. You can't compare him to anyone else because he was the complete player. He had no defects as a footballer: he headed well, he shot well, he was strong, he had no weaknesses. Even today he would be a star. You can't compare him with anyone, not even Maradona. Every era is different but he was on a different level.

Tommy Svensson (Sweden): Above all, Pelé is the one that I remember. Pelé was an all-round player. Very technical, fantastic at reading the game. He was a bit short in stature but made up for it with a great knack for getting up at the right time in aerial play too.

Mario Zagallo (Brazil coach): At the end, after we have beaten Italy in the final, he came over to me, gave me a hug and said, 'We had to be together to win the World Cup for the third time.' It was the best Pelé with the national team.

Ronnie Hellström (Sweden): Pelé was an all-rounder. He could outjump anyone, had a powerful shot, could read the game. The world had never seen a guy like him, even though we got a first taste in 1958. Of the others, I got the chance to play against Rivellino at Råsunda in the summer of 1973. He shot two free kicks that I saved. The ball swerved and changed trajectory. Plus he also used power. That Brazil team was tremendous.

It was a love that grew over the years as players, coaches and fans recognised they would probably never see another player with the same skills or the same dominance. Brazil were only the third team in history to win all their matches on the way to winning the World Cup. The only team to repeat that feat since was Brazil again in 2002.

Piazza (Brazil): Sometimes I find myself looking at my old photos. I have one beside Pelé, the king. Everything was so natural to him. It was so great to play behind them and see those amazing moves that team did. It was lovely to watch even the things that didn't result in goals, such as the move against Uruguay and his header against Gordon Banks. It was a privilege playing for that team, being at the back and watching it all close up. I sometimes thought, 'Just as well I am on their side as it would be so difficult marking them.' I knew that if we let in three then we'd score seven.

Martin Peters (England): If you accept that the man of the tournament must come from one of the finalists, then what other choice is there? Pelé does everything superbly with the possible exception of taking a dive in an opponent's penalty area. He has a lot to learn about that art, though with his skills I can't think for the life of me why he bothers to lower himself to start acting. Let others with only a fraction of his ability make fools of themselves. Pelé has no need of such childishness and he knew by the end of the competition that referees would not be swayed or influenced by amateur dramatics.

Cesar Luis Menotti (Argentina coach in 1978): You have to say what does being the perfect footballer entail? It's Pelé. Physically, he was incredible. He could jump and hang in the air. It was like he had a parachute. And then he did everything, everything. For me he was the greatest in history.

Tarcisio Burgnich (Italy): I thought, 'He's made of skin and bone, just like me.' I was wrong.

Wolfgang Overath (West Germany): I felt a fear, a terrible fear when I looked into those eyes. They were like the eyes of a wild animal, eyes that spat out fire.

Tostão (Brazil): He played with such objectivity. There was no place in his football for excesses, fripperies or fouls. He almost never played keepy-uppy, and he didn't dribble laterally but always towards the goal. When they tried to bring him down, he didn't fall, thanks to his stupendous muscle mass and balance.

Cesar Luis Menotti (Argentina coach): The five best players in history are Pelé, Maradona, Di Stefano, Messi and Cruyff. I don't like to put them in order. But if you really want to know, Pelé was greater than them all. What he did as a footballer was out of this world. He was the greatest in an era of spectacular footballers and he was also the big name in the Brazil 1970 team, the best side I ever saw play.

Arsène Wenger (former Arsenal coach): The chosen one. The king Pelé cemented his own place in history.

Tite (former Brazil coach): You know what I do when someone tries to compare someone with Pelé? I hear but I don't listen. It goes in one ear and out the other. They don't know anything about history, about his quality. They've not tried to follow what he did. Pelé was above all normal standards and I'm not saying that because I am a Brazilian. Those that know history saw the goals, the magnitude, the physical courage. And here I am going to speak as a coach about individual physical merits: the heading, the two-footedness, the ability to pass and make goal chances, the competitiveness, jumping and strength. Find me a weakness, he doesn't have one. So anyone who tries to compare him to others has no credibility.

On a collective basis, the same could also be said for the seleção. As the years have passed, the 1970 side has gone down in history as the epitome of what an attacking football team should look like. Half a century later it is still considered the benchmark against which all other national sides must measure themselves.

Gordon Banks (England): Brazil's performance in the World Cup final of 1970 was a masterclass. On that day Brazil firmly planted their flag on the summit of world football, a peak to which all other teams must aspire. Their success was a triumph for adventurous football of the most sublime quality. The day when the most attack-minded team came up against arguably the best defence in the world. Samba soccer took on catenaccio and effortlessly swept it aside. Brazil's triumph was also that of Pelé and of football in general.

Tostão (Brazil): A great team is when you put together a collective game with individual improvisation and that was what the 1970 seleção did. It is considered the best football team of all time – for many, but not all – because it brought together the collective, organised game with physical fitness and with spectacular individual improvisations. What I mean is that when you have a group of great players, but who are all highly individual, you don't get a great team. And the opposite is the same: there's no point in having a brilliantly organised group if you don't have individual quality.

Bobby Moore (England): Whatever nationality, you could not help but stand in awe of these South American football giants who unashamedly poured forth the pure and basic artistries with an uncomplicated joy.

Roberto Matosas (Uruguay): In Mexico 1970 we just found ourselves against a team that had everything, especially from the middle of the field forward. Only at the 1982 World Cup in Spain did Brazil have as many great players as it did in 1970. It was a great team. I think they influenced coaches around the world who wanted their teams to also play as Brazil did. I think Holland got a lot out of that Brazil.

Although they featured so many greats (or because they did), the professionalism of Brazil's tactics and training before and during the tournament were often overlooked. Many observers believed Brazil won the World Cup because they had the best players. The players themselves knew there was more to it than that. Zagallo's tactical acumen was often underestimated, with Tostão, that most lucid of analysts, describing his work as far ahead of its time.

Tostão (Brazil): Zagallo, for the time, was collective years ahead of the other coaches because in addition to having been a very intelligent player, he was extremely obsessive about tactics, something that back then had always been left in the background. As time went on other coaches passed him but in 1970 he was an extremely important and innovative coach. He used coloured buttons to show us the players' positioning and movement. He demanded that when we lost the ball we must have the three midfielders [Clodoaldo, Gerson and Rivellino] in front of the . . . defenders. If one of the three had gone forward and didn't have time to get back, then one of the front three [Pelé, Jairzinho or me] had to get back to mark. Often that was Jairzinho, who used his pace on the right to get back and form a line of four in the midfield. Zagallo's intention was to repeat the tactical scheme he had at Botafogo, where they marked deeper so as to better counter-attack.

Carlos Alberto Parreira (Brazil): He was a great strategist. Tactically, Zagallo changed the seleção in a way that no one imagined, by giving the team balance, and that was crucial for our triumph.

Anatoly Byshovets (USSR): The tactical formation which they used at that World Cup was perfect for them – the 4-3-3 with Clodoaldo being a central defensive midfielder, who not only broke up the opposition's attacks, but also enabled the attacking functions of Gerson and Rivellino. He was key for that team. That tactical shift from 4-2-4 to 4-4-2 and then to 4-3-3 was a masterstroke! We knew that we had no chance of beating them – I don't think any team in the world at the time had any chances. I would go as far as saying that Brazil's team for the 1970 World Cup was the best team in the history of football.

Tostão (Brazil): Back then, tactics in Brazil were . . . It wasn't like today, when we spend all day talking about tactics on the television, the coaches and everything. Before the World Cup, people were contemptuous of tactics in Brazilian football as it was seen as being of lesser importance. So this was an advance, a very important advance. Lots of things that we imagined would happen were discussed and then actually happened on the pitch. In spite of all this, today's generation – what you hear on television, in bars, etc. – has got it all wrong: there is this idea that the 1970 team was spectacular because the players had the freedom on the pitch to do what they wanted. And that wasn't the case; it was a completely collective game, all organised.

Mario Zagallo (Brazil coach): Our 1970 team was most modern, playing tight football, solid, in a block, defending in numbers and attacking in numbers; it brought together the security and the strength of European football with the kind of freedom that you only see in Brazilian players.

Perhaps even more important was the physical preparation that allowed Brazil to move up a gear when other teams were flagging. Of all the telling statistics from Mexico 1970, one of the most impressive summed up Brazil's superior stamina: of their nineteen goals, twelve came in the second half.

Carlos Alberto Parreira (Brazil): Our training from the start of our preparations until the last game of the tournament was innovative. And that became a reference for football. Even today, they ask about the work we did. For the World Cup, there was about four months of hard work. Every player was given his own specific workload.

Tostão (Brazil): Brazilian football up until the 1970 World Cup was understood to be a game of skill and ball players, but inconsistent when it came to efficiency. It was football that was all about having a good time, putting on a show, but without that winner's consistency. Between 1962 and 1970 European football evolved, especially in England. And Brazil lost in 1966 and we were on the slide. Everyone was talking about how European football was more objective and that Brazilian football lacked strength and physical resilience. But preparations for the 1970 World Cup were great. You know, they got a hold of studies about physical preparations and they drew up programmes for the altitude of Mexico, which was extremely modern for the era. So Brazil, in addition to winning, showed great teamwork, collective football, not just individuality. It was exactly the opposite. So everyone was extremely well prepared physically. It was a revolution in Brazilian football.

Carlos Alberto Parreira (Brazil): The seleção had the stamina to impose themselves, thanks to our physical preparations. That was really clear in the win over England but also in other games in which the team stayed strong in the second half.

For the players who played in that team, the experience changed their life. Even for those who never got a minute on the pitch in Mexico, their lives were never the same again.

Ado (Brazil): It changed my life; wherever I go I am welcomed. But no one recognises me on the street. I always tried to hide away. When people stared at me it really annoyed me. I used to go to the cinema and everyone asked for my autograph, restaurants, too. And I used to think, do I really deserve all this?

Dada (Brazil): I was an ordinary human being before the 1970 title. After it I became a myth; I turned into a saint. The only thing that was missing was them canonising me. Wherever we went we were respected, and people showed us love. I became a personality. It got to the point where I was pinching myself, 'Is that Dada they're talking about really me?'

Pelé (Brazil): There are a lot of videos available and TV programmes that put it on and so I watch the games. I'll tell you something, though: if I'm not careful I always start crying. When I see those players and the people cheering me around, I get all emotional. I'm a sensitive guy!

Tostão (Brazil): Lots of youngsters today, who've only seen the highlights from 1970, say the team is very good, excellent even, but not as good as people make out. The racing driver Nelson Piquet once said he preferred the 1994 team to the 1970 team. Others, generally older people and/or nostalgists, say that the 1970s seleção gets better every time they see it. I understand that. When I listen to old songs from Tom Jobim or Chico Buarque, I like them more.

BIBLIOGRAPHY

Ball, Alan: *Playing Extra Time*

Banks, Gordon: *Banksy*

Charlton, Bobby: *My England Years: The Autobiography*

Dawson, Jeff: *Back Home*

Maier, Sepp: *Ich bin doch kein Tor*

Moore, Bobby: *Moore on Mexico*

Tostão: *Lembrancas, Opinioes E Reflexos Sobre Futebol*

Pelé: *The Autobiography*

Pelé: *My Life and the Beautiful Game*

Pelé: *Why Soccer Matters*

Peters, Martin: *Mexico 70*

Seeler, Uwe: *Danke Fussball*

Stiles, Nobby: *After The Ball: My Autobiography*

Zagallo: *As Lições da Copa*